Keepers of the
Morning Star

AN ANTHOLOGY OF NATIVE WOMEN'S THEATER

Keepers of the Morning Star

AN ANTHOLOGY OF NATIVE WOMEN'S THEATER

Edited by Jaye T. Darby
and Stephanie Fitzgerald

UCLA American Indian Studies Center
3220 Campbell Hall, Box 951548
Los Angeles, California 90095-1548

Publisher: American Indian Studies Center, University of California, Los Angeles
Publications Manager: Pamela Grieman
Assistant Editor: Amy Ware
Editorial Assistant: Anagha Apte
Cover design and layout: Lisa Winger

Printed by McNaughton & Gunn
Library of Congress Catalog No. 2003100128
ISBN 0-935626-56-5

To
Jane Lind and Marjorie Tanin

For their artistic contributions and life-long commitment to
Native theater and Native communities
Aho

Contents

Acknowledgments

Keepers of the Morning Star: An Anthology of Native Women's Theater is a continuation of the UCLA American Indian Studies Center Native American Theater series and joins *Stories of Our Way: An Anthology of American Indian Plays* (1999) and *American Indian Theater in Performance: A Reader* (2002), edited by Hanay Geiogamah and Jaye T. Darby. This series grows out of Project HOOP (Honoring Our Origins and People through Native Theater, Education, and Community Development), a national initiative to advance Native theater artistically, academically, and professionally, housed at UCLA. Project HOOP was first funded by the W. K. Kellogg Foundation as part of its "Capturing the Dream": Native American Higher Education Initiative and is currently funded by the US Department of Education through the Fund for the Improvement of Postsecondary Education (FIPSE). The editors are most grateful to all three of these institutions for their support of Project HOOP. Sincere appreciation goes to Hanay Geiogamah at the UCLA American Indian Studies Center and School of Theater, Film, and Television; Valorie Johnson at the W. K. Kellogg Foundation; and David Johnson at the Fund for the Improvement of Postsecondary Education (FIPSE).

We also thank our colleagues at a number of institutions for their insights during the development of this project and their commitment to Native theater: Paula Gunn Allen, Lionel Bourdeaux, Lucy Mae San Pablo Burns, James Catterall, Duane Champagne, Nancy Farnan, Joy Harjo, Jeff Kellogg, Grace Lee, Margaret MacKichan, Pat Melody, Claudia Mitchell-Kernan, Ted Mitchell, Don Moccasin, Randy Reinholz, Jeanne Bruce Scott, Roberta Una, Edit Villarreal, Della Warrior, Michelle Wester, Albert White Hat, and Russell Young. We remember Lloyd Kiva New for his vision of Native theater and seminal work at the Institute of American Indian Arts.

We are also very grateful to Pamela Grieman and Amy Ware for their dedication and expertise in preparing this volume for publication, to Anagha Apte for her editorial assistance, and to Ken Wade for his research support. Special thanks go to Stacy Barrows, Joanne Bernhaut, Stephen P. Kay, and Scott L. Rosenzweig for their professionalism and care in helping make this book possible. Warm personal thanks go to family members and friends for their encouragement and support throughout this project, especially Joanne Snow-Willstadter, Arif Amlani, Connie Bagley, Cynthia Bloom, Jerri and Robert Smith, Margaret Darby, Robert Willstadter, and Holly and Rachel Sylvers. We honor our grandmothers whose lives and stories continue to inspire us.

We appreciate the generosity of Suzan Shown Harjo for permission to reprint "Morning Star Children," Laura Fragua-Cota for permission to use her painting, "A Song, A Dance, to the Creator for the Harvest of Prayers," on the cover, and Ann Haugo for her bibliography. Above all, we extend profound gratitude to the playwrights—Sierre Adare, Annette Arkeketa, Margaret Bruchac, Marie Clements, Daystar/Rosalie Jones, Diane Glancy, Marcie Rendon, and Spiderwoman Theater—for their powerful words and faith in this project. *Aho*.

Morning Star Children

suzan shown harjo

Morning Star radiates blessings
for Mother Earth
and all the worlds
Her brilliance is
a gift of the Spirit

Maheo sent Morning Star Woman
with Corn and Squash
and Beans and Tobacco
to nourish the People
to feed the Spirit

She delighted the People
as a shining Star Child

She inspired the People
as an Enlightened Elder

She encouraged the People
as an Everyday Woman
sparkling with hope

Maheo told the Cheyenne People:
"The Nation will be strong
So long as the hearts of the women
Are not on the ground"

Dakota and Osage People sing a song, and it is Wakan:
"We are not defeated
While the women are strong"

Messages of Creation
for all Peoples
for all Time

Messages in the hearts of women from Arawak and Acoma
as they turned away from hairy faces
and fixed their eyes on severed hands
and fixed their eyes, and fixed their eyes

Messages in the hearts of women from Washita and Palo Duro Canyon
        as they were stampeded and invaded
        to the sound of ponies screaming in the sunset
        to the sound of screams, to the sound of screams

Messages in the hearts of women from Bosque Redondo and the
Crazy Horse Bar
        as they traded themselves for their children
        as they sold themselves for food and drinks
        as they gave nothing away, as they gave nothing away

Messages in the hearts of women from Warm Springs to Siletz
        as they end a century of missing memory
        as they once again dance in emergence dresses
        as they sing their lost and found song:
                "They Never Touched Me"
                "They Never Touched You"

Messages in the hearts of Native Women

        for all who are touched in unkind ways
        for all who pray to end unholy days
        for all who shelter the disheartened in loving ways

           "They Never Touched You"

           "You Are Blessed By The Morning Star Woman
                And Your Heart Is Not On The Ground"

           "You Are Blessed By The Morning Star Woman
                And The People Are Strong"

           "You Are Blessed By The Morning Star Woman"

           "You Are Blessed By The Morning Star"

           "You Are A Blessed Star Child"

           "You Are Blessed"

"Blessed"

Jaye T. Darby
San Diego State University

"You are blessed," concludes Suzan Shown Harjo, Cheyenne and Hodulgee Muscogee writer and activist, in her powerful poem "Children of the Morning Star" in the preface to this anthology. The word *blessed* articulates an important dimension of contemporary Native women's writing, drawing its power from "traditions of the women," which while reflective of the great plurality of hundreds of Native Nations, diverse traditions, distinctive histories, and centuries-old contests with European encounter, "have, since time immemorial, been centered on continuance" and are inherently life-affirming, according to Paula Gunn Allen, Laguna Pueblo/Sioux writer and scholar.[1] In her seminal book, *The Sacred Hoop: Recovering the Feminine in American Indian Traditions*, Gunn Allen stresses the significance of Native women's writing emanating from positions of strength and grounded in sacred traditions and tribal relationships that honor women. Elaborating woman's revered position in many traditional Native cultures, she writes: "We understand that woman is the sun and the earth: she is grandmother; she is mother; she is Thought, Wisdom, Dream, Reason, Tradition, Memory, Deity, and Life itself. Nos Vemos."[2] Consequently, Gunn Allen rejects both the Judeo-Christian patriarchal construction of women's inferiority and sinfulness and more recent Western feminist theories of subversion, calling them "enterprises that support and maintain the master, feeding his household on our energy, our attention, and our strength."[3] Rather, she advocates writing that is centered on Native perspectives, communities, traditions, values, aesthetics, and issues in all their plurality and complexity, explaining that "principles of self-determination and communitarian or autonomous creativity provide the true loophole of escape" from oppression and offer transformation for Native women, families, communities, and nations.[4] Thus, transformative agency rooted in traditions thousands of years old—not victimization—characterizes recent directions in contemporary Native women's fiction, poetry, and drama.

During the last twenty years, collections devoted to contemporary Native women's fiction and poetry in the United States and Canada have slowly begun to receive the attention these works rightfully deserve. Major anthologies include *A Gathering of Spirit: A Collection of North American Indian Women*, edited by Beth Brant (*Degonwadonti*) in 1984, followed by *That's What She Said: Contemporary Poetry and Fiction by Native American Women*, edited by Rayna Green in 1984; *Spider Woman's Granddaughters: Traditional Tales and Contemporary Writing by Native American Women*, edited by Paula Gunn Allen in 1989; *Writing the Circle: Native Women of Western Canada*, edited by Jeanne Perreault and Sylvia Vance in 1993; *Reinventing the Enemy's Language: Contemporary Native Women's Writings of North America* edited by Joy Harjo and Gloria Bird in 1997; and *Sister Nations: Native American Women Writers on Community*, edited by Heid E. Erdrich and Laura Tohe in 2002. These anthologies present the diversity and richness of Native women's contemporary fiction and poetry.[5] However, publications of drama, for the most part, remain quite limited.

This collection, the first major anthology of Native women's contemporary theater, endeavors to promote Native performance as an evolving art form and seeks to expand the fields of Native theater and women's studies. *Keepers of the Morning Star: An Anthology of Native Women's Theater* includes works from established and new playwrights, including Sierre Adare, Cherokee-Choctaw; Annette Arkeketa, Otoe-Missouria/Muscogee; Margaret Bruchac, Abenaki; Marie Clements, Métis; Daystar/Rosalie Jones, Blackfeet/Pembina Chippewa; Diane Glancy, Cherokee; Marcie Rendon, White Earth Anishinabe, and Spiderwoman Theater, Lisa Mayo, Gloria Miguel, and Muriel Miguel, Kuna/Rappahannock sisters. Their eight plays, drawing on Native storytelling, music, dance, and ceremony from a range of traditions that are fused with western theatrical elements, attest to the innovation of contemporary Native women's theater. While negotiating pressing contemporary Native issues, including family, community, repatriation, sovereignty, urban relocation, and cultural and spiritual appropriation, these playwrights also celebrate the healing power of story and performance. Given the rich array of Native women's theater, we hope this anthology will be the first of many to follow. Other playwrights, such as Elvira and Hortensia Colorado, Linda Hogan, Lee Ann Howe, Vera Manuel, Judy Lee Oliva, and Anna Lee Waters have written important plays that warrant further study and production.[6] This growing body of Native theater opens up new theatrical spaces, broadens boundaries for women's theater, and reshapes contemporary drama by infusing it with compelling stories and new theatrical strategies.

Keepers of the Morning Star grew out of a collaboration and friendship between two women, one European American and one Native, both committed to Native American theater and transformative women's studies. Long conversations at the UCLA American Indian Studies Center between Stephanie Fitzgerald and myself about the power and regrettable continued marginalization of Native women's writing, especially the theater, led to this collection. Inspiration from previous collections of Native women's writing, the playwrights' generosity in sharing their writing, and institutional support from UCLA's American Indian Studies Center Publications Unit and Project HOOP made this anthology a reality.

Each play in this collection responds to an important question raised by Inés Hernández-Ávila, Nimipu/Tejana writer and scholar: "How might the works of Native American women, as mediated sites of recollection and witness, recreate possibilities of discovery and transformation for the readers as well as for the writers themselves?"[7] In the case of the theater, the editors also ask, "and for the audience members?" Thus, while recalling and witnessing the complex interplay of resistance and oppression Native women and communities have endured, each of these plays turns on older Native ceremonial conceptions of agency and transformation that span the millenniums before European contact, from creation stories to the present.[8] These mythic connections to ancestral homes and voices with their multiple resonances enact a kind of theatrical homecoming in contemporary North America—whether in an inner-city apartment, in a dance circle, at a Senate hearing, at a kitchen table, on a high rise, at a Snake Oil show, in a public reading room, or in a graduate student's study. While varying greatly in style, traditions, and subject matter, the works are catalyzed by conceptions of Native spirituality, and by what Gunn Allen describes as "a solid, impregnable, and ineradicable orientation toward a spirit-informed view of the universe, which provides an internal structure to both our consciousness and our art."9 Thus, the order of plays in this anthology follows a circular structure, indicative of traditional oral narratives. The volume begins with Spirit Woman, an Ojibwe ancestor, in Marcie Rendon's *SongCatcher: A Native Interpretation of the Story of Frances Densmore*, and ends with the Abenaki ancestor spirit Molly Ockett in Marge Bruchac's *molly has her say*, attesting to intergenerational continuity that marks much of contemporary Native women's writing.

To enhance the staging and critical study of these works, each playwright articulates her vision through an artist's statement, playwright's notes, and stage directions, offering what Roberta Uno describes as "first voice documentation."10 Throughout the volume, the editors have respected the playwrights' artistic choices concerning the format and style in which they present their work. Consequently, the first thing that may strike readers, directors, and performers is the diversity of theatrical expression throughout this volume.

The opening three plays interrogate Western (mis)appropriations of spirituality, affirming Native spiritual sovereignty by presenting Native traditions that respect ancestors as vital living members of the community. Marcie Rendon's *SongCatcher: A Native Interpretation of the Story of Frances Densmore* interweaves Ojibwe sacred song traditions into contemporary urban life. Rendon, a leading Native writer and activist who combines Native oral tradition with Western playwriting, is concerned with the "interweaving of Native people's spiritual reality coexisting alongside present-time physical reality" (2). By constructing a stage world centered on Ojibwe spirituality within an urban context, this work maintains Ojibwe cultural authority and decenters the privilege of mainstream academic anthropology, especially the work of Frances Densmore, to define the significance of Ojibwe musical traditions.

No Home but the Heart is a dance-drama, an innovative style developed by Daystar/Rosalie Jones, an internationally recognized dancer and choreographer. This work integrates dance and storytelling within the context of theater. Daystar chose "selected events in the lives of her great-grandmother, grandmother, and mother, and tied these events to historical events which affected the resettlement of Native peoples in the late nineteenth century" (81). Through her family story of "displaced French-Cree people from the 'north,' this work acknowledges the universal search for identity, family, and homeland" (81). Employing a panel of ancestors, including her great-grandmother, Susan Big-Knife, as an integral part of the staging, dance, and narration, Daystar takes the audience through the literal and metaphorical search for home of three generations of women from 1837 to 1950. The compelling choreographed sequences attest to the capacity of Native dance to physicalize history, honor family, and lead a person home. The dance-drama concludes with the Jingle Dance, chosen by Daystar because of the Chippewa association with healing.[11] While miles and years away from her homeland, the cadences of the dance and music of the jingles finally bring Daughter home.

Annette Arkeketa, a prominent Native writer and activist, explains that her play, *Ghost Dance*, "is about the repatriation of Native American human remains and cultural patrimony items. It is a story with ancient roots and a contemporary beat that weaves a tragic drama into an ending with hope for our future" (108). Performances of this hard-hitting play have spotlighted repatriation issues: the ongoing conflicts between Native communities seeking proper burials for their ancestors and scientific academics defiling Native human remains as objects of scientific study. *Ghost Dance* lays bare the devastating effects on families and the spiritual denigration of the person whose remains are trapped in boxes and file drawers, thereby exposing scientific practices as sacrilegious and inhumane. The central courtroom scene honors the living presence of ancestors and physicalizes the missing bodies of the ancestors' bones as the spirits of people violently ripped from their graves testify and plead for their return home.

The next two works fuse contemporary and traditional poetics to explore contested conceptions of self and struggles with Native identity and spirituality in a contemporary world. Diane Glancy's *The Woman Who Was a Red Deer Dressed for the Deer Dance* is a poetic exchange between a grandmother and her granddaughter over cross-generational issues of tradition and spirituality. In a recent interview describing her work, Glancy, an award-winning writer, identifies both European modernist and Cherokee spiritual influences. She describes herself "jokingly" as "in the Jackson Pollock school of drama, where you just dribble words here and there, and somehow if you stand back far enough, they connect, a kind of surreal gathering of scenes." She also seeks to include "the seen and unseen world," recognizing that "in the past, the ancestors can show up at anytime; it's a living, fluid narrative."[12] This unique fusion of styles gives *The Woman Who Was a Red Deer Dressed for the Deer Dance* its lyricism and ceremonial power.

Marie Clements, a leading First Nations performer and playwright, developed *Urban Tattoo* as a one-woman performance piece that employs poetic stream of consciousness and multimedia staging to probe the denigration of a Métis woman in an urban setting and her spiritual return to the tribal community. According to Clements, "The impulse came from blood memories, the place of dreams and hope, the knowledge of transformation as a form of survival, and our own deep rhythm that propels us forward despite the gravity of past scars" (206). As a stream-of-consciousness journey, *Urban Tattoo* enacts scarred geographies and psychological dislocations as Rosemarie endures the devastating jolts of urban life—poverty, sexual exploitation, disillusionment, and alienation—and follows her return to the mythic wholeness and balance of her tribal center.

The fifth work, *Winnetou's Snake Oil Show from Wigwam City*, showcases the signature improvisational performance style of Spiderwoman Theater, the oldest running feminist theater in the United States, which was founded in 1975 by Lisa Mayo, Gloria Miguel, and Muriel Miguel. The three sisters get their name from the Hopi Spiderwoman deity and "call their technique of working 'storyweaving,' in which they create designs and weave stories with words and movement, creating an overlay of interlocking stories, where fantasy and power are comically intertwined" (230). *Winnetou's Snake Oil Show from Wigwam City* boldly interrogates the (mis)appropriation of Native people's cultures and sacred rituals by European hobbyists and European American wannabes. A Native agitprop satire, *Winnetou* juxtaposes over-the-top, in-your-face stereotypical constructions of Karl May's German legend of Winnetou as a noble savage in a vanishing race, the Princess Pocahontas cliche, and plastic shamanism with the sisters and Hortensia Colorado performing as themselves. Spiderwoman Theater's enactment of each stereotype becomes an act of recovery, a theatrical phenomenon that Ann Haugo identifies as "not simply a re-appropriation of the dominant culture's stereotype, but a calculated resistance of the stereotype itself, while inhabiting the corporeal form of the stereotype."[13] At the end of the play, Lisa Mayo, Gloria and Muriel Miguel, and Hortensia Colorado step forward as performance artists, taking control of these distortions and defining themselves as Native women.

Through traditional storytelling, the final two works in this collection poignantly restage Native history, invoke the significance of words, and deconstruct European American versions of history. Sierra Adare wrote *Takeover of the Andrew Jackson Reading Room* while she was a Visiting Fellow in Cornell University's American Indian Program "to make the history of the Indigenous Peoples of North America come alive for students" (264) and to address the silences and misrepresentations of Native peoples in mainstream American history. Using a writing club at the Andrew Jackson Reading Room as a framing device, Adare's Native characters literally rewrite history while challenging mainstream American history and Native stereotypes in fiction and history. Although written for college classroom staged readings, and performed in Native American studies courses at Cornell University and other nearby colleges, this play also has the potential for a full-scale production.

Marge Bruchac's *molly has her say* artfully turns on the Abenaki storytelling tradition to remember and honor the voices of Native people of the Northeast. Bruchac, a traditional Abenaki storyteller, writes that this work "focuses on the 'hidden histories' of northeastern Algonkian Indian peoples, and the conflict between Anglo-American written histories of disappearance and Native American oral histories of persistence" (323). Emphasizing the enduring power of story, she explains that this play "was not so much written, as driven, by the traditional songs, the teaching stories, and the voices of the old ones whose spirits are still in this land we call Ndakinna" (318). Molly Ockett, an eighteenth-century Pequawket doctress, and Old Mali, voices of the ancestor spirits, both return to Molly Marie, their disengaged descendant who ironically is completely unaware of her ancestral past even though she is a graduate student of Abenaki history. To counter the mainstream history she is learning in academic texts, they offer traditional stories to help her understand and honor her heritage. Told through the rich cadences and wisdom of Molly Ockett, the play demonstrates how story itself becomes sacred, as only the Abenaki strawberry story has the power to begin to heal centuries-old cruelties and touch the heart of a new generation.

Beth Brant, Bay of Quinte Mohawk writer, describes "Native women's writing as a gift, a give-away of the truest meaning." She believes that creative work is an embodiment of experience and spirit: "Our spirit, our sweat, our tears, our laughter, our love, our anger, our bodies are distilled into words that we bead together to make power. Not power *over* anything. Power. Power that speaks to hearts as well as to minds."[14] Emphasizing the depth of this power, Brant locates the work of many contemporary Native women writers within "an ancient, cultural consciousness," where "the memory of history, of culture, of land, of Nation, is always present, like another being."[15] Each play in this volume, as well as many others by Native women playwrights, bears witness to this power, honors the memories, and celebrates the enduring strength of women in Native life. All women benefit from this gift. *Aho.*

Notes

1. Paula Gunn Allen, *The Sacred Hoop: Recovering the Feminine in American Indian Traditions*, rev. ed. (Boston: Beacon, 1992), 267.

2. Gunn Allen, *The Sacred Hoop*, 268.

3. Paula Gunn Allen, *Off the Reservation: Reflections on Boundary Busting, Border-Crossing Loose Canons* (Boston: Beacon Press, 1998), 174.

4. Gunn Allen, *Off the Reservation*, 174.

5. Beth Brant (*Degonwadonti*), ed., *A Gathering of Spirit: A Collection of North American Indian Women* (Rockland, ME: Sinister Wisdom Books, 1984); Rayna Green, ed., *That's What She Said: Contemporary Poetry and Fiction by Native American Women* (Bloomington: Indiana University Press, 1984); Paula Gunn Allen, ed., *Spider Woman's Granddaughters: Traditional Tales and Contemporary Writing by Native American Women* (Boston: Beacon Press, 1989); Jeanne Perreault and Sylvia

Vance, *Writing the Circle: Native Women of Western Canada* (Norman: University of Oklahoma Press, 1993); Joy Harjo and Gloria Bird, eds. *Reinventing the Enemy's Language: Contemporary Native Women's Writings of North America* (New York: W.W. Norton, 1997); Heid E. Erdrich and Laura Tohe, eds. *Sister Nations: Native American Women Writers on Community* (St. Paul: Native Voices, Minnesota Historical Society Press, 2002).

6.   For more information, see the website for Native American Women Playwrights Archive at Miami University: http://staff.lib.muohio.edu/nawpa/NAWPA.html.

7.   Inés Hernández-Ávila, "Relocations Upon Relocations: Home, Language, and Native American Women's Writings," *The American Indian Quarterly* 19:4 (Fall 1995): 504.

8.   For an in-depth discussion of the ceremonial tradition in Native American literature, see Gunn Allen, *The Sacred Hoop*, esp. 1–117. For an analysis of fourth-wave Native theater, based on these older conceptions of transformation, see Jaye T. Darby, "Re-Imagining the Stage: Tradition and Transformation in Native Theater," *The Color of Theater: Race, Ethnicity, and Contemporary Performance*, ed. Roberta Uno with Lucy Mae San Pablo Burns (London: Continuum, 2002),61–81.

9.   Gunn Allen, *The Sacred Hoop*, 165.

10.   Roberta Uno, Introduction, *The Color of Theater: Race, Ethnicity, and Contemporary Performance*, 8.

11.   Daystar (Rosalie M. Jones), "*No Home but the Heart* and Project HOOP," Multidisciplinary Session: "Project HOOP (Honoring Our Origins and People through Native Theater, Education, and Community Development): Multidisciplinary Directions in Native Theater," Paper presented at the Association for Theatre in Higher Education (ATHE) Annual Conference, San Diego, 25 July 2002.

12.   Quoted in Scarlet Cheng, "Album of a Native American Past," *Los Angeles Times*, Calendar, 2 June 2002, 38.

13.   Ann Haugo, "Princess Pocahontas Talks Back and John Smith Better Listen: Re-presenting the White Imagination," Paper presented at the Association for Theatre in Higher Education Conference, 1995, 1.

14.   Beth Brant, "The Good Red Road: Journeys of Homecoming in Native Women's Writing," *American Indian Culture and Research Journal* 21:1 (1997): 195.

15.   Brant, "'The Good Red Road,'"197, 203–4.

SongCatcher

A NATIVE INTERPRETATION OF THE STORY OF FRANCES DENSMORE

Marcie R. Rendon

Artist's Statement

Almost all of what I write involves the interweaving of Native people's spiritual reality coexisting alongside present-time physical reality. This concept is based on the real-life belief systems of indigenous people that exist as vibrantly today as in the past.

Theatrically, I am interested in combining Native oral tradition with Western playwriting. Historically our storytellers sang, danced, and mimed the history of our peoples in the center of the village. I strive as creator and writer for the same integration my ancestors had of dialogue, music, and movement by using the modern stage and tools of the playwright.

It is also my hope to give voice to characters often silenced: Native peoples, women, children, and those who live in poverty. By giving voice to these people I hope to facilitate access to theater for other Native Americans as writers, actors, technicians, or theater-goers—that for every door opened to me, at least five more will open for other Native people.

All people, throughout time, have recorded historical events of importance to them. Some have done this through song, some through oral storytelling, some through written word, and some by drawings on cave walls. The human need to record for posterity seems to have been around since humans first recognized their own mortality.

SongCatcher

Characters

SPIRIT WOMAN, a spirit, Native woman. With the exception of the casino scene, she is dressed very plainly, maybe just a buckskin dress. She is trying to reach through to Jack to give him "his song."

JACK, modern, young, Native man. Is trying hard to be "traditional" and is searching for his history. Sings on a drum at powwows. Once he discovers Frances Densmore's books he becomes obsessed with her. In last ceremony scene he becomes Midé elder in the past.

BILL, elder Native man. Friend and spiritual consultant for Jack and Chris.

CHRIS, Jack's girlfriend, roommate. Modern, young Native woman. Works for the city's sanitation department. She is strong-willed, with a sure sense of self.

FRANCES DENSMORE, the woman herself. She appears here as a spirit from the past. As a younger woman she is excited about the world, but as the story progresses she becomes more rigid, self-contained.

MARGARET (MAGGIE) DENSMORE, Frances's younger sister, more consistently outgoing and bubbly than Francis ever was. Appears in dream/spirit scenes.

LIZZIE, Frances's lifelong friend. Their relationship gives the hint of mutual attraction.

OLD MAN SPIRIT, an ancient spirit in the spirit world.

MRS. DENSMORE, Frances and Margaret's mother.

FATHER, Native man in dream.

MOTHER, Native woman in dream.

GERONIMO, scene at World's Fair. Is Jack as Geronimo in a dream.

MR. WINDGROW, Dakota man who performs healing ceremony for Frances.

WINONA, Windgrow's wife.

MR. WILLIAMS, Winnebago man who puts love medicine on Frances.

GLADYS, Mr. Williams's daughter.

MAIN'GANS, Midé man who sings his songs for Frances and as a consequence is banned from the Midé lodge and his wife dies.

MAIN'GANS'S WIFE, appears in last ceremony scene.

Setting

Inner-city apartment. Living room and kitchen area are basically one large room. To the back is a door that leads to a bedroom. On the left is a door leading out of the apartment. There is a window in the kitchen. Frances's parlor scenes and some other scenes happen on the stage wings. Lighting is a key component of the scenes, as is Native music.

Playwright's Note

For Native peoples of this continent, stories of social, familial, and historical consequence were passed generation to generation, either through the practice of oral storytelling; the creation of songs, sometimes with accompanying dance movement; or, as in the case of the Ojibwe Midé religious society, pictographs inscribed on birchbark scrolls. The Maple Suger song is a "real" Ojibwe (Red Lake) song, an Indian song with vocables. It is also printed with Western musical notation in Densmore's work.

While much has been written about Frances Densmore, there are few, if any, written accounts of the impact Frances's work had on Native people of the continent. It is through her words that Native songs and customs have been interpreted and passed on as historical fact in Western academic circles. Raised in a staunchly Victorian family and educated at the prestigious Oberlin Conservatory of Music in Ohio, Frances approached her study and recordings of Native music from a Eurocentric perspective. Rather than change her worldview, she tried to fit Native music and culture into her perceptions. Yet historically Native people acquired songs either through fasting, vision quests, or dreams. An individual's song was their sacred possession, not to be sung by others or recorded for posterity, but to be passed orally, generation to generation.

It leaves me, as a Native woman, wondering, "What did my elders think of this woman? How did they perceive her intrusion into their private and spiritual lives? And it is those perceptions that I have explored in this play. First, there is the question: By recording these songs did Frances really capture the spirit of the song, and are they locked up in Washington, D.C.?

This is a belief held by some indigenous people. To them the solution might be to return the wax cylinders to their respective tribes for the surviving generations to learn the songs anew. Others have proposed burying the cylinders much in the same way the bones of Native peoples on display in museums have been turned over to their respective tribes for appropriate burial. Another proposal would have the cylinders recorded onto cassette or compact disc and distributed free of charge to Native peoples.

Another perspective explored in the play is that the spirits of Native ancestors continue to sing the songs in hopes that Native people will once again return to the traditional practices of fasting, vision questing, and dreaming. In this way, the songs will be passed on to new generations.

The second question is: Who was Frances Densmore, really? Was her voluminous output really all her own work? Did her compulsion for perfection in her work alienate her from human connection?

Of more interest to this writer was a story handed down by a Dakota woman, Susan Windgrow, to her granddaughter, Rose

Bluestone. While there are documented references to Densmore having a nervous breakdown, suffering from bouts of melancholy, and overall preferring an isolated lifestyle in which to immerse herself in her study, this story proposes that Densmore was actually the victim of an Indian spell. Given an overall propensity by Native people to believe in "medicine power" either for healing or casting spells, I chose to explore this aspect of Frances's life within the context of the play. Her dependency on her sister, Margaret, is also explored.

In this age of multiculturalism, much larger questions are being asked by this play: From whose perspective is history told? Whose stories get accorded academic credibility? Who determines whose version of history is accurate? How does a history told from a monocultural point of view shape people's perceptions not only of historical times and events, but also people's perceptions of themselves?

According to scholars of Densmore's work, she is to be lauded and remembered as a precise ethnomusicologist who diligently and in the face of much opposition recorded the songs of a dying, vanishing people. To many Native peoples she was an interloper, one in a long line of many who insinuated themselves into Native communities to make a name for themselves at the expense of the people themselves. Rather than viewing themselves as a vanishing race, the Native people of Frances's time were struggling to keep their cultures intact while facing forced acculturation and assimilation policies by the federal government.

When students are told, "Densmore recorded these songs so they wouldn't be lost forever," are they also told about the four hundred years of attempted genocide and extermination that was directed at Native peoples prior to her decision to record for posterity's sake? Are they told that those people did not vanish? The stories, songs, and religions of The People have been passed on to modern-day generations, and for the most part have been passed on to us by our elders who never heard of or read anything by Frances Densmore.

And when Native students hear, "Densmore recorded these songs so they wouldn't be lost forever," the covert message to them is to be grateful to this white woman who preserved their culture for them.

The underlying message is that the real songs are locked up in Washington, D.C., instead of in the hearts and spirits of Native people themselves. It is a systematic erosion of a people's belief in themselves, their own history, and their very existence as a living, breathing, modern people.

Production History

SongCatcher: A Native Interpretation of the Story of Frances Densmore was commissioned by The Great American History Theater in St. Paul, Minnesota. It had its premiere in April 1998. Ron Peluso was the artistic director and Casey Stang was the director. In 2000, the Skywoman Festival presented a staged reading of the play.

Opening Scene

1800s Ojibwe encampment on a warm night. People are sleeping outside. SPIRIT WOMAN *goes through the camp. She stops by three or four individuals and sings fragments of songs to them.*

· Act I

Scene I

Two Native men of today are sitting in an inner-city apartment living room singing a 49 song at a powwow drum. Beside them is a tape player. They laugh as they finish the 49 song.

JACK
   (*Turning on song on tape.*) Hey Uncle, listen to this.

(*They listen for a bit.*)

BILL
   That's an old Red Lake song.

(*Drumming softly with the tape.*)

BILL
   Sounds like that Ponemah song.

JACK
   (*Starting to drum with him.*) Yeah, but this is the really old version.

BILL
   Where'd you find that tape?

JACK
   Charlie Stately's, down at the Indian Center.

(*They listen through to end of song, where* FRANCES DENSMORE's *voice is heard.*)

BILL
   Who's that?

JACK
   Frances Densmore.

BILL

   Who?

JACK

   Some white woman who went around to different reservations back at the turn of the century recording our songs.

BILL

   So that's some guy a hundred years ago singing?

JACK

   Yep.

BILL

   Hmm. You're trying to learn that?

JACK

   Sure am.

BILL

   Off a tape?

JACK

   Sure, why not? She taped a lot of the elders so our songs wouldn't be forgotten.

BILL

   Seems I heard something about that.

(Midé drum image is flashed on theater walls. Pictures of men who sang for her are interspersed with drum image.)

JACK

   Here, I'll play it again.

BILL

   Nah, that's all right.

JACK

   (Ignoring BILL.) I was thinkin it might be cool to learn this older version—show up them boys from Ponemah. Crank out the really old version up at Leech Lake powwow.

BILL

Seems to me like both those songs—the new one and the old one—are Red Lake songs, let them boys have them. You probably got a song in you waiting to come out. Listen for that one.

JACK

Think so? (*Drums softly for a while.*) I don't know, Uncle, my family's idea of good music was Hank Williams and Charlie Pride or hymns on Sunday morning.

BILL

Well, at least they had Grand Old Opry taste, could have wanted you to go to the New York Opry.

We all got a song. We all do. Just gotta get quiet enough to hear it. That's where the old songs came from. The people fasted for their songs or dreamt them. Or a song was given to you.

JACK

Yeah?

(*A twenty-something, young Native woman,* CHRIS, *enters the apartment. She is dressed in a work uniform, and is dirty and sweaty. She looks wearily at the two men on her way to the kitchen. The two men exchange glances, sing softer, finally quit, and finish their drinks.* BILL *gets up to leave.*)

JACK

I know if I don't go to work tomorrow, Chris'll put me on a fast for the rest of the week.

BILL

I'd consider going to work myself then if I were you. Hey, Chris, how's the city sanitation business?

CHRIS

Dirty. What are you guys up to?

BILL

Listening to this tape Jack got down at Charlie's.

JACK

Listen to this Chris— (*Starts to sing old song from Red Lake.*)

CHRIS

Nice, where'd you learn that?

JACK

Off this tape.

CHRIS

Who recorded that?

(BILL *and* JACK *answer simultaneously with the next two lines.*)

BILL

Some white woman.

JACK

Frances Densmore, she recorded a bunch of the elders. Listen.

(JACK *turns on the tape.*)

CHRIS

So that's some guy a hundred years ago singing? Spooky.

BILL

That's what I thought. I'm going down to the Indian Center, catch cover all at Bingo. Later Jack. Chris.

(BILL *exits.* JACK *continues listening to the song, drumming along softly, trying to sing a little with it.*)

CHRIS

Aiye, turn it off. I don't like the idea of some dead guy singing in my living room.

(*There is silence in the room as* JACK *shuts off the tape.* CHRIS *takes off work clothes and puts on jeans and t-shirt.* JACK *drums softly without singing.*)

CHRIS

What'd you do today?

JACK

Not much. Bill came by.

CHRIS

Thought you were going to Daily Labor.

JACK

Guess I overslept.

CHRIS

(*Starting to look through cupboards.*) If you're not gonna work, seems the least you could do is get some food in the house. Christ, I'm starved.

JACK

Go sit down, I'll make somethin (*not getting up, still drumming softly*).

CHRIS

Nah, forget it.

(*She gets herself a bowl of cereal, sits and eats, and ignores* JACK.)

JACK

Look, I'll go tomorrow morning. Wake me when you get up.

CHRIS

Psssh!

JACK

Why you gotta get on my case? We both know the city wanted to hire minorities. That's why you got that fancy old job in the first place. They got an Indian and a woman—two for one. I applied, too, remember?

CHRIS

Right. A day late—cause you had to wait to get paid at the Red Lake powwow.

JACK

(*Trying to humor her.*) Hey, I'm traditional. Not my fault I don't get paid as much to sing as you get to haul garbage.

CHRIS

Gimme a break. Lots of guys work and sing at the drum.

JACK

Yeah, well they grew up hearing the songs. Here I am an old man ...

CHRIS

Right.

JACK

... and don't know half the songs they know. I have to catch up.
That's why I got this tape.

CHRIS

I think those songs are sacred. I don't understand why they let
some white woman record them.

JACK

Dunno. Maybe she gave them whiskey, or somethin better than
commodities to eat.

CHRIS

Yeah, right.

JACK

Well, I'm going to learn it.

(*He turns the tape back on.*)

CHRIS

Real traditional.

(JACK, *disgusted, gets up, puts on hat, and goes to door.*)

CHRIS

Where you going?

JACK

Out.

CHRIS

Why is it that every time you get upset your solution is to walk out
the door?

JACK

Every time I try and learn a little bit more about myself, who I am,
you gotta make smart remarks. I don't need to stick around just
so you can put me down.

CHRIS

How am I putting you down?

JACK

That smart-ass remark about being traditional. I can't help it my family wasn't into the old ways. They were just trying to make a living. Every time I turn around, I gotta prove how Indian I am.

CHRIS

I didn't mean it to sound like that. But being Indian isn't just about learning songs to sing at a drum. I just wish you'd go to work once in awhile. Either work or help out around here a little more.

JACK

I try.

CHRIS

Well, not enough. (*Pause.*) All I'm saying is that being Indian is something you live. It's inside you. You can't learn it from a tape.

JACK

So you're saying I'm not Indian.

CHRIS

Chrii.... I didn't say that.

JACK

(*Exiting.*) You may as well....

(CHRIS *puts bowl in sink, lies down on couch, and falls asleep.*)

Scene 2

Dream: Two scenes simultaneously on stage. It's a warm evening. One is a Dakota encamp-ment. The Dakota side is in shadow. In the encampment, a hunting party has returned home, and the hunters, with drum and dance, are recounting the hunting trip. The only sounds are the drumming, and what is visually seen is the dance of the hunters. The other is the Densmore parlor. A piano is in the room and a young FRANCES DENSMORE *and her sister* MARGARET *are in their nightgowns leaning on the open windowsill listening to the drums in the distance.*

FRANCES
  What is that?

MARGARET
  Heathens! Savages! What if they're on the warpath?!

FRANCES
  Hush.

MARGARET
  What if they come here Fannie and carry us off and make us slaves?

FRANCES
  The Indians don't have slaves, Margaret.

MARGARET
  But they take women captives. Daddy and his soldiers would have to come rescue us!

FRANCES
  Shhh, listen.

MARGARET
  They're getting closer. They've come to scalp us! Maybe we should hide in the cellar! If they try to take us I'll scream and scream.

MRS. DENSMORE
  (*Entering the parlor or voiceover.*) Maggie, hush, quit this foolishness.

FRANCES
  What are they doing, Mother?

MRS. DENSMORE
    Singing and dancing, Frances. Those Indians are interesting
    people with customs that are different from ours, but they will
    not scalp you. There is no reason to be afraid of them. Now you
    two get to bed, go now. Your father will be back from his meet-
    ing shortly and young women your age should be in bed sleeping.
    (*As* FRANCES *and* MARGARET *exit, she calls after them.*) Don't forget to say
    your prayers.

Scene 3

*Dream continues: Dakota encampment and Densmore parlor much later that same night. Again, scenes are happening simultaneously. On the Dakota side, a young man (*JACK*) and woman (*CHRIS*), obviously in love, are walking, whispering, laughing softly, trying hard to be quiet. They are shy with each other. In the Densmore parlor, FRANCES is sitting at the piano. Very quietly she is using the lower keys in an attempt to recreate the drum sounds she heard earlier. In the Dakota encampment, the young man plays a Dakota love song on a wooden flute for the woman with him. The young woman laughs, is shy and embarrassed, and moves backstage away from young man.*

Scene continues: Because FRANCES is concentrating on her attempts to make the piano sound like the drum, she is unaware of the flute song. Frustrated, she softly plays some scales, then begins playing a Brahms's lullaby. The young couple hear the piano. They listen for a pause and the young man begins playing Brahms along with the piano. The young woman giggles and exits stage. Young man listens for a beat, then exits off stage.

MRS. DENSMORE
    Frances!

FRANCES
    Mama, listen!

(*She plays a few bars of her attempt to sound like the drum.*)

FRANCES
    It almost sounds like what they're playing, don't you think?

MRS. DENSMORE
    Almost.

FRANCES

I'm going to listen every night. Pretty soon I'll be playing just like an Indian.

MRS. DENSMORE

I think what you need to do, daughter, is get to bed. You can thump out major chords in the morning when the rest of the world is ready to be awake. Now goodnight.

FRANCES

Goodnight Mama.

(FRANCES *stops playing and runs off stage. Stage darkens.*)

Scene 4

Dream continues: Dakota encampment. Early evening. MAGGIE is seen sneaking up on encampment. MAGGIE has reached the edge of the encampment, where a man and woman are cooking something over a fire. MAGGIE is discovered by the woman.

WINONA

Hey!

(MAGGIE *jumps up to run but is caught by man.*)

WINDGROW

Aaah, a wasichu. Do you want to keep her as your helper or should we have a feast?

MAGGIE

Let me go!

WINONA

Windgrow, stop, you are scaring her.

WINDGROW

Her? She is the one who snuck up on us.

WINONA

It's okay, he's just teasing. Are you lost? Who are you?

MAGGIE

Margaret Densmore, my father is a *general* in the United States Army, you better let me go!

WINDGROW

She is a spy. Or a scout for the United States Army.

MAGGIE

I am not, let me go.

WINONA

(*Handing her a bowl of soup.*) Let her go, Windgrow. Here, as long as you've come to visit, eat. Go on, eat.

MAGGIE

Thank you ma-am. This is very good.

WINDGROW

Should be, newborn chunka.

MAGGIE

Chunka?

WINONA

Don't listen to him. You better eat, then get back home before your parents come looking for you.

WINDGROW

How do we know you're not a spy? What are you doing sneaking up on us?

MAGGIE

We heard some singing the other night and I wanted to find out what you were doing.

WINONA

We were having ceremony. My niece is sick.

MAGGIE

Ceremony?

WINONA

A doctoring. When we get sick we have ceremony and our doctor makes us well.

WINDGROW

He can also put a spell on you. Twist your leg, so you would have to walk like a dog whose foot has been caught in a beaver trap. There's a spy in the army barracks over there, walks like that, cause he was spying on our village.

WINONA

Stop Windgrow! He's just telling you stories, my girl. Our doctor is a good man, he can cure things even your doctor can't. He knows all the medicines and herbs that grow for miles around here.

WINDGROW

So if you ever get sick and your doctor can't cure you, you come back here. You don't need to spy. You want to know something you just come right here, if anyone stops you, tell them you are a friend of Windgrow.

MAGGIE

I better get home. Thank you ma-am for the soup.

WINDGROW

Chunka.

WINONA

You go straight home. It will be dark soon.

WINDGROW

(*As* MAGGIE *walks away,* WINDGROW *whistles.*) Chunka! Come here boy.

(MAGGIE *takes off running with hand over mouth.* WINDGROW *laughs while* WINONA *scolds him.*)

Scene 5

Lights up. Next evening. JACK *and* CHRIS *are on couch in living room.*

JACK

Happy babe? I worked seven hours at Precision Tool today. They might need me tomorrow again. You were supposed to wake me. You're the one who slept right through the alarm. I had to holler three times to wake you up.

CHRIS

I don't know. I work my butt off all day hauling garbage then at night I dream some old white girl thinks she's going to get scalped by Indians. And then another one thinks she's a scout for the U.S. Army. Sometimes I dream so hard I feel like I worked all night.

JACK

Poor babe. Check this out. It's a book written by that woman who taped those songs I was singing yesterday. I went by the library after work.

CHRIS

So that's why supper wasn't ready again when I got home, huh?

JACK

(*Ignoring her.*) She taped hundreds of songs, wrote them all down in these books.

(CHRIS *looks through book.*)

JACK

Check this out.

(*He takes the blanket off the drum, which has Ojibwe pictographs drawn on side.*)

CHRIS

What did you do?

JACK

I copied some of the drawings from the book.

CHRIS

You can't do that. Those are pictographs.

JACK

So?

CHRIS

Those are Midé drawings. You can't just put them anyplace.

JACK

Why not? It's my drum. I think they're cool.

CHRIS

You can't do that. Those are religious drawings. Our elders kept the religion alive through those pictures. They aren't supposed to be public. What if Bill comes over and sees that? You're going to have to paint over them.

JACK

Why?

CHRIS

And get rid of that book, too.

JACK

It's just a book, Chris. They're just drawings.

CHRIS

They're sacred. Our people went to prison or mental institutions for practicing our religion. All this stuff had to go underground. People kept these teachings secret for a long long time because it was dangerous to practice them.

JACK

If you know so much why don't you teach me?

CHRIS

I don't know that much.

JACK

Yes you do. You just never want to talk about it.

CHRIS

I don't know how to talk about it. If you want to learn, then you have to take tobacco to an elder and begin learning that way, not from some book.

JACK

Well, I'm glad she wrote these things down. I try to learn and no one will even talk to me. If they do talk, it's just in riddles. Even though Bill speaks English, sometimes I can't understand a thing he says. Or else he tells me I'll dream about it when I'm ready to know it. I'd have to sleep ten years in order to learn what I've already learned from this book.

CHRIS

But you're not really learning it.

JACK

What do you mean I'm not learning it. I read. The stuff's in my brain. I was a straight-A student, I learn fast.

CHRIS

It's more than that. This is different than learning to read or write. Or getting straight As in calculus at school. It's a different kind of learning.

JACK

Well, my parents didn't tell me this stuff growing up. All they wanted me to do was get good grades, grow up, and get a job. I was the only Indian guy in the whole school. All I knew about being Indian was the guys on the football team calling me Chief. Now I want to learn my history, learn some things about who I really am.

CHRIS

Then you should learn it the right way. Learn it with your whole being. I don't think it's right that she wrote all this down. And it makes me nervous that you even have it here. Who knows what kind of spirits you're inviting in.

JACK

It's not like I'm praying with it. Just reading this isn't going to hurt anything.

CHRIS

Maybe not, but you're opening yourself up, and me, our home, to stuff you don't understand. Don't you remember Bill telling us we have to be careful even with our thoughts. Whatever you put out comes back....

JACK

Okay, I won't THINK about it.

CHRIS

Chrii—

JACK

Well, I'm glad she did this. Besides, all I'm trying to do is learn some songs out of here. I'm not trying to be a medicine man. I just want to learn a song I can call my own.

CHRIS

I'm trying to tell you, it won't be your own.

JACK

Well, I don't think anyone else remembers any of these, especially if they're all dead.

CHRIS

See, see, that's what I mean. That's the kind of thinking that will get you in trouble.

JACK

What do you mean?

CHRIS

Forget it! You're supposed to respect the dead. I'm going to bed.

JACK

I do respect the dead. Maybe one way for me to honor the elders and learn who I am is to learn one of these songs.

CHRIS

I don't think so. And get those drawings off that drum.

(*She goes to bed while* JACK *reads a book, tries to sing some of the songs. He falls asleep with the book on his chest. Stage goes dark.*)

Scene 6

(*Two scenes on stage simultaneously. Dim lights come up on* JACK *who is sleeping on the couch.* SPIRIT WOMAN *stands over him singing softly throughout the following exchange. Off to the other side of the stage, lights come up on* FRANCES *at a desk. This is* JACK's *dream. Only voices, a man's and a woman's, are heard.*)

WOMAN
Jack, are you done with your homework?

MAN
How was football practice son?—Just be proud of who you are, Jack, don't let them bother you.

WOMAN
Best thing to do with those kind of people, Jack, is just ignore them.

MAN
That's right son, show them who's the better man. Being Indian isn't anything to be ashamed of.

(CHRIS's *dream: A younger* FRANCES *is sitting at their kitchen table writing. Jumbo, the elephant, walks past her and into the bedroom.*)

FRANCES (*Voiceover*)
Dearest Lizzie,

I received your splendid letter in due time and enjoyed it highly. Went to Barnum's circus and saw Jumbo awhile ago. Well, after that episode I guess the next event was dancing school. Papa bought me the most beautiful dress to wear when I went down and played for Shaw and his dutifuls one evening ... had a really good time. Then Friday came the Masonic celebration. Annie, Judy, Ella, and I roosted on the Episcopal fence and saw the splendid parade....

(JACK's *side.* SPIRIT WOMAN *is still singing, but moving away from him and beckoning to him to follow her. He sits up in his sleep.*)

JACK
What does she want, Mom?

WOMAN

> I don't know why you ask these questions. Some things are better left in the past.

MAN

> My parents were beat in boarding school to forget this stuff.

JACK

> But she's trying to tell me something.

WOMAN

> It's just a dream, Jack.

MAN

> We have to adapt to the world as it is today, Jack, not be living in the past.

JACK

> But what does she want with me?

(*Light fades.* SPIRIT WOMAN *sings last fragment of song to* JACK *before light.*)

(*Lights come up dimly on two Native spirits—one is a very, very ancient, spirit,* OLD MAN SPIRIT, *and the other is* SPIRIT WOMAN, *crying.*)

OLD MAN SPIRIT

> Spirit Woman, please, they will come back.

SPIRIT WOMAN

> They come back, but they are different. It's almost like they aren't our children anymore. They don't speak Anishinabe. They don't know how to understand their own dreams. They don't fast or go to ceremony so they can hear me when I sing to them.

OLD MAN SPIRIT

> Their world is changing. The gifts we have to give them are the same as always. And they won't forget. They will relearn what they need to. When the Creator made the Anishinabe, it was only our people here, but others came. They took our teachings and locked them up. They took our people away from the natural world. Boarding schools, prisons, adoptive families. They try to

lock up the souls of our people. But the children are strong, Spirit Woman, their spirits are strong. They will come home. There is a natural order to all creation. The eagle still flies.

SPIRIT WOMAN

I keep trying to give him his song. And the only one who is interested is the spirit of this woman Frances.

OLD MAN SPIRIT

That is one spirit who has been searching for peace for a long time.

(*Lights down.*)

Act II

Scene I

Lights up on apartment living room, a few days later. JACK *is reading* FRANCES's *book when* CHRIS *enters from work.* FRANCES's *dress is hanging over bedroom door.* SPIRIT WOMAN *is on opposite end of couch from* JACK.

CHRIS

> Can't you put that thing down? I'm tired of working all day and coming home to find you learning your traditions from some woman who ripped us off in the first place.

JACK

> I am working. Studying. Relearning my history. I went over to the historical society today. They have a whole exhibit up about Frances.

CHRIS

> So now you're on a first name basis with her, huh?

JACK

> She did things other women didn't do at that time. She and her sister traveled by canoe into the woods to go record the elders.

CHRIS

> Bet the women of the village were real impressed to see her pulling up. My grandmothers paddled canoes up and down these rivers for centuries, built them too. Some white woman travels one river up north and gets written up in history. I'm impressed.

JACK

> Come on, that's not all she did. She traveled all over the country recording songs. It was something women didn't do at that time. They got married and had babies.

CHRIS

> It's not something white women did. I'm Ojibwe, we traveled by canoe, with or without kids.

JACK
Well, she got famous for it.

CHRIS
Only because no one ever took any interest in Native women.

JACK
What about "the babe"—Pocahontas?

CHRIS
Right! Only because she saved some white man's butt!

JACK
Alright ... what about Sacajawea? We studied her in seventh grade social studies.

CHRIS
I'm surprised they haven't edited out the part about her doing all that with a baby on her back. If she'd been really smart, she'd have walked them right back into the Atlantic Ocean.

JACK
What's this got to do with Frances Densmore?

CHRIS
Not everything is truth. They were probably just messing with her. If you really want to learn the traditions, talk to Bill. But you better get rid of those Midé drawings before we have him over again.

JACK
Quit worrying so much. Why don't you just teach me?

CHRIS
We're supposed to be partners. You have to learn these things someplace else.

JACK
Well, that's why I got this book.

CHRIS

Some things you can't learn in a book. If you would listen to Bill instead of just trying to get songs out of him, maybe you'd learn more.

JACK

Ah, come on, sit by Jack here. I'll read you our history. If you hear anything that isn't accurate you tell me. So you won't exactly be teaching me. This is filled with songs from our ceremonies. Somebody's gotta learn these. Bring them back.

CHRIS

Nope, that's not for me. I just got off work. I'm hungry!

JACK

Relax. I worked all last week. Got enough food in the fridge to last us a month. Sit down, take it easy.

CHRIS

No. I work, I'm hungry. The least you could do is have some food ready when I get home!

JACK

(*Teasing.*) So what? Now you're a feminist and I'm the house husband? Spose when I met you at the Leech Lake powwow all that coffee you kept bringing me at the drum was just a trap to reel me in?

CHRIS

Yeah right, like I had to reel you in. You were sitting there with your mouth open waiting for the hook to drop.

JACK

And I thought you were a traditional woman. Talking about how you knew how to tan hides and would help me make a drum.

CHRIS

And I thought you knew the traditions, sitting there all big. I don't see you going out and bringing home a deer hide for me to tan. The day you bring one home, that's when I'll make you a drum. In the meantime, could you please have some food made so I can eat when I get home?

JACK

(*Goes into kitchen.*) Okay. Tomato or Chicken Noodle.

CHRIS

I been hauling garbage all day. I want some FOOD.

JACK

A bologna sandwich?

CHRIS

Didn't you buy any real food? I want a MEAL. I'll do it myself. And I don't want those drawings on that drum!

(JACK *gets ready to leave and puts on hat.*)

CHRIS

Who's got an attitude now?

JACK

Not me, I'm just taking some tobacco over to Bill. You told me to ask him if I had questions about things. I dreamt the other night about my family and some woman singing. Seems like she wanted me to follow her. Maybe he can help me remember the song or at least figure out what it was she wanted.

CHRIS

(*Barely audible.*) Maybe if you just listened harder.

JACK

What?

CHRIS

Nothin. Give Bill some tobacco from me and ask him what it means when you see elephants parading around your bed.

JACK

(*Leaving.*) Elephants? And you get on me about not being traditional enough.

(SPIRIT WOMAN *follows him out, leaves door ajar.*)

CHRIS

And shut the damn door when you leave!

(CHRIS *finishes eating. Picks up* FRANCES's *book and reads some on couch and falls asleep.* FRANCES, *in her early twenties, dressed in an 1800s-style petticoat, walks in, sits by* JACK's *drum, picks up drumstick but puts it down and picks up* CHRIS's *cigarettes and lights one up.* CHRIS *wakes up, checks ashtray for burning cigarette, checks knobs on stove. Sits on couch.*)

CHRIS

Sorry, I didn't see you. You sing? (*Asked incredulously.*)

FRANCES

No, not really. I'm studying Indian music.

CHRIS

Studying it?

FRANCES

I find the music fascinating. Within the vocables it appears your people have notes we don't sing.

CHRIS

Really? Got another smoke?

FRANCES

Sure, here.

CHRIS

You're studying our music?

FRANCES

Yes. I am in the process of recording as many songs as I can and storing them for posterity's sake. Few scholars have recognized the validity and importance of capturing these most primitive sounds.

CHRIS

Really?

FRANCES

This is the one habit I've acquired while in the company of your people. I find it most relaxing. I might even venture to say that tobacco might be Native people's greatest contribution to modern civilization.

CHRIS

Well that contribution you're sitting there smoking was given to us by the Creator to pray with.

FRANCES

I'm well aware of the spiritual significance your people place on this plant. If I daresay, given the extent of my research, there are a few things I could possibly even teach you.

CHRIS

Oh, really?

LIZZIE

(*Enters from bedroom, retrieving dress off door.*) Fannie, I'm going to miss you!

FRANCES

My dearest Lizzie, don't be silly, I will write you every week from Oberlin.

LIZZIE

Promise?

FRANCES

Yes, would you lace up this corset?

LIZZIE

Sure. (*Continuing.*) Put that cigarette out before your father smells it.

FRANCES

He'll just think it's his pipe.

LIZZIE

You are the only girl I know who dares to flaunt convention. Darling Frances, what am I going to do without you. You better not get caught smoking at Oberlin. They will surely send you home on the very next train.

FRANCES

Ooh, Lizzie. I will miss you sooo much. You are my dearest friend. How can I go on this adventure without you? I will write you every day, I promise.

LIZZIE

(*Helping* FRANCES *into her dress.*) When you come back you'll be ready to play concerts. Your Papa said Mark Twain is going to speak at Oberlin this year. Do you really get to meet him?

FRANCES

(*While she's talking she pockets* CHRIS's *cigarettes and lighter.*) Lizzie, I think I shall get to meet him. And I will write to you about it just like I write to Margaret, so you just watch for the mail. Mama and Papa are waiting for me. I don't want to miss the train.

LIZZIE

(*Popping candy into* FRANCES's *mouth.*) Your breath smells like a smokehouse!

(JACK *enters apartment.* FRANCES *and* LIZZIE *exit.*)

JACK

Chris, you awake?

CHRIS

What?

JACK

Put that cigarette out before you burn down the apartment.

CHRIS

Dang! I coulda swore that woman you been reading about was sitting here talking to me. I'm awake.

JACK

You sure didn't look awake when I walked in.

CHRIS

She was going on about vocables....

JACK

Come on, you're tired. Get some sleep. You've been working too hard. I'm sorry about earlier.

CHRIS

Yeah, me too. Talk about a waking nightmare. What'd Bill tell you?

JACK

> He said to smudge the house before we go to bed. Go ahead. I'll burn some sage before I come in.

(*They leave.* JACK *finishes smudging, goes into bedroom. Lights down.*)

Scene 3

(*Lights up on Winnebago encampment.* FRANCES *and* MARGARET *are setting up phonograph equipment.* GLADYS *is making some food, quietly listening.*)

MAGGIE

> This is scary don't you think, Frances?

FRANCES

> No, we're not that far from the agency and besides the missionaries know we are here. Nothing's going to happen to us. Why, this village is practically civilized. Even the chief has a Christian name.

MAGGIE

> Well, the women don't seem that friendly.

FRANCES

> It will be okay. I am only going to record the chief.

MAGGIE

> Here he comes. He is striking, don't you think? Do you suppose that's his wife over there?

FRANCES

> I don't know. Shush now. Good afternoon, Mr. Williams, thank you for agreeing to sing for me.

MR. WILLIAMS

> The Father at the mission said you would carry our HoChunk songs to Washington.

FRANCES

> That is right.

MR. WILLIAMS
You are going to put my songs in that box?

FRANCES
In a manner of speaking, yes. You sing and they will be stored in here. Perhaps your wife would like to sing also?

MR. WILLIAMS
This is my daughter, Gladys. She has made some food. You have traveled a long ways in order to share my songs with the people in Washington, it wouldn't be right for us not to share with you. So when we are finished we will eat.

FRANCES
Thank you, we would be delighted to join you in a meal. Should we start? Are we ready Maggie?

MAGGIE
Yes.

(MR. WILLIAMS *takes tobacco out of his pouch and offers it to the four directions.*)

FRANCES
Could you explain to me what you are doing Mr. Williams?

MR. WILLIAMS
I am praying.

FRANCES
The Father told us you were baptized.

MR. WILLIAMS
I am, but the songs I am going to sing are from the old way, so I must honor the spirits who gave them to me—just in case.

FRANCES
Could you tell me the prayer?

MR. WILLIAMS
My translation is not that good. What songs would you like to hear?

FRANCES
What type of songs do you know?

MR. WILLIAMS
(*Flirting with* FRANCES.) Many, many. Songs about the seasons, songs for healing, songs about birth—I know some good love songs, too.

FRANCES
(*Flustered.*) I know, how about a hunting song? Sing a song that will bring you luck when you are hunting.

MR. WILLIAMS
When we are hunting, we must be very still, very quiet. That is not the time to sing.

MAGGIE
What if we started with a song about spring, Mr. Williams.

FRANCES
Yes, a spring song.

(MR. WILLIAMS *sings Maple Sugar song and is recorded. His daughter gives him water when he is finished.*)

FRANCES
Perhaps if you could translate this song, I will write it down so the people in Washington will know the words to this wonderful song.

MR. WILLIAMS
I am singing:
>   Let us go to the sugar camp
>   While the snow lies on the ground.
>   Live in the birchbark wigwam....

FRANCES
Oh.

MR. WILLIAMS
One more song. I will sing you a love song, it is one guaranteed to trap the heart of the one you seek, then we will eat.

FRANCES
Sure.

(Another song is sung and recorded. While they are talking, GLADYS *dishes them up some stew, and as the conversation progresses,* GLADYS *gets more and more irritated.)*

MR. WILLIAMS
You are very beautiful. Your husband must be lonely with you gone from your home.

FRANCES
Oh, I am not married.

MR. WILLIAMS
No? You should stay in the village awhile. Many of the people here could sing for you. We could give you many songs to add to your collection.

FRANCES
They would be willing to do this?

MR. WILLIAMS
Of course, and I would speak on your behalf. You could stay in my house. As chief I have a house like the missionaries. Spend some time with us, some of your people have intermarried with us and after a while have no desire to return to your big cities.

MAGGIE
We appreciate the invitation, but it would not be proper. We are staying at the mission.

MR. WILLIAMS
Proper?

MAGGIE
We are unmarried, surely you can understand how it would be improper for us to stay in your house.

MR. WILLIAMS
Some of your ways I do not understand. A woman in my community is free to make up her own mind. My wife has been gone a number of years. One of your sicknesses took her.

(GLADYS *gets up and takes* FRANCES's *bowl and refills it, while adding something from her pouch to it. She stirs it in and returns it to* FRANCES. FRANCES *has been getting flustered by the talk and eats without thinking.* MAGGIE *has just been eating the bread and barely touching her stew, as if remembering the meal at the Windgrows.*)

MR. WILLIAMS
> I have been looking for a wife and it seems I am related to every-
> one in our village. As I get older I cannot travel like I used to. I
> had a dream that you were coming. I agreed to sing because the
> spirits have sent you.

FRANCES
> We are here on behalf of the Smithsonian Institute. I am afraid
> your spirits have nothing to do with our journey.

MR. WILLIAMS
> There are many things about us that you may not understand. A
> song may be more than just a pretty sound.

GLADYS
> Father, I think you better grab your big stick over there and we
> should head home.

MR. WILLIAMS
> (*Putting his blanket in* FRANCES's *arms.*) Think about my offer. My
> home could give you much more happiness than just my songs.

(*He and* GLADYS *depart.*)

MAGGIE
> Frances! Did he just propose?!

FRANCES
> How embarrassing! I am mortified!

MAGGIE
> The spirits sent you!

FRANCES
> Stop! Enough of this nonsense, help me pack up so we can get
> back to the mission.

MAGGIE

You would be an Indian princess!

FRANCES

I have never been so humiliated in all my life.

MAGGIE

But Frannie! If you married him you would have all the songs you could ever want!

FRANCES

I have you, dear sister Margaret, why should I need anybody else to help me. Please, let us get back to the mission.

Scene 4

Lights come up on SPIRIT WOMAN *who is tightening jars of maple syrup at the sink in the apartment with* GLADYS. OLD MAN SPIRIT *is sitting at the table drinking coffee with* MR. WILLIAMS. FRANCES *is seated by a piano on the side of the stage. She is singing and playing the following song softly throughout the following dialogue.*

FRANCES

> Let us go to the sugar camp
> While the snow lies on the ground.
> Live in the birchbark wigwam
> All the children and the older folk
> While the people are at work
>
> Pour the syrup in the graining trough
> Stir it slowly as it thicker grows
> Now it has changed to sugar
> We may eat it in a birchbark dish
> There is sugar for us all.

GLADYS

I don't know why that woman thinks she can take without giving back.

OLD MAN SPIRIT

They are to be pitied. They are like children who never grew up. What good is the wind if caught in a box?

MR. WILLIAMS
    I thought she might come back.

OLD MAN SPIRIT
    She chose another path. And you, Spirit Woman, must sing the
    songs to future generations.

SPIRIT WOMAN
(*Singing.*)
                I haven't forgotten.
                The wind catches my songs
                Carried on strands of memory
                Children
                Hear me sing

(*Begins singing mourning song as she puts syrup in a basket, then takes Log Cabin syrup
out of fridge and puts it on the counter. Lights down.*)

Scene 5

Lights come up on JACK *and* CHRIS *in the living room, groggy in the morning getting
ready to go to work.* FRANCES *is lying on couch.* MAGGIE *is making tea in the
kitchen.*

JACK
    Thought you were on your moon.

CHRIS
    I am.

JACK
    Then why'd you touch my drumstick?

MAGGIE
    Frances, drink some tea, please?

CHRIS
    I didn't. You think I'm crazy? Next time you leave, leave my cig-
    arettes alone. Support your own habit. What'd you do with my

lighter? (*Picks up pillow from floor, puts syrup back in fridge.*) And clean up after yourself.

JACK

I didn't take that out.

CHRIS

Well I didn't.

FRANCES

Leave me alone.

JACK

And I didn't take your cigarettes. You smoke too damn much.

CHRIS

Come on, I gotta get to work. I don't want to fight this early. Maybe some spirit is hungry for maple syrup on pancakes.

JACK

(*Grabbing her around the waist.*) Maybe it's a sign from the spirits that you'll cook breakfast for supper?

CHRIS

(*Brushes him off, exiting.*) Yeah, right. You want to eat, you cook.

MAGGIE

Frances, you can't just sleep all day again. Get up, what is wrong with you?

FRANCES

(*Sitting up slowly, looking for cigarette.*) Nothing. Just leave me alone, please.

(JACK *stands looking after* CHRIS. *She pops head back in.*)

CHRIS

Aren't you coming?

JACK

I'll catch the city bus.

CHRIS
    Fine!

(*Chris exits.* JACK *looks at clock. Sits back down at table, drinking coffee and reading* FRANCES's *book. Tries singing some of the songs. Phone rings.*)

JACK
    Hey Larry, what's up? Nah, man, I missed the bus. Nah, she was too crabby. She would have just yelled at me all the way there about work-ing more. I'm on my break, too, drinking muck-a-day-mush-ki-ki wa-bo, readin up on my heritage—trying to learn some songs outta this book. Well, stop by after work, tell the boys I'll try to get in tomor-row.... Stop by and we'll crank out some tunes, loosen our throats for the powwow this weekend. Don't worry about it, she'll give me the money to go—nah, she's cool, just working too hard.... Later bro.

(*Takes book over to drum. Tries singing songs.* SPIRIT WOMAN *enters, adjusts curtains at window, opens fridge and puts syrup back on counter. Stands off from* JACK *and sings softly.* FRANCES *turns and looks at her.* MAGGIE *is fussing over* FRANCES.)

JACK
    Damn, wish I had a keyboard. Like we played on piano—sure. What was it told me? Listen for the spirits? All right, you guys, I'm listening, anytime you want to start singing I'm all ears. (*Drums some more.*)

    I don't hear you.

(*Gets up and goes to phone, dials.* FRANCES *gets up and sits at drum with notebook. Drums, starts to write. Gives up and sits.*)

JACK
    (*On phone.*) Bill, Jack here. Say, Larry said he might come over after work and crank out some tunes. Wanna come over for sup-per—I'll make us breakfast—pancakes and maple syrup.... Nah, I was just practicing at the drum myself here, missed the bus to work, I'll catch it tomorrow. Stop by—you want oatmeal and bacon grease, I'll make that for you, too, Uncle.... Alright, bye.

    (JACK *continues.*) It's not even noon. Plenty of time. May as well run out to the casino. (*Goes into bedroom.*)

(LIZZIE *knocks on door.*)

FRANCES
Don't answer that.

MAGGIE
Why? It's Lizzie. She's worried sick about you.

FRANCES
No.

(LIZZIE *knocks again,* JACK *comes running out of bedroom.*)

JACK
Hold on, I'm coming.

(*Opens door.* LIZZIE *enters but Jack doesn't see her.*)

JACK
Damn.

(JACK *goes back into bedroom.*)

LIZZIE
Frances, what is going on?

FRANCES
Nothing.

LIZZIE
This is the third time I have called this week and every time your
mother or Maggie has told me you are ill.

FRANCES
I'm fine, I am just not up for company these days. This last trip
to Wisconsin was very exhausting.

LIZZIE
Frannie, you are my very dearest friend. Tell me what is wrong.

FRANCES
I am telling you there is nothing wrong. I am just tired.

MAGGIE

She has been sleeping since we got back from Wisconsin. And I'm the one cooped up in this house taking care of her while she's too tired to talk to anyone else. I for one am glad to see you Lizzie. Maybe you can talk some sense into her.

LIZZIE

Frannie?

FRANCES

The two of you make me sick. Hovering over me like mother hens.

LIZZIE

You can't mean that Frances. We love you. You are distraught.

MARGARET

Mama took her to the doctor once already. I think she should go back, she just isn't herself.

FRANCES

I don't need to go back to the doctor. He already said I just have a touch of melancholy.

MAGGIE

A touch? Something is wrong, Frances. She sits here and smokes all day, Lizzie. She doesn't even care if Papa knows. She won't even let me fix her hair. She is positively disheveled. I think that man in Wisconsin put a spell on you.

LIZZIE

Man in Wisconsin?

FRANCES

That's blasphemy. Don't talk like that.

LIZZIE

Have you met someone, Frannie?

FRANCES

She is talking crazy. I have met no one. Don't even listen to her. You really need to leave Lizzie. I am not up to company.

LIZZIE

What man, Maggie?

FRANCES

Maggie! You may show Lizzie the door.

MAGGIE

I'm sorry, Lizzie....

FRANCES

Don't you dare patronize me! I am trying to record history! These Indians are nothing but a bunch of schizophrenic ... crazies—with all their mystical ... spirit ... magic, and you are just a couple of silly schoolgirls who know nothing of the real world.

MAGGIE

You can see she's not herself, she doesn't mean what she's saying.

FRANCES

Yes I do, now get out!

(FRANCES *goes to drum and starts beating on drum and singing at the top of her lungs.*)

MAGGIE

Frannie, sister, come on, she has left, come sit.... I'll make you some tea, stop that now....

(JACK *comes out dressed up in boots and ribbon shirt, hair brushed into a neat pony-tail.*)

JACK

(*Exiting.*) Double your money, double your fun.

Scene 6

Lights on apartment go out, come up on a whirlwind of scenes. First, JACK stops to get cigarettes at SA and the woman behind the counter is SPIRIT WOMAN. Then JACK is at the casino, pulling on slot machine, lost in trying to win. SPIRIT WOMAN, dressed like a modern Indian woman, is standing at slot machine next to JACK, humming, singing under her breath. Jack is losing money and getting crabby and shoots annoying glances at SPIRIT WOMAN.

JACK

Damn, it's noisy in here—come on, three sevens, that's all I need, come on baby ... roll!

(JACK *loses the last of his money.* SPIRIT WOMAN *wins. Jack stomps away. He stops at the cash machine and* SPIRIT WOMAN *is there. He stops at the corner store to get butter for supper and* SPIRIT WOMAN *is there. Everywhere he goes,* SPIRIT WOMAN *is trying to get his attention.*)

Scene 7

Apartment later that afternoon. Dishes are piled in the sink as if they have eaten, and the kitchen is in disarray. JACK *and* BILL *are sitting around drum.* CHRIS *is at table working on a crossword puzzle.* JACK *picks up* FRANCES's *book as if he is going to give to* BILL, *then sets it back down and begins singing Red Lake song.*

JACK

When I was driving around this afternoon I heard a radio show about Frances Densmore. This guy named Steve put it together about her. I'm going to call MPR and get a copy of the tape. I figured I could learn some more songs off there.

(FRANCES's *spirit lethargically enters from bedroom, followed by* SPIRIT WOMAN. FRANCES *moves things and* SPIRIT WOMAN *puts them back.*)

JACK

They said in the program today that she got a grant from the Smithsonian to travel around the country ...

CHRIS

In a canoe.

JACK

... and record songs before the elders died. Some elders from Wisconsin are talking about going to D.C. and taking the discs. Get our songs back.

CHRIS

Why don't you just have Jim Northrup bring them back one by one. He's always talking in his column about bringing pieces of the Smithsonian back in his pockets?

JACK

Another elder from Wisconsin wants the wax disks, he thinks we should bury them—like the bones kept in museums. Return the elders home, so to speak.

(*Midé pictograph images flash on theater walls, starting at the back and move to center stage, where they converge on* BILL.)

JACK

(*Continues.*) Larry, you know him? Elder up at UMD? He said on this radio show that Densmore must have had a pretty strong spirit to convince our elders to sing for her.

BILL

(*Looking at pictographs on drum.*) You draw these?

JACK

Yeah, I copied them out of this book.

BILL

Hmm.

JACK

Chris said I should paint over them. She thought you might be offended.

BILL

Some people might.

JACK

You think I should get rid of them?

BILL

Long time ago people would fast, have a dream. From that dream they might learn who their spirit helpers were. Then they would draw that design—maybe on their drum, maybe on a medicine pouch.

(*Midé images start going away from* BILL *as* FRANCES *knocks over syrup bottle in her haste to sit by* BILL.)

JACK

So you think I should get rid of them?

BILL

Each person has their own vision.

JACK

What do you mean?

BILL

You think anymore about fasting?

(FRANCES *sits close to* BILL, *taking out a pen and writing pad.* BILL *watches syrup run to floor.*)

CHRIS

He only fasts when the food shelves run out.

BILL

Think I'm getting a touch of indigestion. Chris, seems you have some hungry spirits here.

(BILL *gets up to leave,* JACK *stands,* CHRIS *jumps up and sets syrup bottle up, cleans syrup off the floor.*)

BILL

Nah, sit down, sing. I'll walk home, helps the stomach.

JACK

I'll walk with you, Uncle.

BILL

Nah, I'm an old man, I need my exercise. Listening to that tape started my own old songs running through my head. I'll listen to them on the way home. You get some rest. Heard they still need help at Precision Tool.

JACK

Yeah, yeah, I'll check it out tomorrow. Thanks Uncle. Later.

(SPIRIT WOMAN *follows* BILL *out.* FRANCES *sits in the chair* BILL *vacated. She takes one of* CHRIS's *cigarettes and stares into space.* JACK *sits back down at drum and sings softly as* CHRIS *cleans up kitchen.* MAGGIE *enters through door.*)

MAGGIE

Come on, Frances, we're going out.

FRANCES

No.

MAGGIE

This time you don't get to argue with me. I found someone who can help you. Come on, we're going.

(JACK *opens book.*)

JACK

Want me to learn a love song for you, babe?

CHRIS

How about helping me with the dishes instead?

JACK

I cooked. Equal division of labor right?

CHRIS

Chrii—

JACK

I was joking. I'll do them tomorrow.

CHRIS

Precision Tool?

JACK

After work. Wish I knew how to read music. She wrote these all down like they were going to be played on the piano or something.

CHRIS

How you gonna write down 'ai ya hey ya' so some white person can read it?

(FRANCES, *getting up angrily to get away from* MAGGIE, *knocks silverware off counter. Both* CHRIS *and* JACK *jump.*)

CHRIS
> What the h—?

MAGGIE
> Get your coat on, we probably won't be back until after dark.

FRANCES
> Why, where are we going?

MAGGIE
> To see someone, an old friend of mine. Someone I met while you were at school. Come on.

FRANCES
> No.

MAGGIE
> If you don't come I'm going to have Father take you back to the doctor. You've been sitting around here for months not doing anything.

JACK
> Okay, miz traditional. Want to tell me how silverware goes flying across the room. Or how someone knocks at the door and then no one is there.

CHRIS
> I don't know.

JACK
> Then I don't know why you always gotta put me down.

CHRIS
> I'm not.

JACK
> Right. You're the one that learned to tan deer hides from your grandma while I was playing center for some all white basketball team and helping my dad combine wheat all fall. Tonto rides John Deere. Whoopee. Now I'm trying to learn some things that I lost and all you can do is put me down.

CHRIS

I don't!

MAGGIE

Come on, Frances.

JACK

"Only when the food shelves run out." "Have Jim Northrup bring them back." What am I supposed to think?

CHRIS

I gotta work in the morning.

(CHRIS *exits to bedroom.*)

JACK

(*Pounding out 49 rhythm on drum.* FRANCES *hurries close and begins writing in notebook.*)

> I don't care who you love
> I can find another one
> Leech Lake, Red Lake
> Mdewakanton Sioux
> I can snag a rich one too

(CHRIS *slams bedroom door shut.*)

FRANCES

Slow down, please. Fascinating rhythm.

MAGGIE

The only thing that brings you to life is Indian music or something about the Indian religion. The rest of the time you just lay around here. We are leaving now!

JACK

> I don't care who you love
> I can find another one
> Pine Ridge, Rosebud
> Fond du lac
> I can snag a poor one too

Oh Christ.

FRANCES
    No ... one more time.

(MAGGIE *grabs* FRANCES *by the arm and drags her out the door.*)

(JACK *pulls a sleeping bag from end of couch and spreads it out. Gets* FRANCES's *book and starts to read. Falls asleep. Lights go out.*)

Scene 8

(*Lights come up on Dakota encampment.* MAGGIE *is dragging* FRANCES *up to* WINDGROW *and* WINONA.)

MAGGIE
    Mr. Windgrow, this is my sister Frances. I've brought the tobacco you requested. If you could, please doctor her tonight?

FRANCES
    Maggie!

MAGGIE
    Frances, trust me.

WINONA
    Sit please, you don't have to worry. Your sister has been worried sick about you. She told us about your trip to Wisconsin. And how your parents have taken you to the doctor and he can find nothing wrong with you.

WINDGROW
    The spirits will take the Winnebego medicine off of you.

FRANCES
    Medicine?

WINONA
    From what Maggie told us, that old man wanted to keep you. Your spirit is still in Wisconsin. My husband will sing and call it back for you.

FRANCES

Maggie, this is crazy.

MAGGIE

Not any crazier than you sleeping for months on end. Screaming at me and Lizzie. Let them help you please? For me?

WINDGROW

This Mr. Williams, he gave you water, food?

FRANCES

Yes.

MAGGIE

And a blanket, too. This one.

WINDGROW

Leave that here. We will burn it. The spirits tell me that Mr. Williams wanted you to stay, but someone else wanted you to go....

MAGGIE

His daughter!

WINDGROW

Whatever you ate was stronger medicine than the old man's love medicine.

WINONA

Come into the house. Windgrow will perform the ceremony and if the spirits wish, your sister will get her spirit back.

(*As they enter house,* SPIRIT WOMAN *and* OLD MAN SPIRIT *are singing. Stage goes dark and lights come up on* FRANCES *walking around in spirit world.* SPIRIT WOMAN *and* OLD MAN SPIRIT *escort* WINDGROW *into spirit world.* WINONA *and* MAGGIE *are seated on the floor of the living room facing the spirit world.* WINDGROW *is in a trance; he is carrying a long hunting knife, the blade of which he is running his thumb over. He follows* FRANCES *around.*)

FRANCES

What do you want? Who are you?

WINDGROW
LoneMan. Your memory is short.

FRANCES
So?

WINDGROW
I sold a song to you.

FRANCES
I paid you well. Leave me alone, can't you see I'm not feeling well.

WINDGROW
You kept us waiting an extra day. You took more than you gave.

FRANCES
You didn't have to sing.

WINDGROW
My family needs to eat. Your men have killed the buffalo. Your soldiers have killed our best warriors and hunters. We need to eat.

FRANCES
Forgive me, none of that is my affair, now please leave.

WINDGROW
The song I sold you—it was meaningless.

FRANCES
What?

WINDGROW
I made it up to get the piece of silver.

FRANCES
You told me it was a healing song.

WINDGROW
I lied.

FRANCES
How dare you try to make a fool of me.

WINDGROW
This knife belonged to Sitting Bull.

FRANCES
I have no money to purchase artifacts today.

WINDGROW
I wasn't offering to sell it to you. I only wanted you to see it.
Someday you will have to pay for all you have taken.

(*As he moves ever more threatening toward* FRANCES, *she runs back and sits close to* MARGARET. OLD MAN SPIRIT *and* SPIRIT WOMAN *sing softly and lead* WINDGROW *back into the ceremony circle. They then retreat, still singing.*)

(*Lights go down, come back up immediately on apartment. There is a banner reading Chicago's World Fair.* JACK *is* GERONIMO—*he is sitting on display, working on something with his hands, humming the song* SPIRIT WOMAN *has been singing to him.* FRANCES *looks, acts fearful of him at first, but then secretively steps behind him and begins writing his song in a notebook she is carrying. As she shuts her book and scurries away.*)

GERONIMO
(*Stands and says.*) How dare you try to steal my soul?

(*Stage goes black.*)

Scene 9

Lights come up on apartment. JACK *looks disheveled, tired, worn. He has a keyboard set up in the living room. He is holding* FRANCES'S *book and trying to play songs from the book on the keyboard. Frustrated, he goes to the drum and tries to sing songs.* SPIRIT WOMAN *is curled up on the couch, patiently waiting. While* JACK *is at the drum,* FRANCES *goes to keyboard and plays one of the songs from the book. Jack gets discouraged and quits and starts to read from the book again.* FRANCES *gets her notebook and begins practicing speech.*

FRANCES
My dear students, a great deal has been said about world fellowship through music, but there are few subjects on which the world is more divided. One man's music is another man's misery. When early settlers and explorers heard the Indians singing there was only one opinion—

it was terrible. Yet the Indians like their music and could listen to it all night—the performance was longer than a Bernard Shaw play.

MARGARET

(*Entering.*) What are you working on Frances?

FRANCES

I have been asked to give a lecture at the Minot High School.

MARGARET

(*Sitting down on couch.*) About your Indian music? Go ahead, I'll be your practice audience. Go ahead.

FRANCES

We should remember that Indian music, to some extent, is like ancient poetry, that was recited, not written down. To be heard, not seen, listened to but not looked at.

MARGARET

That's good.

FRANCES

I have studied Indian music from the human as well as the musical side. I thought here I would play a few bars. (*Goes to keyboard and plays a few measures.*)

What do you think?

MARGARET

It might hold their attention longer than just talking.

FRANCES

That's what I thought. So then I say, Many other composers have used Indian themes for violin compositions, operas, choruses, and orchestra. But let us consider Indian music in the original—as it looks, or sounds, to the Indian. If you were an Indian this would be your music, and we all have a little of the Indian in us.

(SPIRIT WOMAN *leaves to sit at table in kitchen.*)

FRANCES

We all respond to the free outdoor life and the beauties of nature. Indians believed so many happy things about nature—about kind spirits and helpful spirits.

MARGARET

And bad! spirits.

FRANCES

No! That was sacrilegious of you to drag me to the Sioux village. Mother and Father would just die. And the church! Forgive me. If they knew you had taken me to an Indian doctor because you were convinced that Winnebago chief put a spell on me!

MARGARET

He did! He was in love with you! And his daughter was so angry. You remember her face when we left. She put that spell on you.

FRANCES

And I've never eaten in another Indian village since!

(*Knock on door.* MARGARET *answers.* LIZZIE *comes in.*)

MARGARET

Lizzie! Come in.

LIZZIE

(*Whispering.*) How is she?

MARGARET

(*Whispering back.*) Better I think.

MARGARET

(*Louder.*) Let me take your coat.

LIZZIE

Hello, Frances.

FRANCES

Dear Lizzie.

LIZZIE

Today it is "Dear Lizzie."

FRANCES
Well....

LIZZIE
The last time I was here you screamed for me to get out.

FRANCES
It was a touch....

LIZZIE
Touch of what, madness?

FRANCES
My work....

LIZZIE
Your obsession.

FRANCES
Lizzie, you are my most precious friend.

LIZZIE
I wonder, it seems these Indians are the only friends you have.

FRANCES
They are not my friends. This is my work. Maybe someday you will find something that occupies your very soul the way this music seems to have captured mine.

LIZZIE
I thought I had....

FRANCES
What?

MARGARET
Lizzie, sit, have some tea. Frances was just rehearsing a speech she is going to give in Minot. Join us. By myself I am a small audience for her to practice on.

FRANCES
Goodness, no. Lizzie is bored by my field of study.

LIZZIE

I didn't say that. Please continue.

FRANCES

You are mad at me.

LIZZIE

No.

MARGARET

She understands that you were sick, don't you Lizzie?

LIZZIE

Of course. Sometimes I just wonder why your obsession takes you so far from people who care about you.

FRANCES

I have to travel.

LIZZIE

That's not....

MARGARET

Please continue Fran....

FRANCES

This is my career. I must keep my attention focused. All I have is my music.

MARGARET

You have Lizzie and I ...

LIZZIE

Had.

MARGARET

... and your work is in the Library of Congress. What you are doing is very important. Don't start fretting.

(*Aside to* LIZZIE.)

LIZZIE.

Let us hear some more of your speech.

FRANCES

(*While she is talking,* SPIRIT WOMAN *pushes coffee cup off table.* JACK *jumps, looks, is confused, then begins cleaning it up.*)

> Three times in my experience I have recorded rain songs with no desire to have rain. We were having no ceremony and I was not even giving tobacco, but the Indians said it would rain and it did—much to my inconvenience.

MARGARET
> We were drenched!

(CHRIS *enters apartment. Sees* JACK *cleaning up cup.*)

CHRIS
> Decided to do some work today I see.

MARGARET
> Play a song for us Frances.

JACK
> Leave me alone.

(JACK *goes back to reading book.*)

FRANCES
> Ojibwe or Sioux?

CHRIS
> I found a suitcase with 100,000 dollars in it today.

MARGARET
> Lizzie?

JACK
> Uh huh.

CHRIS
> My boss said it was probably drug money and to go ahead and keep it.

LIZZIE
> Either. I must be going shortly.

(FRANCES *begins playing song on keyboard.*)

JACK

That's nice.

CHRIS

Then he asked me to go to the Caribbean over Christmas with him.

JACK

Mmmm.

CHRIS

He asked me to go over to his house tonight and have sex with him.

JACK

Don't you want to have supper first?

CHRIS

You're not even listening to me.

JACK

Am too. You said you wanted to have sex.

(FRANCES *switches from keyboard to sitting at drum and singing.*)

CHRIS

With my boss.

JACK

Yeah, right, since when did you get interested in white men? Quit trying to mess with me. Just leave me alone til I finish this chapter.

CHRIS

That's all I do these days is leave you alone. I can't get a word out of you. You're so wrapped up in Frances Densmore and "songs from the turn of the century." Earth to Jack, it's now 1998.

JACK

Criii—Just leave me alone.

CHRIS

No, I'm not leaving you alone. I am sick to death of working my butt off all day hauling other people's garbage while you sit here day after day playing Indian songs on a keyboard or reading that book.

JACK

I bought that with my own money.

CHRIS

Right, you worked one week and bought a keyboard. I pay for the electricity that runs that thing. You don't help out at all anymore. You must have that book memorized by now.

JACK

I told you, I can't sleep. Every time I try to sleep I hear some woman who keeps singing in my ear and then when I wake up I can't remember what she wants me to remember.

(*There is a knock on the door.* JACK *goes to open it.* OLD MAN SPIRIT *walks in and joins* SPIRIT WOMAN *at the table.* JACK *and* CHRIS *don't see him.*)

CHRIS

So you stay up all night and then are too tired to work. You won't even talk to me anymore. You at least used to have a sense of humor. What's wrong with you?

JACK

Nothing. I'm just trying to learn these songs.

CHRIS

What are you doing?

JACK

Didn't you hear someone knock?

CHRIS

No, no one knocked.

JACK

I heard it.

CHRIS

This is crazy. I wish you would quit fooling around with those songs.

(FRANCES *finishes song at drum.*)

LIZZIE

I am always amazed at how much you know about these quaint songsters, Frances.

FRANCES

Well, I do believe I am the only person who has heard these many songs in their original version. Why, one man alone recorded over 200 songs for me. I have learned to keep my attention focused on my work and to detach myself from the basest of relationships.

LIZZIE

What?

MARGARET

She is talking about her work, Lizzie.

JACK

What do you mean, fooling around?

FRANCES

(*Not waiting for response.*) Another song?

CHRIS

These songs are meant for indigenous ears, indigenous hearts. If non-Indians or just ordinary people like you and me try to interpret them, they'll come out wrong. Some things just aren't supposed to be messed with. Spirits walk in and out of here night and day.

LIZZIE

I am leaving. Good day, Frances. Margaret, I will see you later.

CHRIS

(*Begins smudging apartment.*) I know you want this song, Jack. But this isn't right. Neither one of us sleeps a whole night through, all these crazy dreams. Things get moved around the apartment. Both of us tired all the time.

(FRANCES *and* MAGGIE *move to bedroom to get away from the sage.*)

JACK
You're right, I think I'll go to sleep.

CHRIS
Jack, don't just walk away. Talk to me.

JACK
What's to talk about? You don't want to hear what I'm interested in or what I'm going through.

CHRIS
That's not true.

JACK
I just know that if I could hear this song, and sing it, everything would be okay.

CHRIS
It's not Instant Culture, Jack, you can't pour it out of a box, add water, and poof!—Instant Indian. There's traditional ways you to learn these things.

JACK
(*Entering bedroom.*) So what's there to talk about? Bill says we each got our own vision, our own way. I'm tired.

CHRIS
I can't go on like this.

OLD MAN SPIRIT
Patience. Be gentle. He's right, we each have our own path.

SPIRIT WOMAN
Remember, women hold up half the sky.

OLD MAN SPIRIT
Pray.

(CHRIS *goes into drawer and takes out bundle. Burns more sage in a shell.* FRANCES, LIZZIE, *and* MARGARET *peer from bedroom door as* CHRIS *looks through bundle.*)

CHRIS
Jack, Jack—you sleeping?

JACK
Not now.

CHRIS
Can you come out here.

JACK
Why, what now?

CHRIS
I want to show you something. Come on.

JACK
What?

CHRIS
I want to show you this.

(FRANCES *tries to push closer but is held back by the sage smoke.*)

JACK
Where'd you get these?

CHRIS
Some I got at ceremony. Some, people just gave to me. These feathers are from a Maori man from New Zealand. A lot of their ways are like ours. I met him at a spiritual gathering up in Canada. They pass their songs down generation to generation. My grandma gave me this feather.

JACK
My parents don't have anything to give me.

CHRIS
It's not their fault Jack. They gave you what they thought you would need to survive. I get scared of this stuff sometimes. It's a lot of responsibility to try and follow the traditional ways.

JACK

But at least you have a choice.

CHRIS

Right. I made a choice to go to ceremony. To listen to the elders. To put myself in places where I would learn and people would talk to me. You have the same choice.

JACK

I just feel so stupid. I don't know what to say to the elders.

CHRIS

You're not stupid. You're smart. You're funny. And you're a good singer. You sing better than anybody on your drum. Bill knows that, that's why he teaches you. You don't have to say anything. Just be respectful and listen. If they see you're serious they'll talk to you.

JACK

Bill won't tell me about this song I keep hearing.

CHRIS

Maybe he doesn't know it. Maybe it's not in that book you keep reading. Maybe it's a song just for you.

JACK

What do you mean just for me?

CHRIS

Maybe that's your song. And the spirits keep trying to give it to you but you don't get quiet enough to hear it. Really quiet, inside here. Here, this was given to me by an Aboriginal woman from Australia.

JACK

A stone?

CHRIS

See these markings, it looks like a woman. The woman who gave it to me said that with this rock she could hear the spirits of her ancestors. Here. Maybe it will help you hear your song.

JACK

    From Australia?

CHRIS

    (*Laughing.*) I think indigenous ancestors all reside in the same spirit world. I'll ask Bill to come do ceremony tomorrow night. Come on, I still gotta work in the morning.

(*Lights down.*)

Act III

Scene I

Light comes up on apartment. LIZZIE *and* MAGGIE *are wrapping packages while* FRANCES *sits on a chair smoking a cigarette.* CHRIS *is cooking a feast in the kitchen.* JACK *is sitting on the couch, he is slowly thumbing through* FRANCES's *book and periodically pulls rock out of his pocket. He looks a little less tired and worn.* OLD MAN SPIRIT *and* SPIRIT WOMAN *are standing in bedroom doorway observing goings on.*

LIZZIE

Who are all these packages for, Frances?

FRANCES

I'm sending them up to White Earth. Margaret and I are going up there as soon as the spring rains are over. I want to record some of the old men from up that way.

(BILL *knocks and enters apartment.*)

BILL

(*Wanders carefully through rooms.*) Anin. Chris, Jack. Did you guys get new furniture or something? Seems awful crowded in here.

CHRIS

Nah, I feel the same way, there's no space here.

BILL

It's crowded, for sure.

CHRIS

(*Opening kitchen window some.*) Get some air in here. You guys smell smoke? I'm always smelling smoke these days.

BILL

I don't smell anything.

CHRIS

I think the food's done. You can start setting up, Bill, if you want. Jack, can you help move the furniture back? There's a quilt on our bed you can put on the floor.

(CHRIS *keeps working in kitchen.* BILL *and* JACK *set up living room for ceremony.* FRANCES *is observing them intently.* LIZZIE *hands* GLADYS's *present into Spirit World.*)

GLADYS

What is that woman up to now?

LIZZIE

You are asking me to understand her? Frances, why are we doing this?

FRANCES

When I went into the field in 1906, I did so under escort of missionaries. Now I can send the poor heathens lots and lots of presents through the church society of which I am president. When we go to White Earth, we will stay at the rectory and the missionary will introduce us to the leaders among the Indians and mixed-bloods. He will tell them who I am by reminding them of the presents.

MARGARET

(*Out of* LIZZIE's *earshot as* LIZZIE *takes* GLADYS *another present.*) I knit Lizzie a scarf as a Christmas present. I signed it from both of us.

GLADYS

She doesn't even know us.

LIZZIE

Do you know the people who will be receiving these gifts, Frances?

FRANCES

Goodness no. And I don't wish to. It was hard to learn to "draw the line" and be chummy and cordial with Indians but not let them ever overstep. I must always be on guard to never let them criticize the government nor the white race, nor come across with any sob stuff about the way they have been treated. I am always diligent and do not allow my emotions or personal attachments to cloud my thinking.

(*The men are finished setting the room up.* FRANCES *is drawn back to them.*)

BILL

Okay, granddaughter, we're ready. Can you bring the spirit plate? Jack, you sit in there, Chris, there. Jack, can you tell me why you asked for this ceremony?

JACK

Remember I told you about this dream I keep having? I keep hearing this song way off in the distance, but I can't grab it, or I'll dream it and then can't remember.

BILL

Chris?

CHRIS

I'm worried about Jack. All he does is sing songs out of Frances's book or play them on the keyboard. He hasn't been to work in a month. Like he said, we both keep having strange dreams. I keep smelling smoke. Stuff gets moved around in the apartment.

(*Lights slowly dim as* BILL *begins smudging.* BILL *begins prayer in Ojibwe. Within a few words the stage and theater go completely black.*)

BILL

Gitchimanido....

(*Only* BILL's *voice is heard and that too is drowned out as mournful drum is heard.*)

Scene 2

Spirit lights dance throughout theater, pictographs flash around walls and become stationary as blue light comes up on Ojibwe encampment. OLD MAN SPIRIT *and* SPIRIT WOMAN *are standing with* BILL, *who is dressed as an elder in the past. An Ojibwe woman is sitting in another space, weaving a birch bark basket.* FRANCES *is off in one direction, setting up a phonograph with* MAGGIE *helping her.*

BILL (*as elder from the past*)

Main'gans, you cannot do this. Our ancestors brought these teachings across the great lake, we were instructed to keep them secret, sacred, except for those who have been properly initiated. You sing for the chumakamon-iqway and you put us all in danger.

MAIN'GANS (JACK)
Pssh, you are jealous. Shingobe, from Leech Lake, has his voice in Washington. He is alive. His medicine is still strong.

BILL (*as elder from the past*)
Odjib'we is dead.

MAIN'GANS (JACK)
He was old.

BILL (*as elder from the past*)
We buried him a year to the day after he gave up his most sacred possession, his song. To her.... (*Pointing with lips at* FRANCES.)

(MARGARET *walks over.*)

MARGARET
Mr. Main'gans, my sister is ready. I can't wait to hear your marvelous voice. They will be so pleased in Washington to hear you.

BILL (*as elder from the past*)
You will leave us no choice brother.

MAIN'GANS (JACK)
I will only sing my songs.

BILL (*as elder from the past*)
You will not enter the lodge again.

MAIN'GANS (JACK)
It will be on me.

(MAIN'GANS *follows* MARGARET *to* FRANCES. MAIN'GANS's WIFE *stands with the basket and joins them off to side.*)

MARGARET
And this is Mrs. Main'gans? So pleased to meet you, dear, your husband has one of the finest voices around these parts. Are you ready Frances?

FRANCES
Yes.

MARGARET

Main'gans, sing here.

(MAIN'GANS *sings a few vocals.*)

MARGARET

Wonderful. Stop, here listen. Frances, play it back for him. Main'gans, listen.

(*Song is heard.*)

MARGARET

This is what they will hear in Washington!

MAIN'GANS' WIFE

(*To* MAIN'GANS.) How did it learn it so fast?

FRANCES

I would like to record some Midé songs.

MARGARET

Can you sing us some of the songs from the Great Medicine Lodge? Then your great-great grandchildren will someday be able to go to Washington, and they will hear your voice. Please. This is the most enchanting voice we've heard yet don't you think, Frances? Mrs. Main'gans, you should be so proud of him. Just a couple of your medicine songs, please, my dear Mr. Main'gans?

(MAIN'GANS *sings. His wife goes back to working on basket. As he is singing, pictograph symbols disappear one by one until only about half are left. Spirit lights falter.*)

FRANCES

(*Handing* MAIN'GANS *a quarter.*) I think we have enough for today.

MARGARET

Thank you, Main'gans. How do you say it? Me-gwitch. Your grandchildren will be sooo proud.

(*As* MAIN'GANS *walks toward the other elders, his wife follows. As he approaches them, they one by one turn their backs to him. Alone with his wife, he exits. Lights dim as* MARGARET *hauls phonograph off stage.* FRANCES *sits on tree stump and lights up cig-arette as stage lights dim, then come back up on* FRANCES *still on tree stump. She is*

burning papers and letters in a black kettle.)

OLD MAN SPIRIT
Daughter, what are you doing?

FRANCES
Burning it all.

OLD MAN SPIRIT
Burning what?

FRANCES
Poems, my own songs, letters filled with sentimental rubbish. I don't want people rifling through the attachments of my heart once I am gone.

OLD MAN SPIRIT
I cry for your spirit. The songs you recorded were always The People's. The work you clung to was never yours. Once you've burned the stirrings of your heart, you will be no more.

(*Blue light comes up on Ojibwe encampment.* MAIN'GANS *is standing off by self, in mourning. "Amazing Grace," sung in Ojibwe is heard. The other Midé elders are preparing the body of his wife for burial.* MAIN'GANS *sees* FRANCES *sitting frozen.*)

MAIN'GANS
You! I let you take my songs and now the spirits have taken my wife. My songs, my wife, my religion. You took them all.

(*All spirit lights stop and Midé images disappear at once. Stage and theater go completely black.*)

SPIRIT WOMAN
(*Voice only.*)

> I sing the songs of ages past
> Nothing sacred is ever lost
> No matter what they take
> Our spirits still live on

Scene 3

SPIRIT WOMAN's voice is heard—a strong song. One little light flickers, more spirit lights flicker, Midé images return gradually, drumming is heard. SPIRIT WOMAN and JACK are seen. She is singing his song and he begins to sing with her. Lights come up gradually on apartment until spirit lights and Midé images are no longer evident. As full lights come up on apartment, evidence of ceremony is gone, and the apartment is back in order. SPIRIT WOMAN is sitting on the couch looking at FRANCES's book. BILL is at the door.

BILL
Things should be better now, daughter.

CHRIS
Things seem a lot lighter in here now.

BILL
I heard they're still looking for help at Precision Tool, Jack. You might want to go by there tomorrow.

JACK
Thanks, Bill. I'll check it out.

BILL
(*Tapping* JACK *over heart.*) Sometimes we just gotta remember where to look for what we think we've lost.

(They exit. CHRIS is cleaning up in kitchen. JACK stands by end table, using it as a drum. He softly sings song SPIRIT WOMAN has been singing to him. SPIRIT WOMAN rises to exit and sets book on end of couch before leaving through the door. JACK picks book up.)

JACK
Chris?

CHRIS
Huh?

JACK
You got 32 bucks?

CHRIS

    I guess, why?

JACK

    So I can return this book and pay the overdue fine when I get off work tomorrow.

(CHRIS *throws dishrag at him. Stage goes black.*)

END

No Home but the Heart

(AN ASSEMBLY OF MEMORIES)

Daystar/Rosalie M. Jones

Artist's Statement

The publication of this script has a twofold significance for me. First, after my mother's death in 1987, I felt that the time had come for me to try to tell my own story. In whatever form it might evolve, it was the time to create—to write and to choreograph—a performance work that would call attention to those generations that had to carry the burden of acculturation which took place from early reservation days until what I will call the "tribal renaissance" of the 1960s. That story is the story of our immediate mothers and fathers, and grandmothers and grandfathers. I have used my own family to begin telling those stories.

Second, much of my early work as a dancer, choreographer, and teacher was centered on the creation of dance works for Native youth. Twenty-five years ago there was little material suitable for culturally based production. When I formed my own company, DAYSTAR, the repertoire became an extension of that kind of production: "Contemporary Dance-Drama of Indian America." Although an extensive body of work was done over many years, it has been little recognized. The nature of the work is that dance choreography cannot be "published" in the sense of a script. And it must be said that choreography is usually considered secondary to theatrical production; consequently, it becomes invisible in theatrical literature.

It is my hope that this script will bring a heightened awareness to the importance of choreography in dramatic literature. I hope this script encourages a new genre of Native theatrical production, a genre that celebrates the theatrical possibilities of choreography.

No Home but the Heart
(An Assembly of Memories)

Characters

NARRATOR, a trickster-like storyteller

THE SPECTER OF DEATH, a masked dancer

GREAT-GRANDMOTHER/YOUTH

GREAT-GRANDMOTHER/AGE

GRANDMOTHER/YOUTH

GRANDMOTHER/AGE

MOTHER/YOUTH

MOTHER/AGE

DAUGHTER/YOUTH

DAUGHTER/AGE

TWO AIRPORT FIGURES, masked

CLOG DANCERS #1 AND #2

JINGLE DANCERS

INTERTRIBAL DANCERS, optional

Setting

The time period of the dance-drama takes place within historical times from 1800 to the present. However, there are references to spiritual events which take place outside, and beyond, historical time.

The dance-drama takes place on a bare stage, except for three or four panels hanging upstage, forming the backdrop for the performance. This "Panel of Ancestors" represents the ancestors (specifically, the Great-grandmother, Grandmother and Mother) of the lead character, the Daughter. The director and performers should select appropriate photographs, or realistic drawings of family or relatives, to create these panels. The panel size is three feet wide and seven feet long, produced inexpensively by photo-enlarging the original photographs onto paper rolls. They could also be produced on canvas or cloth. Soft lighting illuminates these panels. The illumination of one or all of the "Panel of Ancestors" is one of the major ways in which a change of scene is depicted. Also, four small rocks, on stage from the first scene, are moved as needed in succeeding scenes. The four rocks "ground" the dance-drama in the presence of the earth.

Scenes

Scene 1.	Great-Grandmother/Youth The Traveling Dance
Scene 2.	Great-Grandmother/Age The Medicine Dance
Scene 3.	The French Connection
Scene 4.	The Specter of Death The Smallpox Dance
Scene 5.	Ten Cent Treaty
Scene 6.	Grandmother/Youth The Clog Dance
Scene 7.	Grandmother/Age The Chair Dance

Playwright's Note

From an early age, Daystar was intrigued by the stories her mother told her about her youth growing up on the Blackfeet Reservation. The stories were random and yet intense in their revelations about family and tribal life on the reservation from the smallpox epidemic of 1837, through the turn of the century, and into the modern day. In creating *No Home but the Heart*, Daystar has drawn from selected events in the lives of her great-grandmother, grandmother, and mother, and tied these events to historical events which affected the resettlement of Native peoples in the late nineteenth century. Because the family's ancestry stems from the displaced French-Cree people from the "north," this work acknowledges the universal search for identity, family, and homeland. In the dance-drama, the Daughter, living in the present day, passes through scenes from the past, in which the embodiments of her ancestors play out selected events in their lives.

This dance-drama relies heavily on choreographed movement of the various women characters. The production's choreographer, or the performers themselves, can create movement for each indicated dance. However, the author/choreographer of this dance-drama is available for consultation about the choreography or the recreation of the extensive choreography involved. The original recorded voiceovers of various characters is also available from the author/choreographer for a user's fee. Contact Daystar at the address or email on the copyright page of this volume.

Production History

The play had a one-performance preview in Grand Rapids, Michigan, and then opened for a two-day run at the Maria Benitez Cabaret, Hotel Santa Fe in Santa Fe, New Mexico, in April 1999. A reworking of the script, and especially of scenes 8 and 9, took place during the summer of 2000. On September 21, 22, and 23, 2000, the revised and expanded production was performed in Hartwell Dance Theater at the State University of New York at Brockport and on January 25 and 26, 2002 at the University of Lethbridge in Alberta, Canada.

In January 2002, the University of Lethbridge hosted Daystar Productions in a one-week residency for its Department of Theater and Dance, culminating in two performances of *No Home but the Heart*. Performers were Sid Bobb (Sto;lo/Metis), Penny Couchie (First Nations Nipissing), Geraldine Manossa (Bigstone Cree), and Daystar/Rosalie Jones. LeRoy Little Bear and Amethyst First Rider coordinated special buses from the nearby Blackfoot Reserve, so that each performance had a remarkable Native attendance. Performances of *No Home but the Heart* also took place at the Yukon Arts Centre, Whitehorse, Yukon, Canada (November 24, 2002) and at the Woodland Cultural Centre, Brantford, Ontario, Canada (March 22, 2003).

My thanks go to colleagues who contributed to the realization of the final production. Ned Bobkoff, DAYSTAR Company associate director, coached the actors in the development of character and stage business, and therefore was credited as a codirector of the production. Special thanks to cast members Stephen Fadden (Mohawk) and Rulan Tangen (Lakota) of the Santa Fe premiere, as well as Santee Smith (Mohawk) and Rose Stella (Tarahumara/Italian) of the 2000 performance run, and Penny Couchie (Nipissing), Sid Bobb (Sto;lo/Metis) and Geraldine Manossa (Bigstone Cree) of the Canadian premiere. The considerable talent and intelligence of these artists were invaluable to the final form of the production.

Preshow Music: *Contemporary synthesized or New Age music, with long sweeping melodies and a touch of nostalgia and a feeling for the past. (Suggestion: "Gathering of Spirits" [6:41] from the album* Cloud Etchings.*) Note that music selections throughout* No Home but the Heart *are only suggestions. For use of copyrighted music in a performance, music rights must be obtained.*

Scene I
Great-Grandmother/Youth
Time: 1800

Stage is in darkness as the voice speaks. The recorded voice of a twenty-year-old woman betrays sadness and confusion.

RECORDED FEMALE VOICE
 I don't remember where I was born.
 Maybe out of a wooden-cart or on a buffalo hunt,
 I don't remember and nobody wrote it down.
 I do know that my sister and me were taken from our parents and raised by the nuns—you know.
 We were taught about what they said was the "true" God,
 but that didn't stop my sister from throwing me away.
 One bright summer day, the two of us were traveling by steamboat down the Missouri River.
 An argument broke out—about something not important anymore.
 There, somewhere on the prairie, I was put off the boat!
 I was never to see my family again.

The Traveling Dance

As the lights come up, we see the Panel of Ancestors prominently displayed along the back cyclorama. Four small rocks are seen placed at random on the outer perimeter of the space. After the recorded voice, and in the silence, a bag of clothing is thrown onto the stage, followed by a second bundle.

Music: *Reminiscent of a windswept prairie. Bell-like sounds mark the sound of a steamship departing. (Suggestion: "Crystal Dawn" [3:40] from the album* Cloud Etchings.*)*

Choreography: *The sound of wind is heard. As the music begins, the figure of the* GREAT-GRANDMOTHER *emerges slowly from behind the Panel of Ancestors. She moves to stage center, with her back to the audience. She has a bandanna tied around her head. She wears a floor-length cotton skirt and a leather, Indian-made cape. She wears moccasins. The dancer portrays the terror of being left in an unknown country, with no means of support or companionship. She traverses the stage in all directions, finally working herself into a frenzy that exhausts her. She collapses to the ground. Slowly she gathers her belongings and her courage. She decides to reposition the four rocks in a diagonal line, down stage right to upstage left. Seeing that she has left her mark, she slowly exits upstage left.*

THE MATRIARCH: Susan Bigknife.
Photo courtesy of the Jackson Family Archive.

Scene 2
Great-Grandmother/Age
Time: 1880

Lights dim to semi-darkness, as the Great-Grandmother/Youth *exits and the* Great-Grandmother/Age *enters. The* Narrator, *offstage left, tremolos softly as the* Great-Grandmother/Age *enters and the recorded voiceover begins. The voice is considerably aged, but not without a sense of humor.*

Recorded Female Voice
> Meet-so-wahk. Ook-ee-mahw. Ah-pi. Is-kwaew.
> Meet-so-wahk. Soo-ne-yahw? Ne-moy-en!
> That man I met on the prairie became my first husband.
> But after a while, he left.
> From then on, I knew I *needed* protection.
> So I always wore a medicine bag and rosary around my neck,
> and the Holy Virgin medal in my vest pocket, next to my heart.
> Lucky for me, because it was my second husband,
> in a jealous rage one day, who tried to shoot me!
>
> Lucky for me, the Holy Virgin medal slowed that bullet and I survived.
> Lucky for him, he got sick and died.
> But it was my third husband who put out my eye.
>
> That's when the spirits spoke to me.
> That's when I learned the secrets of wind and water
> and roots and leaves.
> That's when I learned how to doctor.

The Medicine Dance

Choreography: *The* Great-Grandmother *enters slowly from downstage right, facing upstage, following the rocks as if "following" her younger self exiting upstage left. She enters on the tremolo, and continues throughout the recorded voiceover. She is dressed in old-style cloth reservation dress, belt, head scarf, and moccasins. Around her neck is a Catholic rosary and a medicine bag. A larger bag hangs from her left side. She carries a rattle in her right hand, and a deer antler in her left hand. She is looking for the proper "medicine" place. Shaking the rattle and divining with the antler, she moves*

among the rocks already in place. She kneels and places selected objects at a chosen spot, and then begins repositioning the other rocks around her. Rising, she decides the moment is good, begins shaking the rattle, moving slightly from foot to foot. As she dances, she begins to describe a half-arc around the "place," with the apex at stage front. As she focuses more intently, she breathes more heavily, and expels verbal sounds with each breath, almost singing. The pace and intensity build. At the height of dance and voice, she pauses and stamps one foot on the ground. A bolt of thunder is heard. She stamps again. Another bolt of thunder. Several lightning flashes, and finally, the sound of rain. GREAT-GRANDMOTHER *pulls a yellow cloth from the back of her belt, and begins signaling to the sky with the cloth, waving it skyward once to each of the Four Directions. Satisfied she has properly given thanks, she kneels down, smiling, and dips her hand into the water at her feet. She drinks, gathers her belongings, and slowly exits, pleased with her success.*

Scene 3
The French Connection
Time: 1783

The NARRATOR *has been sitting or standing offstage left. Now he comes center stage, with a knee-length red and black rabbit-skin mantle around his neck. He is dressed in modern style pants, shirt, vest, and moccasins or boots. He may wear a black "reservation hat." He is carrying in a pocket a deck of cards (oversize if possible).*

Music: *Soft, ethereal music plays inconspicuously in the background. About halfway through his monologue, a slow drum beat has replaced the more formal music. (Suggestion: "Morning Rain" [4:00] from the album* Cloud Etchings.)

NARRATOR

1783. That's the year when it all got started—when things first got mixed up. The French king told the fur traders that they had his permission to marry the women of the "new" world ... the Indian woman ... you know, the Cree and Chippewa women. It was okay to marry them because he wouldn't allow French women to cross the ocean. Too dangerous. The French women might get their feet wet! I'll leave it at that.

Now, when the French began to marry these Indian women, they not only learned how to get along with the natives, their relations, the French also learned the secrets of that land ... at least, enough secrets to make a very good living "off the land," as they say. The French gave, in return, guns and playing cards, and religion. A trade-off, of sorts, I suppose.

(*He fingers and shuffles the cards.*)

You know, these cards are useful. They jog my memory about this mixed-up story.

(*Pause.*)

You know, these French people were fighting a cultural war of their own culture. They had their own language, they had their own customs, they had their own *culture*. They had their own way of thinking and they wanted a home of their own in Canada, a province. Well, only problem was that hundreds of them already had Indian wives! What was that going to do for 'em? Ah—but then there was Louis Reil. He was a teacher and a statesman who got everyone organized, as a new people with a new name—Metis. With a new language—Michif. With the Metis, everything was a wonderful blend of the Indian and the French—blended Indian language and French language, Indian customs and French customs, Indian thinking and French thinking.

But the Canadian government didn't like that! (*Mocking each.*) If you were a Frenchman—"Sa Lavee!" If you were an Indian—"Ugh! Me not know!" But you couldn't be both—you couldn't be both! So this mixed up, blended, all-together people along with the full-blooded Cree and Chippewa, and everyone in between, *rebelled*. It wasn't long before the Canadian government (*Gestures "hanging"*) hung Louis Riel. And everyone who supported Louis Riel had to flee across the border into the United States. That meant not only the Metis had to flee, but their full-blooded Cree and Chippewa relatives had to flee as well....

Music: *Mystical sounds of quiet foreboding, such as chanting voices, wind and percussion instruments, begins here, as music for "The Smallpox Dance." (Suggestion: "Moonlight and Jaguar" [7:47] from the album* Little Wolf Band.)

NARRATOR *gestures as if looking out over the vast continent that would become the states he names.*

... into Montana ... into North Dakota ... into Minnesota and into Michigan ... in search of food. For those who fled to the Great Plains, there were slim pickings. It was the late 1880s. The buffalo were gone. And what was left? Smallpox—the Red Death!

Scene 4
The Specter of Death
Time: 1836–1837

Music that has already begun continues. The NARRATOR *moves across the stage and places himself on the floor, near one of the panels. A "bundle" has been preset. Slowly, he opens it and slowly brings out a wooden puppet skeleton, which he props up and manipulates as if it is a lost friend. The Smallpox Dancer,* THE SPECTER OF DEATH, *enters from upstage right.*

The SPECTER *dancer wears a beige, off-white, or red body leotard, covering body and legs. The arms are bare and can be painted, as is the face, with the characteristic "poc" marks of smallpox scarring. Over the painted face is a mask of sallow skin color with "poc" marks. A beige cape with "torn strips" of cloth, fringe, or leather thongs can cover the dancer's upper body. The dancer enters enshrouded with a large blood-red blanket.*

The Smallpox Dance

Music: *Mystical sounds that began in Scene 3 continue throughout the following dance.*

Choreography: *The dancer enters, face and body draped with the red shroud. The* SPECTER *uses large, heavy strides to enter the space, advancing forward on three or four diagonals. The* SPECTER *arrives at down center stage, kneels, and menacingly removes the shroud from the face to reveal the mask. The* SPECTER *slowly stands and begins swaying left and right with the change of musical tempo. With more vigorous movement, the shroud is discarded, and the* SPECTER *dances with ever more frenzied turns, jumps, and falls. Beneath all movement is the hint of seduction. Finally, the mask is removed to reveal the Victim beneath, scarred and terrified of death. The Victim runs to escape its Fate but is caught up in its hypnotic terror. The dance ends with agonized rolls of the Victim toward upstage center, where the dancer becomes frozen into a death image. Lights fade slowly to black and dancer exits.*

Scene 5
Ten Cent Treaty
Time: 1892

The NARRATOR *moves the four small rocks throughout the following monologue until they form a small tight circle downstage center.*

NARRATOR

It was about the second half of the nineteenth century. The United States government decided it wanted all its Indians on reservations—all of them. There was a big movement west. Some guy named Horace Greeley wrote, "Go west, young man." Everybody went! They had to make room for the homesteaders, the farmers, the ranchers, traders, bankers, everybody moving west. The problem was the Indians were in the way. About … 1863, push came to shove. All the Indians who happened to be living on the United States side of the border were told they had to move onto the "reservation." But nobody knew where exactly, or on which land section, exactly.

Remember Chester Arthur? (*Asking an audience member.*) Do you? Chester Arthur—your PRESIDENT Chester Arth…. (*Ironically.*)

The Specter of Death (Santee Smith). Photo courtesy of Jim Dusen, 2000.

Oh, Chet, he was good to us! Now, Chet set up twenty-two "townships" in what would become the state of North Dakota for those Indians who happened to be living in that area. Now, twenty-two townships is about ... 7,500 acres of land. Seventy-five-hundred acres. Can anyone imagine ... a people accustomed to roaming over ... ten million acres of land being confined into 7,500 acres? But Congress wasn't done yet. It wasn't long before Congress—acting under pressure by its "constituency"—decided to reduce the twenty-two townships to ... two. About 200 acres. And that's when things went from bad to worse.

Because it just so happened that the Indian Agent from Washington, D.C. had handpicked thirty-two full-blooded Chippewa to decide who would be eligible for "enrollment." Of course, they chose their own peoples—because, after all, there was less and less land for more and more people. (*Four rocks have now been repositioned.*) Whole families were checked off the roles to reduce the numbers. It got so ridiculous that when a man named Little Shell, a Chippewa chief, returned from a hunting trip with his band, he was told—"Ah ... you don't live here anymore." Sounds like ROTTEN POLITICS to me.

(*A soft, slow drum beat.*)

1893. Washington, D.C. must have had a guilty conscience. They decided to make a financial offer for the land lost by those mixed, all-together peoples. Congress pulled a figure out of the air ... 93,000 dollars for one million acres of land. 93,000 dollars! Of course, they knew all along that they wanted the land, and they wanted it cheap, and that's exactly how they got it. And that "arrangement" became known as the Ten Cent Treaty, because the payment paid for that land amounted to not even a full ten cents an acre.

(*He flips a thin dime into the air. It falls to the floor.*)

Scene 6
Grandmother/Youth
Time: 1900

A dance hall on the reservation. The GRANDMOTHER *and her female companion appear in flounced turn-of-the-century cotton floor-length gowns, each carrying a large feminine handkerchief. The* NARRATOR *makes his character change by donning a French knit hat, or period reservation hat. Over one shoulder he places a powder horn. The stage is empty but well lit before the entrance of the two girls.*

Music: *A period French song. (Suggestion: "Ants, Mosquitoes, and Snowball Fricassee" from the album* Plains Chippewa/Metis Music from Turtle Mountain.)

A young girl's voice, sounding somewhat inadequate in social affairs, but enthusiastic about the opportunity to meet a young man, is heard over the song.

RECORDED VOICE
    Boozoo, Monamie!
    Oh, yes, this is a grand party!
    Have I heard this song before? I don't know, Monamie.
    It's a funny one—something about frogs and crickets and fairy
    coachmen?
    Oh, yes, I see—it is a French song from the old country.
    Dance? Oh, yes, I like to dance.
    Oh, yes, Monamie. I will dance with you!

Choreography for recorded voice: *Two young girls enter from stage left.* DANCER #1 *is the more experienced, pulling out the reluctant younger* DANCER #2. *The* NARRATOR *enters from stage left and comes to center stage. The girls coyly move downstage left to down right. There the two "discuss" the young man; the more experienced will "teach" the younger one how to get a dance partner.* DANCER #1 *approaches the* NARRATOR *up center stage, twirls her scarf coyly and otherwise entices him to dance.*

The Clog Dance

Music: *Fiddle music for a period French/Cree clog dance. (Suggestion: "Quebec Reel" from the album* Plains Chippewa/Metis Music from Turtle Mountain.)

Choreography: *The* NARRATOR *and* DANCER #1 *begin the basic clog step, facing each other, then turning toward the front and dancing directly downstage, then each around to their respective sides, to join again at upstage center. In the meantime,* DANCER #2 *is "learning" the steps at downstage right. She gradually makes her way to upstage center and behind the couple and around in front of them, until she dances directly between the* NARRATOR *and* DANCER #1, *who is now upset by this unexpected turn of events. The* NARRATOR *teams with* DANCER #2, *and they dance as a couple around the stage space.* DANCER #1 *follows them, angrily stomping behind. As they reach upstage center again, all join hands with* NARRATOR *at center. They all dance in a circle, then forward to front stage and back again. The two female dancers join hands and make a figure eight, while the* NARRATOR *begins clapping to spur them on.* DANCER #1 *and #2 continue with more complicated steps. The* NARRATOR *then walks between them and moves downstage to encourage the audience to begin clapping in time with the music.* DANCER #2 *now displays her newfound dancing prowess with her own improvisation at upstage center, as* DANCER #1 *again approaches the* NARRATOR *downstage right, and offers him her scarf as a momento. She quickly exits upstage left, anticipating that he will follow her. Instead, he pockets the scarf and approaches* DANCER #2 *from around the back. He grabs her scarf, and as the music finishes, playfully pulls her off stage right.*

(*The* NARRATOR *returns, breathless and momentarily happy. But he must go on with his story, and continues reluctantly.*)

NARRATOR

Next comes the tragic part. For the next twenty years, the mixed-up, misplaced, and in-between peoples—some full-blooded Chippewas, some Crees, along with the mixed-bloods—moved farther west, trying to find a home, any kind of home. Little did anyone know at the time that the homeless Indian was being created, right before our very eyes.

(*Soft, slow drum beat for thirty seconds.*)

With no reservation and no game for food, some of us went out on the prairie and scavenged for buffalo bones—left over from the carcasses of thousands of dead buffalo. We collected anything we could get our hands on—horns, hoofs, tails. Anything. After that, we had no choice. Since we didn't really belong anywhere, we gathered together as best we could … into caves and tents and sheds, and even into rusted out cars and trucks. Always out of town, left to make do on our own. Nobody knew who we were … and nobody took the time or effort to find out.

Scene 7
Grandmother/Age
Time: 1920

A high-backed wooden chair. The GRANDMOTHER *enters from behind the Panel of Ancestors, after the first three lines of monologue. She wears a floor-length black dress, her hair in a bun and a six-foot-long, two-inch-wide black scarf or cord is draped over her shoulders. It hangs down to her ankles. She slowly makes her way to the back of the chair and places her hands there. Throughout the monologue, she ages as she recalls each child's birth. She is seated on the chair by the last line of the monologue. The voice is recorded; its tonality reflects a woman who has aged beyond her years.*

RECORDED VOICE
How long have I been sitting here?
These days I lose track of time.
But it gives me time to remember how I got here.

It wasn't the way they told us it would be.
They told us that with plowing and cattle
And trapping and trading
We could live a new way.

Living the "new" way was a trade-off of sorts.
We traded elder wisdom—for no wisdom.
There were no doctors, not even aspirin
for childbirth and gunshot wounds and TB and alcoholism.
When the first child was born, I danced.

When the second and third and fourth child was born,
I asked, How could they be fed and housed and taught?
When the sixth child was born dead,
the terrible headaches began.
I buried him down by the lake.

When the seventh child was born, my womb had fallen.
Only by hanging standing upside down, with my feet tied with a
rope to a hook in the wall,
could I not scream.
I didn't dance anymore.

The Chair Dance

Music: *A fusion of western orchestral lyricism and a rather disembodied flute melody. Extremely melancholy, pained, and heavy in quality. (Suggestion: "Tidings" [5:19] from the Theodosii Spassov album* **Beyond The Frontiers.***)*

Choreography: *The* GRANDMOTHER *pantomimes taking two sips from an imaginary goblet placed beside her on an imaginary table. The six-foot-long black scarf draped around her shoulders is used throughout, as a headband, and to symbolically "tie" her legs up above her head. While sitting in the chair, she recalls the days of her youth as a clog dancer, and simulates the basic clog dance steps as she sits in the chair. As she recalls the troublesome headaches, she wraps the scarf around her head. She then rises, walks a few steps, then slowly collapses to the floor. The figure on the floor depicts the pain of childbirth, culminating in the tying of her legs as they are hoisted above her head. This illusion is accomplished with the manipulation of the length of scarf tied to one foot, so that when the feet and legs are in the air (as in a shoulder stand), the* GRANDMOTHER's *feet and legs appear suspended upside down from a hook in the wall. Releasing herself, she returns to the floor, unwinds the black scarf bond, and slowly makes her way to the chair. She sits again, straightens her dress and hair in an effort to regain her dignity, and takes one more sip from the goblet. With deliberation, she rises from the chair, and walks painfully to the exit.*

Scene 8
The Hotel
Time: 1940

NARRATOR *enters from stage right with the chair, places it center stage, and stands behind it.*

NARRATOR
(Delivered in a slow, drawl, cowboy-like, John Wayne voice.)

You know what they say about Injuns, don't cha?

*(*NARRATOR *sits on chair by straddling it, chair back to audience. He continues in a western drawl.)*

They say: "You know how they are. You cain't get five words out of 'em! You's never knows what they's a-thinkin'!"

(NARRATOR *dramatically spits toward stage left, then wipes his mouth. From offstage left, a bed sheet is thrown out, just in front of* NARRATOR. *The* MOTHER *enters briskly from upstage left, wheeling in a squeaky cleaning cart. She is dressed in hotel maid's dress, hair bandanna, and bulky shoes. She manipulates the sheets on the floor with her feet, managing to clean up the spit. She puts the sheet in the cart and exits with determination.* NARRATOR *stands and moves the chair to upstage right.* NARRATOR *continues in his normal voice.*)

So ... we live and suffer in silence.
But that doesn't mean we're not thinkin'.

The Sheet Dance

Choreographic movement continues, based on the MOTHER's *illustrating actions to the* NARRATOR's *story of scrubbing floors, making beds, washing windows, and dusting the rocks (knickknacks). The cleaning cart stays upstage left throughout the scene.*

(MOTHER *returns, carrying a bucket and mop. She proceeds to mop the floor energetically.*)

Well, you can bet ... this mother was thinking.
Yes, this mother was thinking when she took that job at the Flying
B Hotel.
Yes, this mother was thinking when she flushed that
Lysol down those toilets, fifty times a day.
"Caution. Chemicals hazardous to humans and animals."
"Caution: Do not get liquid into eyes, ears, nose, mouth, open
sores, bronchial tubes, or intestinal tract."
"Caution: If contaminated, see a physician!"

(MOTHER *finishes floor mopping, returns to the cart and comes center front with feather duster. After dusting unseen "knickknacks," she kneels and dusts the rocks at center front. She stands and fogs the window with her breath and polishes it with a cloth.*)

Yes, this mother was thinking when she shoveled ice and hauled
garbage and dusted knickknacks, and waxed floors on her hands
and knees for those nice ladies up the hill.

(MOTHER *returns to cart and retrieves the sheet. She manipulates it as if making beds, then sweeps across the floor as if dancing at a fantasy ball, then wraps herself in it, becoming the polishing machine.*)

Yes, she was thinking when she flung those bed sheets out over those beds ten times, twenty times, fifty times a day.

Yes, this mother was thinking, when she push-pulled that seventy-pound, heavy duty, super-duper industrial waxer polisher over those floors at the Bell Telephone Company every night for twenty-five years.

FROOOM to the right, FROOOOM to the left,

FROOOM to the right, to the left, to the right....

(*Continue the last two lines as a rhythmic chant, as needed, for the* MOTHER's *machine movements. Suddenly realizing what she is doing, the* MOTHER *stops and comes out of the sheet, and begins to fold it so that she can carry it under one arm. She moves downstage center, looking longingly out through the imaginary window.*)

Yes, this mother was thinking.

Here's my chance to see the end of the tunnel.

Here's my chance to join those ladies at the top of the hill.

(MOTHER *returns to the cleaning cart, and begins organizing its contents, as if it is fine crystal.*)

Or ... if she couldn't join them, then at least she might have a chance to put out fine china and fine crystal, on a fine table, in a fine home.

Yes, this mother was silent ...

but ... she *was* thinking.

(MOTHER *looks toward the imaginary window, thinking. She then gathers her cleaning items, and wheels off the cleaning cart to upstage left.* NARRATOR *comes down center. He repeats her movements of fogging the window and polishing it with an imaginary cloth.*)

NARRATOR

You know what they say about Injuns, don't cha?

(NARRATOR *smiles, laughs under his breath, and exits slowly upstage right with the John Wayne walk.*)

The Hotel (Stephen Fadden and Rose Stella). Photo courtesy of Jim Dusen, 2000.

Scene 9
Mother/Age
Time: 1950

The recorded voice is that of the MOTHER *in middle age, in full command of herself and her powers. She has made a success of her ambitions. Her voice is heard in blackout.*

I married a good man, and for the next thirty years,
we worked three or four jobs at a time.
Now, signs like "No Dogs or Indians Allowed," were not to be seen in store windows.
We made enough money to build a house next to those nice ladies on the hill.
My child would be educated with the best of them.
For all this, I paid a price.
I knew who I was, on the inside.
But on the outside, I had become the "invisible" Indian.

The Balancing Dance

Music: *Strauss Waltz segues into a singing Native American male voice.*

Choreography: *The* MOTHER *steps into the light upstage center. She is dressed in an ankle-length evening gown, white elbow-length gloves, and elaborate white mask. She begins moving to the strains of the waltz, white gloves gesturing into the air. Occasionally the gesture is "washing windows." She dances downstage, obviously having a good time, enjoying the ball; she waves to friends. The* NARRATOR *enters from upstage right, wearing a full tuxedo and white bow tie; he is carrying a very full wine glass in his gloved hands. They meet and dance as partners. Just as the dancing is becoming truly a fantasy, the* NARRATOR, *without warning, tightens his grip on the* MOTHER, *and confronts her with the following words. The dancing continues as the* MOTHER *creates the illusion of a high wire, walking diagonally across the stage, up left to down right. She balances herself, as if in the struggle to balance her past and present.*

(*The* NARRATOR *follows her movements on the high wire as he delivers a series of derogatory comments.*)

NARRATOR

Whatayamean, full blood? You know your grandma wasn't full blood!

And she wasn't full-blood Blackfeet neither!

Everybody knows she was some other tribe. Like Chippewa, or Cree, or something like that.

And that other half had some foreign blood mixed in with it ... like Irish or German or French or—Italian!

Enrolled? Ha, ha. You expect to be enrolled with that kind of mixed-up blood?
That's right next door to the MONGREL DOG category if you ask me.

(MOTHER *loses her balance on the high wire and nearly falls, but she manages to reach the other side quickly, and alights from the high wire. She glares at* NARRATOR, *then suddenly throws liquid from the wine glass in his face. The Native American chant has already begun. The* NARRATOR *is stunned into a stationary, butler-like statue. The* MOTHER, *in disgust and suppressed rage, methodically removes her white mask and the white gloves one at a time, and disparagingly places each over his unmoving arms. From*

his jacket she removes a rattle and walks toward the center Ancestral Portrait. The back-
ground music has segued into a Native song. She turns and begins a round dance step in
a small circle, singing softly. The singing grows louder as she dances downstage toward the
audience, continuing sideways toward right stage. Her voice overpowers the male voice of
the recording, which fades out. She stops nearly at the curtain and finishes her song, now
in full voice. The song closes with four vigorous shakes of the rattle and a triumphant
woman's call. Immediate blackout. All exit.)

Scene 10
Daughter/Youth
Time: 1970

Lights up on NARRATOR, *who is now center stage, right foot on a small stool, a half*
mask propped on his knee so that it is facing the audience.

NARRATOR:

But life went on for these mixed-up families, with tradition and
without tradition. Some traditions were preserved, some were
lost, and some new ones created, from those mixed-blood families. In this generation, a "Renaissance of Remembering" is taking place. Children are asking questions about who they are and
where they came from. It's time for the truth, the whole truth,
and nothing but the truth. It's time to remember. In remembering—
we live!

(NARRATOR *puts on the mask as he moves downstage left, facing audience. He begins a*
repetitive gesture, in which he rhythmically checks the time on the watch, left wrist, then
right wrist.)

Mistaken Identity Dance

A bustling, noisy airport. Recorded sound effects of jet planes taking off. The
DAUGHTER *enters from upstage left, wearing modern pants, shirt, and a loose-fitting*
summer jacket. She is carrying an airline ticket and newspaper. The DAUGHTER *is about*
to experience being recognized as only an "exotic," not as an indigenous person.

Choreography: *The* DAUGHTER *moves downstage right to check an airline monitor, then moves to center stage to sit on the stool. She opens the newspaper to read. A third figure enters from upstage right, crosses to behind the* DAUGHTER, *then to the* NARRATOR, *tapping him on the shoulder, with a gesture to the* DAUGHTER *as if to say, "Look at this!" Third figure moves downstage right and freezes in position. The* NARRATOR *moves toward the* DAUGHTER *on the first recorded voice line, "Excuse me." Thereafter, the choreographed movements of the trio should convey a rude inquisitiveness, bordering on an unconscious racial antagonism toward the* DAUGHTER, *initiated from the recorded voice sequence below.*

RECORDED VOICES (*Continuous after airplane sounds recede into the distance.*)

> Voice #1: Excuse me, young lady. I couldn't help but notice you. You look so Oriental!

> Voice #2: I hope you won't mind my asking. What's your nationality? Race? Origin? Genetic association? Ethnic grouping?

> Voice #1: Who are you? Where do you come from? Are *you* American?

> (*The* NARRATOR *and second masked figure create humorous tableaus behind the* DAUGHTER.)

> Voice #3: Are, you—Japanese? Chinese?

> Voice #3: Pakistani?

> Voice #1: Excuse me, ma'am. You look so Korean!

> Voice #1: I hope you don't mind my asking....

> Voice #2: I hope you don't mind *my* asking. Are you from Hawaii?

> Voice #3: You must be Filipino!

(*The* NARRATOR *and second masked figure remove* DAUGHTER'*s coat and wrestle for it in a tug of war.*)

> Voice #1: You have such an exotic face ... but I can't reconcile the face with the height!

> Voice #3: I know. You're from Madagascar!

(*In response to this last remark, the* DAUGHTER *mimics a karate blow, which sends the second masked figure falling backward into the arms of the* NARRATOR. *He/she recovers to a standing position. Undaunted, the two masked figures slap their palms together as if to say "Aha!" They spread their arms like airplane wings, and swoop away like birds. They walk/fly/dance off the stage.* DAUGHTER *remains on stage.*)

Scene II

Daughter/Age
Time: The Present

The Remembering Dance
Part I

The DAUGHTER *is left on stage alone. She retrieves her coat and puts it on. Music in an up-tempo, jazzy style begins.*

Music: (*Suggestion: "The Road to Mugla" from Theodosii Spassos' album* Beyond the Frontiers.)

Choreography: *She moves about the stage, gesturing her anger at her treatment by the masked figures, mocking them. Her movements are based on natural rhythmic gestures of clenched fists, angry pacing about the stage which bursts into jazz-like or hip-hop movements. The stool is used as a dance prop, such as threatening to throw the stool at the audience, swinging it over her head, moving in circles with the stool, etc. Gradually her movements become more expansive and free, expressing her own sense of self. Finally, she looks up into the surface of the stool as she holds it over her head, and she sees her own image, which she then compares to each of the photographs in the Panel of Ancestors. She begins to recognize them, and her relationship to them. She begins to see her own identity. With this realization, she calmly sits on the stool, thinking.*

The Remembering Dance
Part II

Music: *A flute melody.*

The voiceover is the DAUGHTER, *speaking softly and confidently.*

RECORDED VOICE
    I am not "half" anything.
    I am the sum total of my ancestors.
    I am my mother. I am my father. I am my Grandmother. I am my Great-Grandmother.
    I am the living legacy of the woman who survived the Red Death of 1837.

Choreography: *The* DAUGHTER, *sitting on the stool, is moved by the memory, and reprises the dance movements of her* GRANDMOTHER's *clog dancing. She finishes, back to the audience, and slides her body head first to the floor, with legs in the air, reminiscent of the* GRANDMOTHER's *birthing dance. She rolls over onto the floor, facing upstage. She sees again, the Panel of Ancestors. She stands slowly and moves toward the center panel with the words "I am the living legacy...." She turns to face front after the word* 1837.

(*The* DAUGHTER *comes forward, and carries the stool down front. As appropriate, the* DAUGHTER *can also sit on the edge of the stage.*)

DAUGHTER

My mother left this world in the middle of winter, four days before the New Year. An old Blackfoot woman at the funeral said she heard the sound of wings beating in the air. It sounded so good, she said, that it almost drowned out the words of the priest. My mother was buried that same day, down by the lake, under a cool aspen tree. Four days after that, a letter arrived. It was addressed to her:

DEAR APPLICANT:

YOU HAVE BEEN DETERMINED TO BE A DESCENDENT OF THE PEMBINA CHIPPEWA PURSUANT TO THE PROVISIONS OF THE ACT OF DECEMBER 31, 1982, PUBLIC LAW 97-463.

SIGNED, SINCERELY YOURS,

SUPERINTENDENT, DEPARTMENT OF THE INTERIOR, BUREAU OF INDIAN AFFAIRS.
UNITED STATES OF AMERICA

(*The* DAUGHTER *folds the letter until it is almost postage stamp size. She then carefully places the folded letter into the medicine pouch around her neck [invisible until now], which she removes and lovingly places downstage left. A dreamcatcher will be placed here by one of the* JINGLE DANCERS *at the end of the next scene. Satisfied with the completion of her story, the* DAUGHTER *surveys the storytelling scene, and then slowly leaves the stage, exiting preferably on a straight forward path through the audience.*)

Scene 12
No Home but the Heart
The Timeless Present

The Spirits Dance

The NARRATOR *enters, picks up the stool, and moves downstage left where he places the stool.*

NARRATOR
In a time long past,
Lived a man whose daughter had become very ill.
Months passed.
And she did not get better.

Choreography: *A single* JINGLE DANCER *enters from upstage right. She enters not with the traditional step, but with high, soft steps, as if tiptoeing. She gestures at first, with a feather fan in one hand, and a dreamcatcher in the other. She steps softly, gently, moving right and left to stage center. She faces center front in affirmation, and then begins dancing toward the left with a round dance step.*

Three more dancers join, preferably entering each from a different direction. As they join together and continue dancing, they vary the step into the old time Jingle step and then into the modern step, in sequence. They dance and gesture as appropriate to the words of the NARRATOR, *building in strength, and then fall back into the quiet, soft stepping. The dance is done in silence, except for the sound of the jingles.*

One night,
A certain man heard in a dream the *sound* of the spirits.
As the sound grew louder,
he saw it was the spirits dancing.

(Three more JINGLE DANCERS *enter, each entering every second or third line given below.)*

When he awoke, he told his wife of the dream.
They talked and prayed about that dream.
And when the time was right,
Four girls were selected.
This man's wife made regalia for those girls
So that they would honor his dream.
When all was ready and the appointed day arrived,

The girls danced
As the spirits had danced.

(All four dancers dance as a group for two to three minutes. As the dancers slow to a walking step, each places a dreamcatcher at predetermined points, approximating four directions, around the stage.)

Ever since then,
We have danced in this way,
As the way to pray
For all those who are suffering from abuse,
Or from loneliness.
Ever since then,
We have danced in this way
As the way to pray
for all those suffering from any sickness,
Whether it is in the past or the present or yet to be.
Ever since then,
We have danced in this way
As our way to pray.

No Home But The Heart (L to R: Daystar/Rosalie Jones, Rose Stella, Santee Smith, and Stephen Fadden). Photo courtesy of Jim Dusen, 2000.

(The JINGLE DANCERS *exit quietly througout the last four lines. Slow fade to black.)*

Optional Finale

Full stage lights up. Various intertribal dancers enter, dancing with spirit and energy, in a dance of celebration of their ancestry, history, and way of life.

END

Ghost Dance

A Play

Annette Arkeketa

Artist's Statement

Ghost Dance is an intellectual, emotional, and personal experience for me. *Ghost Dance* is about the repatriation of Native American human remains and cultural patrimony items. It is a story with ancient roots and a contemporary beat that weaves a tragic drama into an ending with hope for our future. This play was created to show all communities how disturbing the robbing of our ancestors' graves is and how it affects Indian people.

As an activist, writing is my contribution to facilitating change in our society. Writing is my weapon to combat the social injustices that indigenous people battle daily. I write to expose the popular culture to indigenous issues and concerns. I have been active in the repatriation of Native American remains since 1991 on national, regional, and local levels. I have witnessed, researched, and experienced the many dimensions of repatriation issues, which involve spiritual matters, political advocacy, and scientific debate. I write on these matters because the indigenous perspective is important and necessary.

The repatriation of Native American remains is a culturally sensitive issue for many tribes. I have been blessed with beautiful friends, great contemporary heroes/heroines, and a patient family. The following are the many people who shared and supported my visual dream of *Ghost Dance*, and taught me about repatriation through political activism, spiritual participation, academic essays, books, articles, and personal stories:

Jana and Cricket Rhoads; Tulsa Indian Actors' Workshop; Thunderbird Theatre; Pat Melody and Jennifer Attocknie; Marla Red Corn; Angie Hamilton; Richard Hill Sr.; Peter Jemison; Jim Northrup; Tessie Naranjo; Lawrence Hart; Gordon and Connie Yellow Man; Walter Echo-Hawk; Roger Echo-Hawk; James Riding In; Ron "Sam" Little Owl; Pamina Yellow Bird; Lee Lone Bear; Maurice Eben; Dr. Dorothy Lippert; the late Dr. Kimball Smith; the late Dr. Jack Jackson; the late William Tall Bull; Hamon Wise; Floyd Young Man; Suzanne Shown Harjo; Sierra Adare; Dr.

William Huie; Dr. Cornel Pewewardy; Juanita Pahdopony-Mithlo; Harry Mithlo; Shiloh Perkins; Ray Hernandez; Don Patterson; Steve Russell; Paul Shunatona; Ruth Soucey; Janet Johnson-Peatross; Wordcraft Circle of Native Writer's and Storytellers; Otoe-Missouria Buffalo Clan; American Indian Ritual Object Repatriation Foundation; my husband Al Rendon; my children Levi, Jonathan, and Stephanie; my parents the late Ben Arkeketa and Mary Arkeketa; and my sisters Susan, Tricia, Kim, Ginger, and Jenise.

Ghost Dance

Characters

ARTIST, Indian male

BOY, eleven-year-old Indian

GIRL, nine-year-old Indian

HOKTI BUFFALO, thirty-year-old Indian female attorney

GRANDMA, Mrs. Chief's Blood, Hokti Buffalo's grandmother,
    Indian

GRANDPA, Mr. Chief's Blood, Hokti Buffalo's grandfather, Indian

LORI BUFFALO, fifteen-year-old Indian, Hokti's sister

ALCOHOL SPIRIT, female

LARRY, thirty-year-old white man, Hokti's ex-boyfriend

LOCUST, thirty-year-old Indian Two Spirit, male, Hokti's cousin,
    tribal historian, may also be ARTIST with an older demeanor

SHERLOCK, Dr. Fields, fifty-five-year-old white man, archaeologist,
    wears suit with bow tie

DR. BEN BISON, thirty-five-year-old Indian male archaeologist,
    wears suit and ponytail

WILD BILL, thirty-five-year-old tribal chairman, attorney, judge,
    Vietnam veteran, very handsome

JONATHAN, tribal member

MR. WHITE, auctioneer, white man

SENATOR JAMES, chairman of congressional committee, male

SENATOR TURNER, Senate committee member, black female

STANDING WOMAN, eighteen-year-old Dakota woman

PLUME, six-year-old Cheyenne girl

NEE, ancient ancestor

Setting

I recommend a three-tier-type stage to make the staging more interesting and resourceful for the scene changes and to accommodate the
actors/actresses; however, I encourage the creative talents of the directors
and their production experts to develop a setting that is accommodating
and necessary, given their space and budgets. I don't know what it is like

to be a director, but I have confidence that if a director wants to work on *Ghost Dance*, he or she has ideas of his/her own that will take on a life of their own to tell the story of repatriation.

One of the questions posed during the consultation with the cast and crew at the Gilcrease Museum during the 2001 reading was "What is the era of this setting?" I explained that this story had no boundaries for an "era." Repatriation is an infinite problem. The times fluctuate with our contemporary times, future, past, future-past-present-future. These are the "time zones" I have experienced with repatriation.

Playwright's Note

Ghost Dance can be presented as a full-length drama or staged as a reading performance. The monologue of STANDING WOMAN has been used in drama competitions and also as an audition monologue. The reading performances of *Ghost Dance* have recently been used to open up a dialogue about reburial issues in Native communities. After the performance, the producers usually have a panel of repatriation educators, spiritual leaders, and advocates to answer questions the audience may have about repatriation.

This is a story with fictional settings and characters, but with symbolic significance regarding Native communities and repatriation. I encourage the creative talents of directors. I recommend a set design that facilitates a smooth transition for set changes. As always, my greatest concern is that each word is spoken clearly and loudly enough for the audience to hear, but with enough finesse that the natural rhythm of the dialogue is maintained throughout the play.

Production History

In the summer of 1999, the actors from the Tulsa Indian Actors' Workshop first read *Ghost Dance*. In January 2001 Elizabeth Theobald Richards directed a public reading of *Ghost Dance* at the Gilcrease Museum in Tulsa, Oklahoma. The play has also been read at Tulsa Unversity May 2002 by the Tulsa Indian Actors' Workshop in collaboration with artist Shan Goshorn's photography exhibit of her Earth Renewal Series on Repatriation.

Act I

Theater is pitch black. The sound of a shovel digging and cold wind sets the tone for the opening scene.

Opening Scene

The ARTIST *is painting symbols on a brick wall. The outline of a buffalo robe is on the wall. He is spray-painting symbols ancient and new on the wall inside the outline of a buffalo robe. The* BOY *and* GIRL *are passing by and stop to look at the symbols. They are curious and want to know what he is doing. He explains that he is telling the story of the Indians. They want to know about the Indians. They have only heard stories. There are no longer any Indians. What happened to them?*

BOY
> What are you spray-painting? What do these lines mean?

ARTIST
> The story of the Indians.

GIRL
> What do you mean? What happened to them?

ARTIST
> See here. (ARTIST *points at hand print.*) This is where they made their mark, before they became no more. This is to show you that they once walked these streets, drove past in their Mustangs and Broncos. Kind of like an autograph. Now it is a fossil tag.

BOY
> You mean they had cars and trucks?

ARTIST
> Some of them did. Others had bus fare or relatives who gave them gas money to drive them around.

GIRL
> The Indians in the movies had horses and lived in tipis. Did the soldiers kill them all?

ARTIST

(*Sizing up the inquisitive little girl.*)

No, the soldiers didn't kill them all, although they tried … you don't need to know. Besides everyone is glad they are gone. They are especially glad to be gone, they don't have to suffer as human beings any longer. Hey, don't you have to be running along? Isn't it time for your nap or cartoons or something you *just* have to watch on TV?

GIRL

Naps are for babies an' old people.

BOY

Tell us more about the Indians? Where did they go and why are they glad to be gone?

ARTIST

It is a long story. You two run along; you probably have better things to do.

BOY

No, we just have homework to do. We have time!!

GIRL

Tell us! Tell us! I want to know right now!

ARTIST

OK, OK. When I begin this story I want you to listen carefully. I will only tell you once. So you must remember everything exactly as I tell it. It is a true story. Got that? If you change the words around, you are not listening.

GIRL

Huh?

BOY

I'm lis'ning? I'm lis'ning?

ARTIST

You must listen with your heart open. It is useless to only listen with your ears. When you open your heart, you will hear and you will remember the words exactly.

GIRL

Does that mean we will know what happened to the Indians if we listen with our heart open? Wouldn't that hurt?

ARTIST

Yes, sometimes it does hurt.

BOY

Ssshhh, be quiet, let him tell the story. We have to know the words 'xactly.

GIRL

Yeah, 'xactly.

ARTIST

Long time ago, around the turn of the century, there were a group of people. They were called Human Beings, People of God, or what most people know them as, Indians. There were lots of these folks, for as far as the eye could see. There were tall ones, short ones, round ones, lean ones, happy ones, and not so happy ones. There was one particular one, Hokti, who wasn't so happy and had become very ill ... she was in the hospital....

Scene I

A hospital room. HOKTI *is lying on a bed with* GRANDMA, GRANDPA, *and* LORI *gathered around.* HOKTI *has slipped into a coma.* GRANDPA *starts singing a traditional prayer song.*

LORI

No Grandpa, Hokti doesn't know the songs anymore.

(GRANDPA *sings louder.* HOKTI *gets out of the bed with the family standing up looking at the body on the bed, they do not see her. She is listening and observing the reaction of her family at the news she is dying.*)

HOKTI

Lori, I do know the song.

GRANDMA

Grandpa, she's not ready to leave us. I won't believe it. Hokti will pull through this, I know she will.

HOKTI

Grandma, I am right here, I am still alive!

(*The* ALCOHOL SPIRIT *enters and is laughing at* HOKTI. HOKTI *looks at the* ALCOHOL SPIRIT *and realizes she is looking in a mirror. The* ALCOHOL SPIRIT *talks to her and laughs mockingly.*)

HOKTI

Why are you laughing at me?

ALCOHOL SPIRIT

Because, you are dead. Diseased, terminated, checked out, and nobody cares. (*Starts laughing again.*)

GRANDMA

Hokti, I know you are there. Whatever it is troubling you, leave it behind, leave it behind. Come back to us.

LORI

The doctor says there is no hope. Now she won't suffer. Now *we* won't suffer.

From left: Marla Red Corn as Hokti and Jana Rhoads as Alcohol Spirit. Photo by Tom Fields, 1997.

HOKTI

Lori, how could you say such a thing?

GRANDMA

Be quiet. She can hear you.

LORI

She can hear us?

GRANDMA

Yes Lori, she hasn't left us....

LORI

(*Interrupting* GRANDMA *and speaking directly to* HOKTI.) Hokti, go to the Spirit World, you won't be sick anymore. God will take care of you. Now you won't be so unhappy. You won't make Grandma and Grandpa unhappy. (*Hesitantly.*) You ... you won't come home drunk anymore.

(LORI *starts crying;* GRANDMA *holds her to comfort her.*)

HOKTI

Oh Lori, I am so sorry.

LORI

You aren't the same Hokti. I miss my sister, but you're not my sister. My sister would never hurt any of us.

(LARRY, HOKTI's *boyfriend breaks in frantically on the scene; he goes to* HOKTI's *bedside.*)

LARRY

Is it true? Is she dead?

HOKTI

Larry, how sweet, you came to see me.

ALCOHOL SPIRIT

(*Laughs again.*) Yeah Larry, here we are, ready to party.

GRANDMA

Larry, please leave, we want to be alone with Hokti.

LARRY

But, but, Hokti loves me. How can I leave? Besides, she owes me money! I have all the documents here. If you will just sign here, Mrs. Chief's Blood....

HOKTI

What??? Larry, how could you?

GRANDMA

Get out!

LARRY

(*Agitated and an obvious cocaine abuser.*) Mrs. Buffalo, you don't understand, if she is dying, there are insurance benefits to discuss. She owes me!

HOKTI

What!? I owe you? For what?

ALCOHOL SPIRIT

For drinks!! A round for everyone!

HOKTI

(*To* ALCOHOL SPIRIT.) Ssssh! Be quiet.

ALCOHOL SPIRIT

Just one, one for the road.

GRANDMA

My granddaughter is dying. How dare you come in here and demand that she owes you anything.

LARRY

(*Tries different approach.*) But Mrs. Chief's Blood, I, I ... I love her.

HOKTI

You love me?

ALCOHOL SPIRIT

He does love you. He just said it!

HOKTI

Yes, that's just it. He just said it. Now that he thinks I am dead.

LARRY

Besides, you don't know the sacrifices I have made for your granddaughter. I got her hired after she got fired from J & A Associates.

HOKTI

You are such a liar. My grandfather got me that job.

GRANDMA

You are a pitiful young man. Go home, son. The only one that owes you are your people. They owe you a better example of how you need to get away from all those things that poison your mind. Please leave. (*Clutching her chest as if in pain.*)

LORI

Grandma, are you OK?

(GRANDMA *nods at* LORI, *reassuring her that she is fine.*)

LARRY

Old woman, you can't make me leave, and I won't....

GRANDPA

Yes, she can make you leave. And, you will. We are tired of you waiting shameless like a vulture for my granddaughter to die. But she is not dead and she's not ready to die. We are here for her. God is here with her. Now leave or I will call the police.

LARRY

You can't throw me out of here.

GRANDMOTHER

I will give you one minute. (*Picks up the phone to call security.*)

LARRY

You don't know who you are talking to. I need these papers signed.

(GRANDPA *takes the papers from* LARRY *and tears them up.* GRANDMA *is talking on the phone to security.* LARRY *realizes he must leave.*)

LARRY

    I'll be back for my money. (*As he exits sounding desperate,* LARRY's *voice trails off.*) She owes me, she owes me big time.

(ALCOHOL SPIRIT *is laughing.*)

HOKTI

    Hey, I am getting pretty tired of you and your laugh.

ALCOHOL SPIRIT

    Why? It is yours, everything about me is yours.

HOKTI

    (*Talking to the* ALCOHOL SPIRIT.) You're not me. I don't even know who you are.

ALCOHOL SPIRIT

    Sure you do, take a real good look. I'm the one who comforts you when you are alone. You love me when you are afraid. You drink me to show people you can be real tough. You love me more than life itself. I am always there for you.

HOKTI

    (*Taking a look.*) How can you be me? You look bloated. Your eyes are bloodshot and your hair; it is so brittle. Your skin looks like an old piece of leather. (HOKTI *looks at the body on the bed and realizes it is herself.*)

    Why is my skin so yellow?

GRANDMA

    Lori, Hokti is not dead. She is still here, I know she is. I can feel her.

LORI

    But Grandma, I don't think she is happy here. She used to be so beautiful. What happened to her?

GRANDMA

    She is still beautiful, Lori. You must not give up on her. She will come back and she will be more beautiful.

LORI

I used to want her to come home, but now she shows up and all she wants is money from you and Grandpa. Then I hear you cry; it makes me angry at her.

HOKTI

I had no idea, Lori.

LORI

I want our life back the way it used to be, when we were all together we laughed and talked about everything.

HOKTI

So do I, Lori, and I'll make sure....

ALCOHOL SPIRIT

(*Sympathizing in a sarcastic manner.*) Me too, Lori, me too....

HOKTI

(*To* ALCOHOL SPIRIT.) Don't you dare say her name.

ALCOHOL SPIRIT

(*Mumbling.*) Oh no, never again.

LORI

Hokti, you don't talk to me anymore. What did I do? I am sorry for whatever I did.

HOKTI

Lori, you didn't do anything. This is not your fault.

LORI

She used to help me with my homework and comb my hair and we would tell each other secrets. She would say, "Now this is a sister secret, and those are sacred." (LORI *and* GRANDMA *console each other.*) I miss my sister.

ALCOHOL SPIRIT

Hah! Who needs that sacred sister stuff? I know all your secrets, and I won't tell. They will be sacred with me.

HOKTI

Oh God, what have I done?

ALCOHOL SPIRIT

You need a drink Hokti. I am here for you like I have always been. I comfort you when people tell you you're no good. Like the time your partner lost that case with the Williams Company and he blamed it all on you.

LORI

We used to go to Sweet Water Pond and tell our dreams.

ALCOHOL SPIRIT

I'm there for you when you meet all those people who talk to you like you are not as smart as they are.

HOKTI

Stop! I don't want you here. (*Turning to* LORI.) Oh Lori, I forgot about those times. They were always special.

LORI

We were going to be the best basketball players.

HOKTI

The best dancers.

LORI

The best singers.

LORI AND HOKTI

(*Like a familiar chant.*) The best at everything.

HOKTI

We said we would make Grandma and Grandpa so happy that they will bust with pride when people ask "Mr. and Mrs. Chief's Blood, is that your granddaughters?"

ALCOHOL SPIRIT

Oh gads, now I need a drink!

LORI

We would say, Grandma and Grandpa can't act too proud, or people will say, "Oh those Chief's Bloods sure do like to boast about their granddaughters." But we would make you so proud of us, you and Grandpa would brag anyway.

GRANDMA

I am proud of you, Lori.

HOKTI

I am, too.

LORI

But Grandma, we were going to do it together, forever; she promised, she promised.

HOKTI

I did promise.

LORI

You and Grandpa always told us. We are Indians, we always keep our word. We do not lie.

ALCOHOL SPIRIT

Now you really need a drink.

HOKTI

God, help me!

ALCOHOL SPIRIT

Come on Hokti, she's a little brat. Always questioning why you didn't go see her. We had better things to do!

HOKTI

I missed the state basketball playoffs; her team won. I promised her I would be there.

ALCOHOL SPIRIT

You promised her a lot of things. What's the big deal? You were the life of the party that night. Besides, your family and the whole tribe went to the basketball game. She didn't need you.

HOKTI

I promised them I would meet them there. I told Lori if they won I would take her team to go eat pizza. Instead, they called me the next day and wanted to know where I was. I lied to them; I told them I had to work late, I had a deadline.

ALCOHOL SPIRIT

You've lied to them plenty of times. What's the big deal? Hey, when we get out of here, I know a really cool place we can go.

HOKTI

I missed work the next morning, too damn hungover to go in. Then when I did get to work I got fired.

ALCOHOL SPIRIT

But you found another job right after.

HOKTI

Only because my Grandfather recommended me to one of his business associates.

ALCOHOL SPIRIT

At least they were nicer than the first firm that fired you. Boy, we were under a lot of pressure there.

HOKTI

Shut up!

ALCOHOL SPIRIT

Light, draft, vino? You definitely need me.

HOKTI

Dear God, please help me. Please dear God, take this awful craving away.

ALCOHOL SPIRIT

I can't go away, because I am you. You love me.

HOKTI

Oh God, no! You are not me. I am not you, or am I?

ALCOHOL SPIRIT

Everyone thinks you're dead, but I know you're alive.

HOKTI

Not Grandma, not Grandpa; they haven't let go of me.

ALCOHOL SPIRIT

But that's not enough, Hokti. They won't be around forever. I will. I am here always, forever.

LORI

Grandma, Hokti said she would always be there for me forever and ever; she said that meant a long time. I was afraid one time. I asked her what would we do if anything happened to you or Grandpa? I would be alone. She said not to worry she would be here for me.

HOKTI

What have you done to me? You are not me! I have more pride than what you have shown me!

ALCOHOL SPIRIT

(*Laughing.*) And your best pride is when we are all together, me, you, and lover boy Larry, partying over at the Two-Step Saloon.

HOKTI

Larry, the man of my stupid dreams comes in worried about money I owe? What a jerk. We're attorneys for christ's sake. What kind of attorney would ask their grandparents for money? Coke heads and alcoholics.

ALCOHOL SPIRIT

We have had some fun.

HOKTI

And we have had some times that were not so fun. How could you take advantage of me like that?

ALCOHOL SPIRIT

Because you're eeeeaaaasssyyyy. Remember, you said so yourself.

HOKTI

You are right. But, it isn't that way now, and it won't be again. I let you pull me down to that level, no more. Get out.

ALCOHOL SPIRIT

What are you going to do? Call the police? Arrest me? Huh, I'm not leaving. You need me.

HOKTI

No, you need me. Now get out.

(HOKTI *starts pushing the* ALCOHOL SPIRIT. GRANDMA *and* GRANDPA *stand beside the bed and begin to sing again.*)

ALCOHOL SPIRIT

(*Losing ground.*) But, I'm your best friend. you can't shut me out. I refuse to leave. I am everywhere. I'm around the corner. I'm in all the big advertisements. I'm a movie star. I'm your best commercial. You can't get rid of me!

HOKTI

You are nothing and nowhere. You no longer live through me anymore.

ALCOHOL SPIRIT

I'm your history, your present, your future.

HOKTI

(*She pushes the* ALCOHOL SPIRIT.) You are a false image, you are not my history and you are not my future. Now get out. God damn you, get out. I'd rather be dead than to have you back.

ALCOHOL SPIRIT

You are dead without me.

HOKTI

I am dead with you. Now go. I hate you, I hate you.... Dear God, help me!

ALCOHOL SPIRIT

(*Exits.*) You can't get rid of me; I'll be back.

(HOKTI *returns to the bed and begins to stir.*)

HOKTI
(*Mumbling.*) Help me, help me.

GRANDMA
We are here baby girl, we are here....

(HOKTI *sits up and makes regurgitation motions and sounds.* GRANDMA *helps her sit up. Lights fade.*)

LORI
I thought you were dead.

HOKTI
I was Lori. I am alive now. (*Realizing she has the chance to apologize.*) I am sorry baby girl. I love you with all my heart. (*She hugs* LORI.)

LORI
I was afraid.

HOKTI
You don't have be afraid anymore. When you were born, I vowed I would protect you. I felt important — I became a big sister. You are so precious to me. I never wanted anything to hurt you and I am the one who hurt you. I promise Lori, I will never hurt you again.

(LORI *pushes away from* HOKTI.)

HOKTI
Lori, I know I made you promises I didn't keep. That will not happen again. I will show you. I will not let anything or anyone ever come between us.

LORI
(*Hugging* HOKTI.) I want to believe you.

HOKTI
I know you do. And I know I can't expect you to now.

LORI

What about when you come home? Will you be like you were before? Will you be, you know....

HOKTI

Drunk? You can say it Lori, what I put you and the rest of the family through ... there will be no more of that.

GRANDMA

Granddaughter, I am thankful. You will be fine.

HOKTI

Lori, I heard everything you said.

LORI

Please Hokti, I only meant....

HOKTI

It isn't your fault for having those feelings. God knows I haven't been the best sister. I will make it up to you, you'll see. I won't be going back to that evil spirit again. I want to live!

GRANDPA

And you will. Aho!

(*Lights fade and come up on* ARTIST, LITTLE GIRL, *and* LITTLE BOY, *who look at brick wall with artist making a symbol of healing and throwing out the evil alcohol spirit.*)

GIRL

Is that what happened to all the Indians? Did the evil alcohol spirit get them?

LITTLE BOY

No, didn't you see that she turned the alcohol spirit away?

ARTIST

That was *one* of the struggles the Indian People had to battle with and they had other bad spirits to deal with.

(*End of scene. Lights fade.*)

Scene 2

Museum scene. There is an exhibit show titled FACTS: MORE INDIAN DEAD WAREHOUSED AND STORED IN MUSEUMS THAN LIVING TODAY. HOKTI, LORI, *and* GRANDPA *walk in while the tour is taking place.* DR. BEN BISON *and* WILD BILL *are in display cases. The stage is set up on three different levels. The displays are set up staggered.* DR. BEN BISON *is lying down, face up, dressed in a suit and tie. His display case will be down front center stage.* WILD BILL *is standing up in a judge's robe, up center stage. These characters are on display to make a public comment about Indian museums as modern-day Indian tombs and mortuaries across the nation. The display cases resemble coffins.*

LOCUST
(*Recognizes* HOKTI, LORI, *and* GRANDPA *as they come in the museum.*) Sister, you've come home! (*They all hug;* LOCUST *begins to lulu, then* HOKTI, *then* LORI *joins in.*)

HOKTI
Locust? You look so good (*Referring to his make-up.*) You look better than me! I'm jealous.

LOCUST
It does no good to be jealous sister. I've always looked better than you! Hah! (*They both laugh.*) Oh, it is soooo good to see you. Grandpa, Lori, right this way. We will visit later. I am working this little gig today.

GRANDPA
OK grandson.

LOCUST
(*Stops in front of case that is next to* DR. BEN BISON *exhibit. Animates his actions as he composes himself.*) This one you may recognize. He looks a lot like that actor that was abandoned in a Hollywood movie by his best friend, a white Cavalry soldier. You movie buffs may remember. (*He narrates dramatically.*) The situation got rough at the end of the movie; the Cavalry is about to ride in and massacre the tribe, so the white guy leaves and writes it in his diary…. Took up a whole reel of film to show what a good friend he had become;

then he rides off through the timbers, over a beautiful mountain with his woman into the sunset, leaving us poor Indians to the Cavalry to fend for ourselves. End of movie. Now how do you like them apples? Won all kinds of little gold Oscars, even had the Indians liking it ... they started adopting all the white movie stars.... This next one....

(*He is interrupted by* SHERLOCK.)

SHERLOCK
(*Examining* DR. BEN BISON *with a measuring tape, measuring his face and speaking to the audience with authority.*) This is definitely a Choctaw. Look at the contours of the cheekbones.

DR. BEN BISON
Wrong, wrong, wrong.

(*The talking exhibit startles the crowd.*)

DR. BEN BISON
Choctaw cheeks my butt.

(*He turns over and sticks his buns up in the air, then lets out a big fart. The tour crowd backs up except for* SHERLOCK. LORI *and* GRANDPA *laugh.*)

HOKTI
How disgusting!

LORI
(*Thinks it is funny.*) He made a big fart.

LOCUST
Oh, for heaven's sake!

DR. BEN BISON
(*He is on a sarcastic roll.*) Now tell me about these cheekbones, Sherlock?

SHERLOCK
(*Exaggerates an inhale and exhale.*) Beans, corn, and (*sniffs the air*) some sort of spice.

DR. BEN BISON
Garlic. You clever devil, you.

SHERLOCK
I thought you were dead. I mean, I at least thought you were wax.

DR. BEN BISON
You mean you wish I were dead. Sorry I ruined your morbid infatuation.

SHERLOCK
How dare you.

DR. BEN BISON
No, how dare you. No Choctaw blood here, Sherlock. I'm not going to tell you what tribe I am, because you won't believe me anyway. You will just wait till I am dead. Dig me up. Study my cheekbones. Decide you know that I am a Choctaw, ate corn chips, frybread, popcorn, beans and flavored myself with garlic. Then you will dust me with radioactive carbon, say I'm a few thousand years old, set me on a shelf for half a millennium, write a paper, and move on to the next dig.

SHERLOCK
(*Flustered.*) You rude ... crude...!

DR. BEN BISON
Now, that is a fact. Good show, Sherlock. Run along, you are missing the rest of the tour.

(DR. BEN BISON *sees* GRANDPA *and* LORI. *They recognize each other and give a sign of recognition.* HOKTI *is following the rest of the tour.*)

LOCUST
Yoo hoo, over here, now stay with the program.

LOCUST
Lori, our baby girl (*puts his arm around* LORI), is one of our most talented weavers. She was taught by our grandmother. She weaves exquisite clan belts for our babies. She begins the belts when word is sent that we have an expected child in the tribe. Bet'cha didn't know that, Sherlock.

SHERLOCK

(*To audience.*) Ahh yes, the umbilical cord doctrine.

LOCUST

We are fortunate to have some of her belts on display today.

LORI

Grandpa, you let Dr. Bison show my belts?

GRANDPA

Yes, Lori, your Grandma gave specific instructions to Dr. Bison to treat these belts like they are the most sacred thing in the whole world. I'm sure he'll return them in tip-top shape, or he'll have to answer to Grandma.

LORI

Uuuuuhhh, Dr.Bison, it won't be good to deal with Grandma if anything happens to my belts.

DR. BEN BISON

I know, Lori. Don't you worry, yer Grandma loves me.

LORI

Not as much as she loves me.

SHERLOCK

Mr. Locust, do you have any of your belts for sale?

LOCUST

Sorry, Sherlock. The belts are only for our tribal members. We do have other things for sale at the casino. Drop by, you may get lucky.

(*Everyone faces* LOCUST, *and* SHERLOCK *touches the belt, looks around suspiciously, then takes out a magnifying glass and examines the material.*)

DR. BEN BISON

Don't worry Lori, ole Sherlock here won't steal your belt. He waits until it is in the grave before he steals. He makes more money when he steals from the dead, by selling the grave goods to museums and auction houses.

SHERLOCK

Do I have to continue to endure your insults?

LORI

How can you sell things that you steal from graves? Why would you do that?

SHERLOCK

My name is not Sherlock. Dr. Bison, would you please quit harassing me.

DR. BEN BISON

No. Answer the young lady! Tell her how you make your living from the most helpless, the dead.

SHERLOCK

I will not address the issue of those things here.

DR. BEN BISON

Those *things* are human beings. And those things you have picked clean from their bones are their personal belongings. Tell her there will be an auction this Thursday of things that were looted by your company's excavation team.

SHERLOCK

Why, I have no idea what you are talking about.

DR. BEN BISON

Huh! I tracked the inventory history to your company.

LOCUST

Now gentlemen, you are interrupting the best part of the whole exhibit. This handsome hunk is Wild Bill. He's a judge and our tribal chairman. He just makes me want to … lulu.

LORI

Wild Bill, how did you get that name?

WILD BILL

By shooting at trespassers hunting illegally on our tribal lands. Scared the poop out of those poor poachers. That kind of helped calm the Nam nerves I acquired while serving in the Marines. My Grandpa was disappointed because he said I could shoot better than just grazing the earlobes and nose tips off those trespassers. He said the rabbits were relieved I took to shooting at the two-legged. I was getting pretty good, only one day I caught one trespasser a little too close to the temple, grazed him, my sight was off a wee bit. I figured I better aim at something else before I hit one between the ears. I decided to heal those frazzled trigger-happy nerves with a good healthy dose of law. I went to law school. Law school took my mind off of target practice and those Vietnam nightmares. Gave me a whole new set of nightmares, called Indian law. I got my law degree.

LOCUST

We call him and the tribal police "Sovereign Keepers." Don't cha love it?

WILD BILL

And hey, Sherlock, I like boiled meat, potatoes, frybread, and cherry Kool-Aid. Eeeeh-hah, you can't beat food like that.

LORI

What happens to the trespassers after you shoot them, Wild Bill?

WILD BILL

A few show up now and then at the federal court house, when I sit in for judges who take a vacation from the bench. When I recognize them, I ask them what happened to their earlobes or nose tips. They swear they had a fight with some sort of wild animal.

We put an ad in the local paper asking for the owners to claim their nose tips and earlobes at the tribal police station. Nobody ever comes in to claim them. We bury them out back.

DR. BISON

Sherlock, now there are some remains you can come after, only you probably won't get much money for them, unless you write a paper to explain "The Trespass Man Movement at Turtle Falls Reservation." Then that might generate some sort of supply and demand for your vulture vending.

SHERLOCK
Dr. Bison, our firm is very reputable and....

DR. BISON
They are a reputable Indian grave-robbing business. You have more remains of our ancestors in your county repositories than we have living here on this reservation.

SHERLOCK
They are not your relatives, they are from a different tribe than the Indian people that live here at Turtle Falls....

LOCUST
I'm the tribal historian, for your information, Sweetheart. (*Looking at* SHERLOCK) Those people you have sitting on your shelves exposed to the cold surroundings in your warehouses are my relatives.

SHERLOCK
According to my findings, your people have only been in this area for the last fifty years. Prior to that you were camped 200 miles north of here.

LOCUST
Tell me Dr. Sherlock.... What tribe are you?

SHERLOCK
Uh, what an absurd question. I am not Indian.

LOCUST
No, no, no ... I am not saying you are Indian, silly. I want to know, who are your people? You used to be indigenous from somewhere! Don't you know?

LORI
Duuuhhhhh.

GRANDPA
Lori, ssshhhh, listen.

SHERLOCK
Why (*stammering*), I, I'm Irish, German, and French.

LOCUST
How do you know that?

SHERLOCK
Why, my mother told me.

LOCUST
What town in Ireland, Germany, and France are you from? Do you speak any of those languages from those countries?

SHERLOCK
Why good heavens no. How should I know what town in Ireland, Germany, or France? That was at least two generations ago. I was born and raised in the United States. I am an American.

LOCUST
So you don't know what town your ancestors are from, what communities, much less your native language? How pathetic, you don't know who you are, yet you stand here surrounded by the beautiful indigenous people of Turtle Falls trying to tell us who we are?

SHERLOCK
Why, no. Yes. Well, I never thought about it.

DR. BEN BISON
Obviously.

LOCUST
Well, Sweetheart, you are definitely too much for me. I write about my clan and the activities we have. Contrary to popular belief, we have a written language. It is something *you* will never see, we protect it so *you* won't exploit it. What I write is how we live and how we have lived for centuries. Get it Sherlock? Then our children won't have to read an untrue history of our people.

SHERLOCK
My friend just recently wrote a book about the history of your people; it is called....

LOCUST
Is he from our tribe?

SHERLOCK
Well no, of course not; but he spent last summer here with the Two Star family and....

LOCUST
Well then, how the hell do you think your friend knows anything Sweetie? Hello? We do not authorize anyone to write about our people except our own historians. There are seven clans in our tribe. We each have our own clan functions. Your friend's book is a fraud to the public. How can he say he knows our history when he isn't even a member of our tribe?

SHERLOCK
A fraud? How can you say that? Why Rome Book Industries is one of the biggest publishers in the country. They certainly would know what is credible.

LOCUST
Not to us. And that is what matters.

SHERLOCK
Now wait a minute. My friend is a good writer and has written many books about Indians. I think he might even be part Cherokee.

(*All the Indians start laughing.*)

SHERLOCK
Why are you laughing?

WILD BILL
Sounds like we have a trespasser!

(*End of scene. Lights fade, with the sound of a gun shot whiz.*)

Scene 3

Kitchen of HOKTI's *grandparents.* HOKTI *is settling in as she has moved back with them after the hospital ordeal. She is greatly disturbed by* DR. BISON's *behavior at the museum.*

HOKTI

Grandpa, why did we have to stop by the museum? That man was rude and disgusting.

GRANDMA

Sounds like you and Dr. Bison were up to your old tricks? Did he have Lori's belts in a safe place?

GRANDPA

(*Chuckling.*) He had a "for sale" sign on it. Ten bucks, nobody wanted them.

GRANDMA

Good.

GRANDPA

Oh Ben, he sure is silly sometimes, but he gets his point across. I made some prayer sticks, with little pink and blue plumes. I gave them to Ben to give out to the white people so they would go home and pray. They wouldn't take 'em when he gave them away, so he stuck a price tag on 'em and they sold like hot cakes. They like stuff like that. I saw Sherlock buy one before he left. Ben said that some of 'em bring 'em back. They say they don't work. He charges 'em again and sends the same stick back home with 'em.

HOKTI

They pay again, Grandpa? That's ridiculous.

GRANDPA

Sure, kind of like those wicker and metal plates I see over at the mission. It comes back and people put money in it to pay for their prayers.

GRANDMA

Oh, you and Ben are always trying something on those poor white people. They are some way Grandpa, you shouldn't be making fun of them.

GRANDPA

No Grandma, it isn't like that at all, we just want to see how they react. We are doing a study on the white man.

HOKTI

Field notes and all?

GRANDPA

Sure, Ben is an archaeologist you know. He has to create experiments.

GRANDMA

More like experiences. You two are some way.

GRANDPA

This is research Grandma, we're going to write a book about the white man, called "Too Much for the Average Indian."

HOKTI

Grandpa, *you're* too much for the average Indian. (*Changing the subject.*) Grandma, it feels good to be home again. (*She inhales the aroma of the kitchen.*) I missed being home. I missed the smell of your kitchen. Why is it that only grandparents can have a kitchen that smells so comfortable? I went home with Angie Rain one time to her reservation, and we stayed with her grandparents and their home smelled like this.

GRANDPA

You can only smell those smells on grandmas. Aye, grandmas smell good. But you can't get that smell until the little grandchild runs around here all sweaty and sticky from running and playing.

HOKTI

But you old guys add the extra spice.

GRANDMA

Yeah, old spice. Aye.

GRANDPA

Don't forget, you have to be here.

HOKTI

I am here Grandpa. I don't know why I ever left and for so long.

GRANDPA

You had to leave Hokti. You had too much to learn, you just forgot that we're still here for you.

HOKTI

I know Grandpa. I learned more than I wanted to know. I am the one who is some way.

GRANDMA

Don't regret anything you have been through Hokti. You're home now and that's what matters.

HOKTI

And I thank God for that. I need help Grandma, I need to stay here for awhile. I need time to figure out what I want to do.

GRANDPA

Hokti, you stay here as long as you need to. (*Chuckling.*) If you start wrinkling up and getting white hair, then maybe you'll need to start thinking it is time to move on.

GRANDMA

You stay as long as you like. You don't need our help as much as you need the Creator's help. Don't ever forget that. You are never alone. We are only here to remind you of that. We love you granddaughter, we'll always be with you. There is nothing that can take that away.

HOKTI

I know that now Grandma. How could I be so stupid and blind about that?

GRANDPA

You were under the influence of an evil spirit, Hokti. You was easy prey. Good people are easy prey for evil.

HOKTI

How did you know? That's what I dreamed when I was at the hospital.

GRANDMA

A messenger was sent to you, so you could see what you were battling with.

HOKTI

It was real, Grandma. I was afraid. I was afraid mostly because I could see myself. I could see the terrible things I put you and Lori through. And the song Grandpa sang, I remember that song. You told me one time that the song would make the spirits come home and make us strong again and the buffalo would come back.

GRANDPA

Yes Hokti, it makes our spirit strong. It's a ghost song.

GRANDMA

We used to sing that to you girls when you would get sick or feel sad.

GRANDPA

Remember when Dog Tired died?

HOKTI

How could I forget? That old basset hound was so bent and broken from chasing rabbits, skunks, and cars. I used to ask him what he was going to do with the cars if he ever caught one.

GRANDPA

(*Chuckling.*) When we buried him, you sang that song big and loud. I thought all our relatives were going to come back from the spirit world and give Dog Tired back to you. Your little heart was so hurt. But my heart was happy to hear you sing like you did. I sang that song in the hospital to remind you and to remind myself of that time. You did get stronger, you put your little friend in the earth and you spoke to the Creator and asked the Creator to take care of your little friend. That is why I sang that song in the hospital. I knew you would speak to the Creator and ask for help.

HOKTI

I did ask the Creator for help. And I returned.

GRANDMA

Hokti Buffalo has returned.

HOKTI

Yes Grandma, I have returned. (*She hugs her grandparents.*)

GRANDPA

The words to that song are about our ancestors and how they go
to the spirit world to watch over us and they will return when....

(*The conversation is interrupted by a knock on the door.*)

GRANDMA

Grandpa, it's Locust.

GRANDPA

(*Answers the door.*) Grandson, come in, we were just sitting down to
eat, come join us.

LOCUST

(*Shakes hands with* GRANDPA.) Hello, good to see you Sweetie. (*Gives*
GRANDMA *a kiss on the cheek.*) You been feeling all right Grandma?
Taking your medicine?

GRANDMA

Yes, Grandson.

LOCUST

(*Gives* HOKTI *a kiss and hug.*) Hey, Hokti babe, good to see you
home. (*Turns to* GRANDPA.) I have a message for you Grandpa.
(*Speaks formally.*) There is to be an emergency tribal council meeting this evening at 6 o'clock. We need you there to discuss the
tribal leaders' decision about ceremonial burials.

GRANDMA

We will have time to eat and attend the meeting.

LOCUST

Sorry Grandma, I'm the camp crier tonight. I won't be able to
stay but I will take some of that fabulous frybread. I have to run
and find Dr. Bison. He will be addressing the council.

GRANDPA
    Here grandson (*handing him some bread*), we will be right along.

LOCUST
    Oh how lovely this bread looks, Aho! (*Exits.*)

(*End of scene. Lights fade.*)

Scene 4

Tribal council members seated at front of general council. The room is noisy as folks talk at once to one another. WILD BILL *pounds a gavel and brings the meeting to order.* LOCUST *has a laptop computer and is recording the meeting. He gestures, making facial and subtle body expressions to animate emotion, concern, and seriousness as the meeting unfolds.*

TRIBAL CHAIRMAN
    Ladies and gentlemen, I would like to call on Mr. Chief's Blood at this time to give the invocation to officially open this meeting. Mr. Chief's Blood will you please give the invocation.

GRANDPA
    (*Gives brief invocation in his native language.*) Creator, be in our hearts and minds as we gather as your children to seek your guidance. Ho!

CAST
    Aho!

WILD BILL
    Folks, we are called here tonight because of all the controversy and issues surrounding the looting of our cemetery. Seems no matter what we do, we cannot keep looters out of our cemetery.

JONATHAN
    (*Standing up and interrupting.*) Looters? I thought we was here to talk about the casino, not this grave stuff.

LOCUST
    Oh, Jonathan, sit down, that meeting is tomorrow night.

WILD BILL

(*Pounding gavel.*) Order, order. Sorry Jonathan, we rescheduled that meeting because of the occurrence last night. Mr. and Mrs. Two Hearts' son's grave was dug up and looted last night. (*The crowd gasps.*) As you know, Jason Two Hearts was buried just last week! The Sovereign Keepers are doing everything they can to find out who did this terrible crime. They have put a patrol unit around the cemetery twenty-four hours a day. Tonight we are here to address this situation. Our elders have already met and want to speak about this.

JONATHAN

(*Addressing the audience.*) Tom, Sara, I am very sorry to hear this, (*looking at* TRIBAL CHAIRMAN) but since you mentioned thievery, we better talk about criminals taking our thunderbird and spiderweb neon lights from the casino!

WILD BILL

Yes, Jonathan, I promise you we will look at those issues tomorrow.

LOCUST

That isn't a spider's web, it's a dreamcatcher, sweetie.

JONATHAN

Oh hey-la, whatever they call 'em, never seen anything like those 'till those wannabes started showing up around here. Used to be anybody who looked white, like them, said they were white folks! And they were proud of it! Now everybody wants to be an Indian. Now everyone is dream catching. Stealing them too, like that! (*Sits down.*)

(*The crowd is restless and the* TRIBAL CHAIRMAN *pounds the gavel and gets control once again.*)

WILD BILL

Please, let's continue. I have asked Dr. Ben Bison, our tribal archaeologist, to speak to us about this incident. I know a lot of you have questions about why this is happening. Dr. Ben Bison, please.

DR. BEN BISON
Thank you, Mr. Chairman.

JONATHAN
Hey Ben, ain't archaeology legal grave robbing? Ain't that what you guys do?

DR. BEN BISON
Yes, Jonathan, you could say that and I will tell you why.

DR. BEN BISON
What has happened last evening has been occurring since 1492.

JONATHAN
In 1492, you know who sailed the ocean, when it used to be blue.

HOKTI, LORI, LOCUST
(*Directed at* JONATHAN.) SSSShhhhhh!

DR. BEN BISON
But most of the recorded history of grave looting activity is from journal accounts from 1776. These recordings cite prolific activity of our people being exhumed from their graves. The deceased have had their jewelry, clothing, toys, and sacred personal items removed from their graves.

Federal policies to collect dead Indian bodies for the study of diseases was solicited by the Army in 1862. In 1867 there was an Army memorandum sent out to the field doctors to document the age and sex of skulls. Then in 1868, the U.S. Army Surgeon General went a step further and directed the medical officers to collect Indian skulls. This unleashed a massive collection of Indian skulls that were collected by army soldiers and personnel, bounty hunters, and other scavengers of our dead.

JONATHAN
Wait now, Doc, federal policies? You mean like it's on the books to do all this skull collecting as a bounty?

DR. BEN BISON

Yes, Jonathan. Not only skull collecting but mining for our burial items and clothing became popular when Thomas Jefferson was president. He looted the mounds near his Monticello estate. The federal government has endorsed the major activity of looting graves since then.

JONATHAN

Why us? Are the Indians the only ones that have federal policies that allow the government to do this?

DR. BEN BISON

Yes, our race is the only race that has to deal with this absurdity. We are big business and a way of life for museums and other institutional archaeology labs, like state universities. In some federal policies we are labeled as "archaeology property." We aren't even considered to be human beings. The anthropology and archaeology societies of this country say we are their property.

LOCUST

Dr. Bison, if we are the only race being dug up by these policies, wouldn't that be considered racist?

DR. BEN BISON

Yes. I call it institutional racism.

LORI

And don't they know that messing with graves and burial things will come back to them in bad ways?

DR. BEN BISON

Most of the people that do these sorts of activities don't believe the way we do. They are more interested in their studies of what they will find and how they can compile their data of measurements and analysis. They are not concerned with the spiritual consequences.

JONATHAN

How much do they get for us Doc? (*Makes sign language for money.*)

DR. BEN BISON

It depends, Jonathan. Some folks who pay (*makes sign language for money*) are private collectors, others are museum folks, archaeologists, or other collecting professions like auction houses. I did a sample study of a report I had on one auction house and the amount of sales ran into the millions.

JONATHAN

You mean we are worth more dead than alive!

DR. BEN BISON

Yes, Jonathan, we are worth more dead than alive.

JONATHAN

No wonder I can't get a decent doctor for my mother. She's ill you know. They can't seem to diagnose her illness. She said they won't be able to. She wants to go see an Indian doctor. But I told her, Mom, we are casino Indians now, no one goes to see the Indian doctors anymore.

DR. BEN BISON

Folks, because of this body snatching, there are now more Indian remains lying in museum repositories, state and federal repositories, and private collections than there are Indians alive in this country.

(*The crowd is restless.*)

WILD BILL

Mr. Chief's Blood will now address the council.

GRANDPA

(*Very emotional speech.*) It has been decided by the leaders of the seven clans that this community beginning the next new moon, for those of us who make our journey on to the next world, we will begin by cremating ourselves. (*The crowd gasps in surprise.*) If we do this then there will be no cause for anyone to disturb our journey to the next world. We will no longer have our ceremonial burials as we know it.

It has also been decided we will no longer be a tribe, we will no longer hold our traditional ceremonies. We will no longer say we are Indians. What will remain of us will only be ashes.

(*The crowd gasps; there is much outraged commotion.*)

GRANDPA

This is what the leaders have decided, so be it.

(GRANDPA *returns to his seat slowly. The crowd is now restless. The chairman is pounding the gavel.*)

LORI

No! no!

HOKTI

What kind of solution is that?

LOCUST

So what are we if we are no longer Indians?

JONATHAN

What about the casino?

LORI

What about the harvest ceremony?

HOKTI

Grandpa, what are you saying? How can we say we are no longer Indian?

(GRANDPA *stands up once again; the crowd gets quiet.*)

GRANDPA

(*Addressing the crowd firmly.*) When we allowed our ancestors to become a science project, put in a box on a warehouse shelf, viewed as a museum exhibit, or on someone's coffee table to be used as an ashtray, that is when we ceased to be Indian. Human Beings. One of our own children's journey was disturbed just last night. How can these things happen? How has such an act been allowed to continue? You heard Dr. Bison, these type of atrocities have been occurring since Columbus landed. And what have we done to stop them? We must ask these questions ourselves. Why ask ourselves? Because nobody is going to care how we treat our dead, our children, ourselves, with the respect and dignity we deserve as human beings, unless we care first.

We have failed to protect our ancestors who gave us the right to call ourselves Indians. How can we be expected to care for ourselves or our children if we forget those who gave us those beautiful gifts we call our culture? Our way. The way of The People. You tell me, what kind of way is that for us to allow the desecration of basic human dignity? And the most helpless and defenseless cannot even depend on us to protect them.

LORI

Grandpa, I will never say I am not Indian. Never, that means forever.

LOCUST

I can't say I am not Indian? What will the neighbors think? How absurd, how obscene, it is genocide. Whatever it takes to make our community stronger, I will do.

You and the traditional leaders must reconsider what you are saying.

LORI

Grandpa, I would rather die than do what you ask.

HOKTI

What you are asking us to do is to commit cultural suicide. (*The audience is quiet.*) How can you Grandpa? We are still alive, still here, we want to live. You have to show us how we can change this terrible situation.

(*Each member in the house stands up and demands that the traditional council reconvene and reconsider. WILD BILL pounds the gavel. The traditional leaders are discussing together what is going on.*)

GRANDPA

(*Stands up.*) Our traditional leaders are here and we have heard you. We will remain The People, Human Beings, now and forever. We are in a battle for human rights. We need your help, we expect it.

Aho!

(*Crowd responds,* Aho!)

(*Lights fade and come up on* BOY, GIRL, *and* ARTIST. *Downstage left or right. They are engrossed with the speech of* MR. CHIEF's BLOOD. *The* BOY *and* GIRL *are alarmed and frightened.*)

GIRL

That is awful. I wouldn't want anyone to dig me up and take my bones and clothes.

GRAFFITI ARTIST

They take your toys, too.

GIRL

Why? I love my toys. My grandma and grandpa give me good toys. What does cremate mean?

BOY

That is when they burn you up after you die and you become ashes. (*Looking at* ARTIST.) What are you doing?

ARTIST

(*Drawing.*) Way back in the days before cars and television, when The People lived in their communities in the old ways, they took care of their people when they died. If they were out on a hunting expedition and would die, the people would carry them back, to make sure they were buried with their people, their ancestors. Their mothers, or daughters, sisters, grandmothers, would dress the dead in their most beautiful clothing, place with them the articles they would need to make the journey to the next world. The men would have their tools or weapons, the women would have their tools and beautiful articles of things they made. The children who died would have their toys that they loved.

Some of the ancestors were placed on scaffolds, some were put in canoes, others were placed in trees so that the environment would claim them. Then The People would bury their bones after all the flesh was gone from their bones. The ancestors sing:

> We belong to this earth
> We belong to this earth
>
> Our lives are sacred forever
> Our lives are sacred forever

(*End of scene.*)

Scene 5

DR. BEN BISON's *office.* DR. BEN BISON, HOKTI, GRANDPA, and WILD BILL *are discussing leads on who dug up Jason Two Hearts' grave.*

DR. BEN BISON
  Whoever did this didn't mind leaving their signature all over the place. They have fingerprints and footprints. They're at the lab working on a match.

HOKTI
  Grandpa, the meeting tonight and what you were saying about us not being Indian anymore. It is all so unreal.

GRANDPA
  Hokti, meet Ben Bison. Ben meet Hokti.

DR. BEN BISON
  Well, welcome to the real Indian world, Hokti. Where have you been, asleep?

HOKTI
  I remember Dr. Bison. He was on exhibit at the museum.

DR. BEN BISON
  I remember you when you graduated from high school, the valedictorian. I just started graduate school; it has been a long time....

HOKTI
  (*Interrupting* DR. BISON.) Listen, Dr. Bison, I am trying to under-

stand what is going on here, what is happening, and yes, if you want to know, I have been asleep. You and your crude remarks and gas attacks are not what I would call a rational means to educate the non-Indian world about our people. Is that the best you can do? I heard no real solutions from you this evening when you were addressing the council.

DR. BISON

Oh, so you don't appreciate my approach about these repatriation issues. Well, I apologize, but don't come into my office and talk to me like I am someone who doesn't understand. Like I am some white man. I know this situation all too well. I have made my life's work studying and acquiring the necessary skills to address these issues on a professional level and from my own intuition of how these things need to be addressed. My intuition comes from the good nurturing I had in my upbringing. Very much like yours from my grandparents, my parents, my people. The only solutions I have are to help our leaders understand what is going on, so they can give us the wise direction that has maintained our survival. So, Ms. Buffalo, what have you done for your people lately?

HOKTI

(*Embarrassed and mad.*) I came back to them.

DR. BISON

You came back? Sounds like you did your own repatriation effort. How does it feel to be back where you belong? (*Pause.*) I am sure there is no substitute. So how long did it take you to get back where you belong?

HOKTI

Too damn long.

DR. BISON

Sounds like it.

GRANDPA

She took the long way around.

DR. BEN BISON

We are all taking the long way around. The desecration of Jason is one overt criminal act that we must stop from happening again. We must stop the warehousing of our ancestors in institutions, repositories, and people's homes.

HOKTI

Yes, but....

DR. BEN BISON

We are the only people who continually have to go before Congress and testify so that federal laws will be made to give us equal protection. You are an attorney. You should know this.

HOKTI

I know you're right. It's just that I never thought about all this before.

DR BISON

Welcome home. Do you think it was a coincidence that you returned home at this time? The ancestors have brought us all home. They are tired and want us to protect them. *They* want to come home. You are a practicing attorney?

HOKTI

Yes, but....

DR. BEN BISON

But what? Either you are or you aren't.

HOKTI

But I ... I am on vacation.

GRANDPA

Yes, she is Ben, and she's the best.

DR. BEN BISON

Vacation? From what? Being Indian? We have many legal problems here that we are going to need help with when it comes time to prosecute these people for their crime against Jason Two Hearts. We have other issues. We have a congressional hearing coming up next week that we need to attend to testify concerning repatriation. The process is taking too long. There are too many arguments over who has control over our people. The scientists, the museum people, the pot hunters all want to gain control over our ancestors' remains of what they call "culturally unaffiliated remains."

HOKTI

I am a corporate attorney, Ben. I am not a trial attorney.

DR. BEN BISON

Did you pass the bar in this state?

HOKTI

Well, yes, but my expertise is in finance and....

DR. BEN BISON

Then you can stand up in court and defend our people.

HOKTI

You are throwing these things at me so fast. I need to research and study the facts and look at different cases concerning repatriation.

DR. BEN BISON

There are no cases or precedents Hokti. We are setting precedents. Our ancestors are probably laughing at us now for the way we argue with the white people over technicalities, and b.s. issues to repatriate our dead. All they want is to be returned to the earth. It is time. We have to follow through. If we cannot protect our ancestral remains, how can we say we care about ourselves, our people, our children? We are letting people who don't even know where they are from control our lives....

(Interruption, knock on the door. It is WILD BILL. He enters the office.)

DR. BEN BISON

Wild Bill, come in.

WILD BILL

I need your help, Ben. We just got word that the Double Dealers auction tomorrow night has our family's medicine robe. It was taken by the archaeologists during the dam excavation from my grandfather's grave. He used this robe to doctor our people.

DR. BEN BISON

We knew about the auction Wild Bill. I will make some phone calls to see if the auction house can pull the robe from the list and give it back to you.

WILD BILL

I doubt they will do that Ben. Remember how the turtle clan tried to get their drum back last November?

DR. BEN BISON

Yes, you're right. I will call anyway. They have a new attorney working for their auction house. If I explain the situation there might be a chance. In the meantime, we need to plan to attend this auction.

WILD BILL

My clan will be at the auction.

HOKTI

Are you sure the robe belonged to your Grandpa?

WILD BILL

Quite sure Hokti. Even if it weren't my family's, I would help any family get this robe back to its proper place.

HOKTI

How do you know they took it?

WILD BILL

My mother was told this by some of the people who watched the excavation team that did the field study for the dam that was being put in. They watched them remove bodies, toys, clothing, bundles, and fans. They also watched them disrobe my grandfather. They took all his clothing off. They laid him out naked on the bare ground. They took his fans and other worship articles. Mom was grief-stricken. We managed to get back his clothing, fan, and pipe; now we have found the robe and we need to get it back to him.

HOKTI

How did it wind up at an auction house?

WILD BILL

Someone took the robe from the repository where the robe was kept. We have sketchy details about how this happened. I promise you, we will find out how it became an auction item.

GRANDPA

Wild Bill, this is what we will do to get your grandfather's robe back.

(GRANDPA *places his arm around* WILD BILL *and they exit out the door discussing the plan, lights fade.*)

(*End of scene.*)

Scene 6

Auction House in big metropolitan city. There are many bidders and the auction house is very elaborate. The bidders are non-Indian and wear suits and dresses. It is obviously a lucrative business. They carry their auction bid numbers with them. WILD BILL and DR. BISON make one last attempt to have the robe pulled from the auction bidding. They are speaking to the auctioneer who is shaking his head no.

WILD BILL

I will speak to your attorney, Mr. White, that is why I am here. You seem to be selling an item that has been stolen from my family, and we want it taken off of the auction sale.

MR. WHITE

Oh, here he is now. Larry Smith. Oh, Larry, could you come over here, please?

LARRY

Yes, may I (*he sees* HOKTI) help you?

HOKTI

Larry, what are you doing here?

LARRY
Hokti, I thought … thought you were….

HOKTI
Dead? Sorry to disappoint you.

DR. BEN BISON
You two know each other?

HOKTI
Too well. Larry, we are here to get this #64 item off the auction block. The auctioneer here says you will have to approve the withdrawal of the item. So, take it off.

LARRY
I can't take it off just because *you* people want it off. What is the reason?

HOKTI
It belongs to Judge Wild Bill's family. It was stolen from his deceased grandfather by the archaeologists during the excavation that was done when they put the dam in. We want it back.

LARRY
I will have to check with the Double Dealer trustees; they are not here. I am not usually here but they heard that there might be some protest over some of the items being auctioned so they sent me here. I cannot remove the items unless they give me permission.

HOKTI
You need their permission? For what? The robe was stolen. Don't they know they could have criminal charges filed against them?

MR. WHITE
(*Begins the auction.*) Ladies and gentlemen, please take your seats. The bidding is about to begin.

HOKTI
You take that robe off of the auction block, now.

LARRY

No way. Not after the way your family treated me when I visited you in the hospital.

HOKTI

You thought you could get my power of attorney, you spineless slime.

WILD BILL

(*Walks up to* HOKTI *and puts his arm around her protectively.*) Hokti, is there a problem with our request?

HOKTI

Yes, Judge.

LARRY

Judge (*nervously reaches out to shake hands*), what an honor to have you with us this evening.

GRANDPA

Hokti, come on, we don't need anything from your friend. We can do this ourselves.

LARRY

Mr. Chief's Blood, just what do you think you can do? Tear up the auction sheet?

GRANDPA

No, son, I can bid.

(WILD BILL *and* GRANDPA *lead* HOKTI *away from* LARRY.)

HOKTI

Grandpa, what are you talking about?

GRANDPA

We need you with us, Hokti. The bidding is about to begin and your friend is not going to help us.

(HOKTI *stands with the rest of the clan members as they stand in the back of the room.* LORI *and* GRANDMOTHER *show up. Everyone is there as they watch the auction begin and the robe is brought to the podium by* LARRY *who intentionally wants the robe to be bid first.*)

HOKTI
(*Talking to* WILD BILL.) What a jerk.

WILD BILL
Hokti, Larry seems to be missing an earlobe.

MR. WHITE
It has been requested that we begin with item #64. This is a rare buffalo robe that has various markings and ancient symbols that comes to us from the collection of an anonymous client. This robe dates back to the early 1800s in antiquity and has been preserved in immaculate condition. Do I hear....

(WILD BILL *leads his group to the front of the audience of auction bidders. They file in and stand in front of all of the bidders. The auctioneer continues with his request for bids. It is a tense moment.* HOKTI *stands in the back of the room watching as her family and the rest of the clan members walk to the front.*)

MR. WHITE
Do I hear $800 for this priceless robe?

(*The crowd is silent and some get up and leave.*)

MR. WHITE
(*Nervously.*) Do I hear $500? Ok, how about $300? $200?

(LARRY *stands up and begins to protest but* WILD BILL *stands beside him.*)

WILD BILL
(*In* LARRY's *ear.*) What happened to your earlobe?

LARRY
It was a hunting accident.

WILD BILL
Yes it was. (*He puts his hand firmly on* LARRY's *shoulder and makes him sit down.*)

LARRY
Yes, your honor.

MR. WHITE
Do I hear $100?

LARRY

Fred, may I have a word with you? (*Looks at* WILD BILL *cautiously and stands up to go talk to* MR. WHITE.) May I?

MR. WHITE

(*Nervously.*) Of course, Larry.

(LARRY *and* MR. WHITE *speak to each other quickly.*)

MR. WHITE

Ladies and gentlemen, there has been a mistake. The robe will be removed from the auction. It is learned that the robe belongs to Judge Wild Bill's family. Judge, please, the Double Dealer Auction House would like for you to come forward and take your robe. Of course, this means we won't be, can't be held responsible for any criminal violations....

LARRY

(*Interrupting.*) Ahem, Fred, let them have the robe. I'll handle any legal issues.

(*The room is silenced. The bidding is over.* WILD BILL *signals for* DR. BISON *to come get the robe.* DR. BISON *wears a mask, gloves, and a smock over his police uniform. He then inserts the robe into a plastic bag. The women begin to lulu and the men give war cries.*)

(*End of scene.*)

Scene 7

DR. BEN BISON's *office. They have just returned from the auction.*

DR. BISON

Tell the Sovereign Keeper lab folks to wear gloves, masks, and protective lab coats, Wild Bill. There may be arsenic on the robe. When they are through with their preliminary analysis, tell them to check for other hazardous chemicals.

HOKTI

Hazardous chemicals?

DR. BISON

Yes, Hokti, not only do we have to worry about all the looters, the law, the attorneys, we have to worry about arsenic poisoning after we get our remains and items back. The archaeologists and museums use arsenic as a pesticide and other chemicals to preserve the items. Adding insult to injury, once we get our patrimony and funerary items back we must decontaminate the items of these poisons.

WILD BILL

Thank you all for your help. Dr. Bison, I must be getting home. I have things I need to prepare before we put the robe back with my grandfather.

HOKTI

Wild Bill, wait. I need to apologize to you for not walking up to the front with you and Grandpa today at the auction house. I didn't know what to expect, or what to do. I feel bad because I didn't stand with you.

WILD BILL

You do not need to apologize, Hokti. I am glad you were there. You did help, in a good way.

HOKTI

But, I didn't do everything I needed to do. I was halfway about it. I have never been that way. (*Turns to* GRANDPA.) You always told me not to be halfway about my decisions, not to be wishy-washy.

GRANDPA

I also taught you to do what you think is right. If you don't fully understand what is going on, then you shouldn't do anything. You aren't ready. You did the right thing.

HOKTI

I do know one thing. I am very proud to be your granddaughter. I'm sorry for all those awful times we have had. I wanted to cry when I saw you standing up there with that white man. I thought how dare he treat my grandfather like that. And Lori was right there with you. At least she has the guts her older sister lacks.

GRANDPA

You *were* there with me Hokti. I am proud of you.

(HOKTI *and* GRANDPA *hug.*)

DR. BEN BISON

Hokti, we need your help. Monday we have to go before Congress to testify why we should get the remains back that are classified as culturally unidentifiable human remains. It is an archaeological movement to take control and possession of our people who have not been culturally identified with any tribe and to claim our ancient ancestors.

HOKTI

(*Reluctant.*) Wild Bill can do this.

WILD BILL

I won't be able to be there Hokti. (*He takes* HOKTI's *hand and faces her, then strokes her cheek affectionately.*) I have a case that I will be hearing next week. I will brief you on compliance and lack of compliance and the federal laws pertaining to these testimonies.

HOKTI

Grandpa, I don't feel ready for all of this.

GRANDPA

You will be ready.

HOKTI

I need to interview witnesses. I need to research the law.

GRANDPA

Don't worry, I will get the witnesses.

WILD BILL

I will be in my office in the morning, Hokti. I also want to know more about your friend, Mr. Larry Smith. It seems I recall a complaint concerning his ethical standards from your grandmother. You know I sit on the State Bar review board for complaints and grievances.

HOKTI

She couldn't have complained about his ethical standards because he has none.

WILD BILL

How did you get mixed up with someone like him in the first place?

HOKTI

(*Hesitant, then relenting.*) You know how it is in law school, Wild Bill. We started out as study partners. We helped each other get through some tough tests. Then we wound up as partying partners after the exams. After graduation and the bar exam we stayed as partying partners. But that is all over now. When you have a boyfriend like that while you're under the influence, it is hard to see the reality of the whole mess.

WILD BILL

I know how things can be a mess. Right, Mr. Chief's Blood?

GRANDPA

Yes, you have both been to hell and back. (*Takes their hands and reassures them.*) That part of your life is behind you. Now let's get to work.

HOKTI

Grandpa, who are you going to call as witnesses?

GRANDPA

I have been communicating with the witnesses since Dr. Bison has told me about these hearings. Don't you worry. They are expert witnesses.

HOKTI

I hope not a bunch of archaeologists.

GRANDPA

No baby girl, not a bunch of archaeologists.

(*End of scene.*)

Scene 8

HOKTI's *room at her grandmother's home. She is asleep and has a dream. She wakes up and looks in the mirror.* ALCOHOL SPIRIT *is looking back at her.*

HOKTI

Leave me alone.

ALCOHOL SPIRIT

Oh, so you acknowledge that I am here.

HOKTI

Acknowledged. Now leave.

ALCOHOL SPIRIT

Pretty good trick, coming back to life. We need to celebrate that one. They'll probably put you on one of those TV talk shows. Good lord, look at you! You need a drink, honey.

HOKTI

No, I don't need a drink.

ALCOHOL SPIRIT

Big day Monday, going before those congressmen and women. We got all weekend, Hokti. Hah, they are going to laugh at you for your lack of preparation. You don't even know who the witnesses are.

HOKTI

Grandpa knows who they are. That is good enough for me.

ALCOHOL SPIRIT

Well, he sure put you on the spot. Remember the last time you trusted someone else to show up with the information? You got fired because they didn't show! (*Laughing and mocking.*) You can trust me, I'll be there....

HOKTI

Get out!

ALCOHOL SPIRIT

Oh, I'm not going anywhere. You craved me, that is why I came back. You know you're going to bomb out. That's why you need me, to get through tomorrow, the weekend, Monday. You can call in sick. Or better yet, you can show up with me and we will show them we work together real good. What will it be Hokti? Scotch, bourbon with a chaser? Or hey, we have resources here. I know there is a bottle of mouthwash or cough syrup somewhere in this place.

HOKTI

I'll show you what is in this place. I'm in this place. Now get out.

ALCOHOL SPIRIT

You wanted me.

HOKTI

Maybe I thought about you, but now that you're here I can see how disgusting you are.

ALCOHOL SPIRIT

(*Losing ground.*) But Hokti, I....

HOKTI

Get out and leave me alone!

(GRANDMA *comes to her bedroom.*)

GRANDMA

Hokti, are you OK?

HOKTI

Grandma, it came back, it came back. That awful alcohol spirit. I had a dream that I was back at my old apartment and we were partying. I had an awful craving for the taste and I woke up and the spirit was here in my room.

GRANDMA

But you ran it off.

HOKTI

Yes, I did.

GRANDMA

Let me tell you, Hokti. One of these days, Grandpa and I will not be here when that awful spirit comes around. But you can make it leave. Every time it gets easier. And over time it will leave you alone.

HOKTI

I can't bear to think of you or Grandpa not being here with me.

GRANDMA

You hear people say all the time that the people you love will be with you in spirit. It is true. As long as you're here on this earth until the Creator brings you to join us in the spirit world. Even old Dog Tired will be there. That is why it is important to have people understand when we die, we journey to the spirit world, our bones return to our mother earth and we are born again in our children.

HOKTI

Grandma, I'll do my best to help everyone understand. I am anxious about the hearings. I don't know who Grandpa is calling for witnesses. I have been busy with Wild Bill, going over the laws and procedures for compliance, and ... It isn't hard to understand, but there are some things that need to be better defined.

GRANDMA

You'll do fine, Hokti.

HOKTI

Grandma, what do you think of Wild Bill? He is so handsome, funny, and smart. When we were together today, we talked about what needed to be done at the hearings. Then we talked about you and Grandpa, his parents, what the tribe needs. I think he wants to snag.

(They both laugh.)

GRANDMA

Hokti, I have known Wild Bill since he was in his mama's belly. She is blessed with a wonderful son. He went through some rough times after he came back from Vietnam, but he finally found the peace he needed in his heart to survive that "trip to hell" as he calls it. (*Smiling and stroking* HOKTI's *hair.*) Monday will be an extra-ordinary day for sure. Your grandpa will be with you. I'll be here waiting for you. Let your heart speak; you'll do fine.

(*End of scene.*)

Intermission

Act II

Scene I

Senate Hearing Room. The Senate Committee is set stage right. They appear indifferent, expressionless. Some wearing bifocals. HOKTI *is standing with* DR. BISON *at a table before the committee, obviously agitated and looking around. She has a witness list and is questioning* DR. BISON *because there are no names associated with the list. There are only numbers. She is upset because her Grandpa has not yet appeared with the witnesses.*

HOKTI
Ben, this is not like Grandpa. He always makes his appointments promptly. Lori and I call him Grandpa Early when he makes us rush to be somewhere on time! Where is he? And what kind of witness list is this? There are no names. There are only numbers. Why are there only numbers?

DR. BEN BISON
(*Surprised.*) These are accession catalogue entries.

HOKTI
What? Accession entries? Isn't that what the archaeologists use to catalog their excavations?

DR. BEN BISON
Exactly.

HOKTI

This entry says this person is a human skeletal remain, adult age about sixty-three represented by a left femur and miscellaneous fragments.

DR. BEN BISON

This one says female human skeletal remains, age eighteen to twenty-five, represented by cranium mandible, one partial humerus.

HOKTI

Oh my God Ben, this one is a ....

(SENATOR JAMES *pounds the gavel.*)

SENATOR JAMES

Ms. Buffalo, are you ready to begin your testimony? I understand you have some opening remarks. You will have a few minutes to present your remarks and then we will begin our testimonies. Are your witnesses ready?

GRANDPA

(*Entering stage left.*) Yes, we are, Mr. Chairman.

(GRANDPA *enters with the witnesses. They are the actual victims of graves or from incidences of war or other causes of death that brought them to be remains considered for repatriation. They are dressed in traditional Indian clothes. There is a young woman, a girl, and an ancient elderly man. There can be more. They are dressed in many different tribal dresses, some wear bandages from wounds. A backdrop with slide photographs of Native American people from the 1800s grouped together could add a more dramatic effect. It is obvious they are ancient people. This scene is the most powerful scene of the play. It should in no way be treated as surreal.*)

(HOKTI *realizes that her witnesses are ghosts. She changes her posture from unsure to reassured as she watches the witnesses file in. She realizes she must be strong.*)

HOKTI

Mr. Chairman, we are ready to begin.

MR. CHAIRMAN

(*Surprised by the witnesses.*) Please, please begin.

HOKTI

Mr. Chairman, members of the committee, I am here today on behalf of the Indian people, who refer to themselves as The People or Human Beings. Today you will hear the testimony of witnesses who have been treated unjustly and who suffer from a double standard in this country. These are the expert witnesses. The actual victims of the piracy of our Native American graves. We are here today to testify before you that these victims have been identified as "culturally unidentifiable human remains" by the archaeological society of this country. What this label does is prevent these witnesses from being properly buried by our society. The witnesses you will be hearing from today will tell you themselves they resent being labeled as culturally unaffiliated and looked upon as property. We are here to plead they be returned to this earth with a proper burial as the universal law of humanity would expect.

(*Spotlight on each witness as they speak.*)

HOKTI

Our first witness is Catalog No. 736-2,97BLI0.

STANDING WOMAN

I am Standing Woman. I died on the prairie when something inside my body burst here. (*Holding her side.*) The pain inside would not stop. I knew I was going to die and asked my relatives to dress me in my elk hide dress. The one my grandmother made for me. She was there crying to see my life slip away. I cried, too, as she helped me dress. My mother wanted me to wear the knife pouch and awl pouch that she made for me when I was a little girl learning how to dress and sew buffalo skins. They made me the moccasins with the porcupine quills across the feet for my journey to see my relatives. My friends and relatives cooked my favorite meal of corn, venison, chokecherries, and buffalo. They placed these things above my head to take with me on my journey so I would not get hungry as I passed to see the world where our ancestors wait for us to join them. My mother and grandmother gave me many messages to take to our ancestors.

My father tried in vain to save me. He cried when he realized I was dead. He tore at his flesh and gashed his arms and legs in vain. My mother and grandmother cut their hair. I wanted to be buried there. We had spent so much time there together when I was young. I love how the wind blows the buffalo grass. I feel the spirits there when I run and play with my brothers and sisters. My mother and father wanted to take me home with them, but I wanted to be on the prairie, to be part of the earth where the buffalo and other animals crossed.

They buried me there, placing rocks they had gathered to cover me so the wolves could not dig me up. Then they traveled home to our village.

Several days later soldiers came upon my grave. They uncovered me. Right away they undressed me and started to cut on my body. They cut my breasts off and moved my body from the place where I was put by my mother and grandmother. They took off my leggings, moccasins, and my hair medallions and necklace that I had around my neck. One of the soldiers cried out and said what they were doing was wrong. The soldiers who made a good time with my things ignored him. There was another soldier who looked sad and turned away. He told them to stop cutting my body after they cut my hair for a scalp trophy.

My body lay there for the wind to carry the smell of death to the wolves who came to investigate. When they arrived, they would not touch my body because of the desecration. They mourned with their howl. They ate only the buffalo meat and venison. They moved my body back to the grave by gripping my feet with their jaws and my hands with their jaws. They used their feet (*she demonstrates how they used their paws to cover her*) and tried to cover me with the dirt that had been discarded by the soldiers.

The soldiers were on their way to my people's camp. When they arrived they attacked our camp. The soldiers who did this unholy act to my body were wearing my things around their necks. My family saw my necklace. They killed the soldiers.

After the battle, my family went to where I was buried. The wolves were still there surrounding my little shallow grave. My family chased them away and came to me. They realized the wolves protected my grave and tried to bury me again. My family took my body and dressed me again. They carried me to be with our other people and placed me on a scaffold. After the flesh was no longer visible on my body, they buried me with my dress and camp utensils I would need in the world of our ancestors.

After several years, they moved their camp because the soldiers would not leave them alone. Then after many years my bones were dug up by white people. They separated my bones from the dress and other things my family had buried me with. One of the people who dug me up put my things in a bag you could see through. He took these things to his home and put them in a large glass case for many years. Then he took them to a place where they were put on a structure that looked like a human being, and there were white people who would come and look at my dress and moccasins. I saw my people come and look at my things through a glass window. I pitied them.

There was another man who took me to a strange place and began to draw on my bones. He placed me in a box, and I stayed there for many more years. Sometimes there would be someone who would open the box and smudge me with a light mist with a strange odor that would make the air difficult to breathe. Then they closed the box. My bones are still in that box. I want them back in the ground where they took me from. I cannot rest until they are there.

HOKTI
  Calling witness Catalog No. 736-3, 28ABII.

(A young girl appears dressed in Cheyenne traditional dress. She has a gunshot wound on her forehead.)

PLUME
  I am Plume. My Grandpa is Morning Star. We ran from the soldiers in the snow every day. I was hungry. I was afraid. Mama kept telling me to be strong. I could feel she was afraid, so I ran even harder. Finally, we quit running. Uncle and Mama and the oth-

ers, we stopped running. The soldiers came at us and Uncle and the others fought them but the soldiers killed them. Mama and me laid in a big hole in the earth with the other women, holding hands like this (*she imitates their action*), singing the strong heart songs. The soldiers came. We sang louder. I closed my eyes and sang louder; they shot me here (*touching her forehead*). They shot Mama. It was cold. They took me out of the hole with Mama and laid us on the ground. A man took my doll Mama made for me. Why did he take my doll? Then they put me on a wagon. I was sent here. Why? Why did they take my clothes? Then everybody looks at this (*points to bullet hole*), and they touch it. I want to go home. I want my mama.

HOKTI

She is talking about the flight of Dull Knife's people from Fort Robinson in 1879. This child has not had a proper burial ever. She was separated from her people when her remains were removed to the museum in Washington, D.C. The records say she is classified as being culturally unaffiliated.

(NEE *steps up to the witness spotlight. He is ancient and wears a shirt, breechcloth, leggings made of buckskin with natural paint; his jewelry is made of stone and shell.*)

NEE

(*Looking at the congressional panel.*) I look at you and can say—you are a good man or you are a bad man.

(SENATOR CHILDERS *sits up uneasily.*)

NEE

You are a man that thinks (*touches head*) here (*touches the center of his breastbone*) like that. (*An old expression that signifies that it is an understood statement.*)

(*Looking at* SENATOR CHILDERS.)

I look at you and know you are a good woman. You have children and grandchildren.

(*Looking out at the audience.*)

I look at you (*beat*), my granddaughters and grandsons, and am glad you have not forgotten me. (*Beat.*) The strangers who took me up from our Mother (*uses sign language to describe*) like that, did not have the proper teachings of how to be a human being.

(*Looking at the congressmen and women.*)

How can you argue for what is right?

My grandson calls me. (*Looking at Grandpa.*) He needs me. I am here for my grandchildren. I am the one who taught them where our proper place is. When we go on to the spirit world, our flesh is wrapped by our mother. When you remove us, you uproot a sacred child who has been taken from his mother, her mother, without permission, like that.

My flesh is the mountains, valleys, prairies, desert.
My hair the feathers of our winged relations.
My voice is the wind you hear daily.
My hands (*shows the lines of his hands to the audience*) and feet
the indelible track of all you remember.
I am you.
A human being.

Grandchildren, I see how you live, separating yourself from this earth. The more you hold for yourself, the more you separate as people of God, then you forget what is real and not real. You shut yourselves away in your homes indulging yourself with "things" that take you from your mother. You have forgotten how to give back. You call me unreal, a ghost. I came here today to remind you that I am real.

I am more real than anything you will ever know upon this earth. No matter how hard you try to make things right here on earth, it can never be right unless you treat the ancestors of this mother earth with respect and honor.

Aho!

(*Spotlight fades on* NEE.)

HOKTI

Ladies and Gentlemen, it is important to understand in addition to these witnesses' testimony, there are over 2.5 million remains and even a million more in funeral objects that were taken from Native American gravesites.

My next witness is Dr. Ben Bison, tribal archaeologist for the Turtle Falls Band.

DR. BEN BISON

Distinguished congressmen and women. The argument we often hear is that the American Indian people are used as science projects for the sake of science under the umbrella of education. The truth is, of all the millions of remains you have in these institutions, less than 10 percent have been used for these so-called educational triumphs. Most of the information taken has been interpreted by non-Indian people who have skewed the data to fit their hypothesis.

I am an archaeologist. I studied the same educational doctrines and developed methodology according to the Western political thought of the schools who teach this science. I wanted to study this science much for the same reason other archaeologists want to: to preserve the historical records of this continent. But I resent the fact that they only study our people for some pipe dream that they are going to make a significant impact on the human condition that everyone will benefit from. This is a Euroegotistical patronizing pile of buffalo chips.

For centuries these human beings have rested in institutions with no one taking the time even to look at them for scientific research. Yet, they fight to keep them. Like treasures they can't part with. The archaeology community is afraid of losing some sort of control because they have built a profession and institution upon our ancestors' bones and possessions. So they try to fool the public with an educational outcry.

The educational sham is a farce for several reasons. One, the inventories are so massive you would have to hire an army of archaeologists to do all the scientific studies this country thinks they do. Secondly, the real thrill for archaeologists is the find of the site where they excavate, write a grant, do the excavation, file the remains, then it is on to the next dig. Thirdly, the ethical scientists that do actual studies and documentation will ultimately repatriate their subjects of study. These individuals are few and far between. They work hard to help everyone understand that not all archaeologists are racist grave looters.

HOKTI

The justification to continually degrade and study our people, rob our graves, and then say we have no control over our dead is a serious and terrible injustice. This racist policy is a direct violation of our constitutional rights under the clause of equal protection. It is also an infringement upon our religious freedom.

Another injustice was imposed upon us with the term "culturally unidentifiable human remains" in Public Law 101-601. This term disassociates our ancient ancestors from their descendents. I am an Indian before I am anything else in this world. These ancient human remains belong to this earth, not to the archaeologists or other scientists who insist they own our ancestors.

We are in a cultural war and our recourse is cultural suicide. This means we have to change our traditional burial customs. Today our elders are telling us that we will no longer have a proper burial, but we will now be cremated when we die. This is our solution to stop the grave looting. If we are ash, there is nothing to steal. We do not want our children and grandchildren to suffer offenses and be put in ludicrous situations to plead for our dignity as human beings.

SENATOR JAMES

This is not a courtroom trial, but a hearing to see if there is a case and if it can be settled. Yes, there is a case and it can be settled. It is hereby ordered on this day that all Native American people removed from their places of burial shall be returned to their rightful resting place.

(*A commotion starts in the court room; chairman hits gavel.*)

SHERLOCK

But Your Honor, what about the scientific testing that still needs to be done?

SENATOR JAMES

Address this hearing by stating your name.

SHERLOCK

My name is Dr. Fields, I am an archaeology professor at....

SENATOR JAMES

Good lord, don't you get it? The science project is over.

SHERLOCK

But Senator, we do have ethical standards if that is what you are talking about?

SENATOR JAMES

Dr. Fields, tell me and this committee where you were you born and raised.

SHERLOCK

Why, what does my background have to do with this? Why is it that everyone is so concerned about where *I* come from? Have you been talking to Mr. Locust?

SENATOR JAMES

It has everything to do with what is going on here. Now answer the question, where are you from?

SHERLOCK

I'm from Missouri, born and raised, where my parents and grandparents are from.

SENATOR JAMES

Are your grandparents still alive?

SHERLOCK

No sir, they are both dead and my parents are deceased, too.

SENATOR JAMES
    Are they buried in Missouri?

SHERLOCK
    Yes sir, on our family farm. We have a little family....

(*Interrupted by* SENATOR JAMES.)

SENATOR JAMES
    Are you sure they are still buried there, Dr. Fields?

SHERLOCK
    Yes sir, quite sure.

SENATOR JAMES
    Tell me why you are sure Dr. Fields, or better yet, tell the Indian
    people that are here today why you can be so sure your family are
    buried in Missouri on your family farm. And then tell our audi-
    ence why their family members are not buried where they were
    laid to rest.

SHERLOCK
    I'm not sure we are talking about the same thing, sir. I mean,
    there is more to it than what you are saying.

SENATOR JAMES
    You are right. It is called a double standard. You are sure about
    your ancestors' remains, and we are here discussing their ances-
    tors' remains. The problem is your profession. It has ignored the
    constitutional rights of the Native American people.

SHERLOCK
    But the scientific data that we have gathered have helped them to
    understand their culture better. The genetic studies show....

(*Once again* SENATOR JAMES *interrupts.*)

SENATOR JAMES
    Tell me the significant contributions your profession has made to
    help the Native American people.

SHERLOCK

Well, we have established historical data when they seek federal recognition. Our records are used to help determine if their tribes will gain federal recognition or to establish sacred sites.

SENATOR TURNER

How many cases have you gone to court to speak in their behalf for federal recognition?

SHERLOCK

None, madam, but I studied under Professor Harold, the nationally renowned state archaeologist and he has testified numerous times with data concerning Indian tribes.

SENATOR TURNER

What did he testify?

SHERLOCK

In one report he cited that his research proved that one of the sacred sites they wanted to claim was not a sacred site.

DR. BEN BISON

That was our Canyon Bluff site, Senator. He is correct. Our people wanted the site protected from trespassers while we make our annual pilgrimage. Our people have been making their pilgrimage there since creation. Professor Harold was hired by land developers who wanted to put a housing development at the Canyon Bluff area. He carbon-dated a piece of charcoal that was found at a camper's area and declared our ancestral worship area as having been there for only fifty years. We have gone to federal court and there is an injunction pending concerning the Canyon Bluff site development.

SENATOR JAMES

So based on that analogy, Canyon Bluff has only been there fifty years?

SHERLOCK

No sir, just the site where the Indian people pray.

SENATOR TURNER

Dr. Fields, when you die, what type of funeral service will you have?

SHERLOCK

Well, I hardly think that is an appropriate question for me.

SENATOR TURNER

And why wouldn't it be appropriate for you?

SHERLOCK

Because we are here to discuss culturally unaffiliated remains.

SENATOR TURNER

Exactly. Now please answer the question.

DR. FIELDS

Well, I have left specific instructions that there will be no funeral service, and I will be cremated.

(*The crowd gasps.*)

SENATOR TURNER

Cremated? Don't you find that ironic, Dr. Fields? You, a scientist who makes your life's mission analyzing dead people, will be cremated when you die?

DR. FIELDS

It is my preference.

SENATOR TURNER

Is cremation a religious rite for you?

DR. FIELDS

Why no ma'am, religion has nothing to do with it.

SENATOR TURNER

What religious denomination do you belong to?

DR. FIELDS

I don't have a religious preference. I believe that question is irrelevant. Whatever happened to separation between church and state?

SENATOR TURNER

Dr. Fields, just so you will understand a few things about me, since I now understand a few things about you, I want you to know that I, too, am a doctor, of social science. I am also an attorney-at-law, and I am a senator of these United States. I took an oath from the time I was a young girl to eradicate the social disease called racism. As an attorney for civil rights, I took an oath to protect my clients against discrimination. As a United States senator, I took an oath and made a promise to my constituents that I would make sure that justice would serve all the people. Finding and confronting the perpetuators of this social disease can sometimes be difficult, but never impossible. I am confident today that I have found one of the hosts of this terrible social disease. I can now prescribe a treatment and work on a cure. Your testimony today has convinced me that the road to healing for our Native American people can begin today. May God have mercy on your soul.

SHERLOCK

But, I don't think you understand the dilemma you will be putting the science community in if you repatriate all the bones.

SENATOR JAMES

That is all, Dr. Fields. Please be seated.

SHERLOCK

But....

SENATOR JAMES

Be seated Dr. Fields, or I will have you escorted out.

(SHERLOCK *sits reluctantly.*)

SENATOR JAMES

Ms. Buffalo, do you have any closing statements?

HOKTI

Yes, Mr. Chairman, ladies and gentlemen of the committee, it is clear that there has been a serious injustice here. Science is not above law or humanity. In a civilized world, we must always be cautious of not becoming too enamored with ourselves that we close our eyes to basic human rights. Based on the testimony of today's witnesses who are inappropriately labeled culturally unaffiliated remains, we ask that you amend the term to Native American remains and expeditiously repatriate them.

SENATOR JAMES

I will also add to your statement that this committee finds our archaeological institutions guilty of racism, grave robbing, and fraud. We find the American public guilty of the same for allowing this to happen. If this were a civil court, the plaintiffs would surely enjoy the wealth of millions. In this case, the plaintiffs have only asked for one thing, to be treated humanely and justly.

Members of this committee, I move we return all the Native American people to a place of burial, and strike the words "culturally unaffiliated remains" from Public Law 101-601 and replace it with Native American human remains. All Native American human remains shall be repatriated.

SENATOR TURNER

I second the motion.

SENATOR JAMES

All in favor?

SENATOR TURNER

Aye.

SENATOR JAMES

Anyone opposed?

(*Silence.*)

SENATOR JAMES

Motion passed. So be it. This hearing is adjourned!

(*End of scene. Lights out.*)

Scene 2

GRANDPA *and* HOKTI *return home. When they get home,* GRANDMA *has suffered a stroke. She is dying.* LORI **and** LOCUST *are with her.* GRANDPA *rushes to her side immediately.*

HOKTI
We took the first flight back that was available. How is she?

LOCUST
She is not doing so good, Sweetie.

GRANDMA
(*Weakly.*) I want you to dress me in my elk teeth buckskin. Bring me my scarves. I want the black one to wear around my neck.

LORI
No, Grandma, I don't want you to die. (*She begins to cry.*)

(LOCUST *and* HOKTI *open a trunk and bring her dress and scarves. The take out her leggings and moccasins, necklaces, and a fan. They dress her.*)

GRANDMA
Everyone out, I need to speak to Grandpa and Hokti.

(MOTHER *and* LORI *exit.*)

GRANDMA
Hokti, you will help your Grandfather cremate me. I don't want some person who is not part of this family to handle my body after I die. You will have to be strong for Lori. She needs you now more than ever.

HOKTI
Cremate? No Grandma, no, I can't bear this. We won, Grandma. We won, you don't have to do this.

GRANDMA
You won a major battle today Hokti, but you haven't won the hearts of the people who still want us after we are dead.

HOKTI
But they have to leave us alone now, Grandma.

GRANDMA
Listen to me, Hokti. What has been won today is the beginning of change. We are depending now on the minds and the hearts of the people to change their views, their doctrines, their feelings towards us. Some will change overnight. Others will take one, maybe two generations before their children will understand what is right. Some will never understand what they have done is wrong. Do as I request. I don't want our children to forget after I die that I still need their protection.

HOKTI
I'll protect you.

GRANDMA
I am going to join my mother and father. It is time. You have to be strong, Hokti. If you must cry, cry with your family here. But when you go outside of this home, do not show your grief. You must be strong. You must do this. I have decided how I want to leave this world. Now you must help me.

(HOKTI *exits, and* GRANDPA *and* GRANDMA *hold each other until the lights fade to black. A slow drum beat begins and a scaffold burial is under the spotlight.*)

(GRANDPA *sings a song that is mournful and chilling; the cast joins in, their faces painted with mourners paint.* HOKTI, MOTHER *[if hair is long], and* LORI *have visibly shorter hair.* GRANDPA *should have shorter hair also if his hair is long. They are placing food, water, and other burial offering items on the scaffold.*)

(*Then the sound of fire is heard. The scaffold is burned.*)

ARTIST
(*Makes sign for cutting his hair.*) Long time ago, Indians would cut their hair when people die that they loved and cared for.

GIRL
But your hair will grow back, won't it?

❈

ARTIST
Yes. As the years pass, the pain that you feel in your heart begins to heal and your hair grows back.

GIRL
I feel pain right here (*touching her heart*), I want my heart to heal. Cut my hair.

BOY
Cut my hair, too.

(*The* ARTIST *cuts their hair. He rubs paint on their faces. Mourners are still crying.*)

Scene 3

The theater is pitch black. There is the sound of shovels digging in dirt; it begins faintly and becomes louder. We hear voices of grave robbers.

MR. WHITE
Hey, Larry, we hit it. Help me bring it out.

LARRY
Geez, this mother is heavy.

MR. WHITE
Just a little more. Damn, Larry, use your muscles.

LARRY
Hey, we got it.

MR. WHITE
Open 'er up. Here, crowbar that side.

(*They use a flashlight as they open up the coffin.*)

LARRY
What the hell is this?

(*The* GRAVE ROBBER *is sifting ashes from the coffin.*)

MR. WHITE
It's goddamn ashes.

VOICE OF POLICE
(*Over a loudspeaker.*) No, it is the law. Hands behind your head.

MR. WHITE
Hey, you can't arrest us. There was nothing but ashes. Tell them, Larry!

LARRY
(*To* MR. WHITE.) Shut up!

VOICE OF POLICE
Looks like we have some trespassers.
You have the right to remain silent....

(*Lights fade.*)

Closing Scene

The ARTIST, BOY, *and* GIRL *stand and examine the brick wall. There is artwork of fire inside the outline of the buffalo robe.*

ARTIST
This is the story of the Indians.

BOY
It is our story.

ARTIST
Why is that?

BOY
We are the generation Grandma talked about. This is our story and everyone's story.

GIRL
We will make sure everyone is treated with respect. We are Human Beings.

ARTIST

    How will you do this?

BOY

    We will tell this story as you have said it, 'xactly.

(*The* ARTIST, BOY, *and* GIRL *dip the palms of their hands in red paint and touch the wall leaving their hand prints inside the outline of the buffalo robe over the fire symbol.*)

(*Lights fade.*)

END

The Woman Who Was a Red Deer Dressed for the Deer Dance

Diane Glancy

Artist's Statement

My deer dress is the way I felt, transformed by the power of ceremony.

This dramatic/poetic piece is an intermixing of ethnographic material. The story of *Ahw'uste* was taken from Doi on *Ahu'usti* and Asudi on *Ahw'usti*, *Friends of Thunder, Tales of the Oklahoma Cherokees*, edited by Frank and Anna Kilpatrick (Norman: University of Oklahoma Press, 1995), pieces of the old language (Cherokee), and contemporary materials (the granddaughter's life in the soup kitchen and dance bars). It is a dialogue/monologue between a grandmother and her granddaughter, both arguing against the other for her own way of life. The grandmother talks about stories and the Spirits and the red deer dress she has made to feel more in tune with *Ahw'uste*, a mythological spirit deer. The granddaughter talks about the problems of a contemporary life, including her experiences with several men. The grandmother continues talking about *Ahw'uste* and the Spirits, who in the end, she realizes, let her down. "Damned Spirits," she hits the table with her fist, "didn't always help us out. Let us have it rough sometimes," she says as she talks of hunger and the uncertainty she faced in her life. The granddaughter says she has to look for work, which she can't find, and says she doesn't have time for the *Ahw'uste* and the Spirits, and longs for more practical help from her grandmother. In the end, the granddaughter enters some of her grandmother's world and says, "You know I've learned she told me more without speaking than she did with her words."

The play began when I saw a red papier-mâché dress titled, "The Crone," made by a friend, Carolyn Erler, a fabric artist. I liked the dress so much, I had to write a dramatic piece to go with it.

Production History

The Woman Who Was a Red Deer Dressed for the Deer Dance was presented at The New Dramatists, 424 West Forty-Fourth Street, New York City, by Mutt Rep, Don Wilson Glenn, director, with Siouxsan Monson and Barbara Kidd Calvano, September 14, 1995. That year it was also presented at the Walker Art Center in Minneapolis, with Diane Glancy and Carolyn Erler, November 11, 1995, and the American Indian Community House, 404 Lafayette Street, New York City, Siouxsan Monson, director, with Siouxsan Monson and Margarita Promponas, December 7, 1995.

The play was later presented at Raw Space, 529 West Forty-Second Street, New York City, by the Sage Theatre Company, Barbara Kidd Calvano, director, with Barbara Kidd Calvano and Alexis Iacono, December 27–30, 1998, and January 2–4, 1999; the Associated Writing Programs Conference, State University of New York, Albany, with Anne E. Wood and Ingrid Lazerwitz, April 16, 1999; and the Birch Wathen Lenox School, New York, New York, Marilyn Schulman, Director, November 18–19, 1999.

The Woman Who Was a Red Deer Dressed for the Deer Dance

In this I try. Well, I try. To combine the overlapping realities of myth, imagination & memory with spaces for the silences. To make a story. The voice speaking in different agencies. Well, I try to move on with the voice in its guises. A young woman & her grandmother in a series of scenelets. Shifting between dialogue & monologue. Not with the linear construct of conflict / resolution, but with story moving like rain on a windshield. Between differing & unreliable experiences.

GIRL
Have you heard of *Ahw'uste*?

GRANDMOTHER
I have but I've forgotten.

GIRL
They said they fed her.

GRANDMOTHER
Yes, they did.

GIRL
What was she?

GRANDMOTHER
I don't know.

GIRL
A deer?

GRANDMOTHER
Yes, a deer. A small deer.

GIRL
She lived in the house, didn't she?

GRANDMOTHER
Yes, she did. She was small.

GIRL
They used to talk about her a long time ago, didn't they?

GRANDMOTHER
Yes, they did.

GIRL
Did you ever see one of the deer?

GRANDMOTHER
I saw the head of one once. Through the window. Her head was small and she had tiny horns.

GIRL
Like a goat?

GRANDMOTHER
Yes like that.

GIRL
Where did you see her?

GRANDMOTHER
I don't know. Someone had her. I just saw her. That's all.

GIRL
You saw the head?

GRANDMOTHER
Yes, just the head.

GIRL
What did they call her?

GRANDMOTHER
A small deer.

GIRL
Where did you see her?

GRANDMOTHER
What do they call it down there?

GIRL
Deer Creek.

GRANDMOTHER
Yes, that's where I saw her.

GIRL
What did they use her for?

GRANDMOTHER
I don't know. There were bears there too. And larger deer.

GIRL
Elk maybe?

GRANDMOTHER
Yes, they called them elk.

GIRL
Why did they have them?

GRANDMOTHER
They used them for medicine.

GIRL
How did they use them?

GRANDMOTHER
They used their songs.

GIRL
The deer sang?

GRANDMOTHER
No, they were just there. They made the songs happen.

GIRL
The elk too?

GRANDMOTHER
Yes, the elk too.

GIRL
And the moose?

GRANDMOTHER

Yes, the moose.

———————

GIRL

It was like talking to myself when I stayed with her. If I asked her something she answered flat as the table between us.

Open your deer mouth and talk. You never say anything on your own. I could wear a deer dress. I could change into a deer like you. We could deer dance in the woods under the redbirds. The bluejay. The finch.

U-da-tlv:da de-s-gi-ne-hv'-si, E-li'-sin
Pass me the cream, Grandmother.
My cup and saucer on the oilcloth.

How can you be a deer? You only have two legs.

GRANDMOTHER

I keep the others under my dress.

———————

GIRL

It was a wordless world she gave me. Not silent, but wordless. Oh, she spoke, but her words seemed hollow. I had to listen to her deer noise. I had to think what she meant. It was like having a conversation with myself. I asked. And I answered. Well— I could hear what I wanted.

When I was with her I talked and never stopped because her silence ate me like buttered toast.

What was she saying? Her words were in my own hearing?—
I had to know what she said before I could hear it?

———————

GRANDMOTHER

I don't like this world any more. We're reduced to what can be seen.

GIRL

She fought to live where we aren't tied to table and fork and knife and chair.

It was her struggle against what happens to us.

Why can't you let me in just once and speak to me as one of your own? You know I have to go into the *seeable*— Live away from your world. You could give me more.

———————

GIRL

You work the church soup-kitchen before? You slop up the place and I get to clean up. You night shifts think you're tough shit. But I tell you, you don't know nothing. I think you took my jean jacket. The one with Jesus on the cross in sequins on the back. Look— I see your girl wearing it I'll have you on the floor.

Don't think I don't know who's taking the commodities— I'm watching those boxes of macaroni and cheese disappear.

I know it was you who lost the key to the storeroom and I had to pay for the locksmith to change the lock. They kept nearly my whole check. I couldn't pay rent. I only got four payments left on my truck. I'm not losing it.

———————

GIRL

She said once, there were wings the deer had when it flew. You couldn't see them but they were there. They pulled out from the red deer dress. Like leaves opened from the kitchen table—

Like the stories that rode on her silence. You knew they were there. But you had to decide what they meant. Maybe that's what she gave me— the ability to fly when I knew I had no wings. When I was left out of the old world that moved in her head. When I had to go on without her stories.

They get crushed in this world.

But there're still there. I hear them in the silence sometimes.

I want to wear a deer dress. I want to deer dance with *Ahw'uste*—

———————

GIRL

What does *Ahw'uste* mean in English?

GRANDMOTHER

I don't know what the English was. But *Ahw'uste* was a spirit animal.

GIRL

What does that mean?

GRANDMOTHER

She was only there for some people to see.

GIRL

She was only there when you thought she was?

GRANDMOTHER

She had wings too. If you thought she did. She was there to remind us— You think you see something you're not sure of. But you think it's there anyway.

GIRL

Maybe Jesus used wings when he flew to heaven. Ascended right up the air. Into Holy Heaven. Floating and unreachable. I heard them stories at church when I worked the soup-kitchen.

Or maybe they're wings like the spirits use when they fly between the earth and sky. —But when you pick up a spirit on the road, you can't see his wings —he's got them folded into his jacket.

GRANDMOTHER

They say rocket ships go there now.

GIRL

The ancestors?

GRANDMOTHER

Yes, all of them wear red deer dresses.

GIRL

With two legs under their dresses?

GRANDMOTHER

In the afterworld they let them down.

GIRL

A four-legged deer with wings —wearing a red deer dress with shoes and hat? Dancing in the leaves— Red maple, I suppose. After they're raked up to the sky? —Where they stay red forever only if they think they do?—
Sometimes your hooves are impatient inside your shoes. I see them move. You stuff twigs in your shoes to make them fit your hooves. But I know hooves are there.
Why would I want to be a deer like you?
Why would I want to eat without my hands?
Why would I want four feet?
What would I do with a tail? It would make a lump behind my jeans.

Do you know what would happen if I walked down the street in a deer dress?

If I looked for a job?
I already know I don't fit anywhere— I don't need to be reminded—
I'm at your house, grandma, with my sleeping bag and old truck—
I don't have anyplace else to go—

———————

GIRL

(*Angrily.*) OK dude. Dudo. I pick you up on the road. I take you to the next town to get gas for your van take you back when it still won't start I pull you to town 'cause you don't have money for a tow truck. I wait two hours while you wait. Buy you supper. I give you love what do you want? Hey dude your cowboy boots are squeaking your hat with the beaded band. Your CB's talking to the highway the truckers the girls driving by themselves that's what you look for. You take what we got. While you got one eye on your supper one eye on your next girl.

I could have thought you were a spirit. You could have been something more than a dude—

GRANDMOTHER

The leaves only get to be red for a moment. Just a moment and then the tree grieves all winter until the leaves come back. But they're green through the summer. The maple waits for the leaves to turn red. All it takes is a few cold mornings. A few days left out of the warmth.

Then the maple tree has red leaves for a short while.

GIRL

(*Angrily.*) I can't do it your way, grandma. I have to find my own trail— Is that why you won't tell me? Is that why you won't speak? I'm caught? I have no way through? But there'll be a way through— I just can't see it yet. And if I can't find it, it's still there. I speak it through. Therefore, it is. If not now, then later. It's coming. If not for me— then for others.

I have to pass through this world not having a place but I'll go anyway.

GRANDMOTHER

That's *Ahw'uste*.

GIRL

I'll speak these stories I don't know. I'll speak because I don't know them.

GRANDMOTHER

We're like the tree waiting for the red leaves.
We count on what's not there as though it is because the maple has red leaves —only you can't always see them.

GIRL

You'd rather live with what you can't see— is that the point of your red leaf story?

GRANDMOTHER
I was trying to help you over the hard places.

GIRL
I can get over them myself.

GRANDMOTHER
I wanted you to look for the red leaves instead of the dudes on the highway.

GIRL
A vision is *not* always enough—

GRANDMOTHER
It's all I had.

GIRL
You had me— Is a vision worth more than me?

GRANDMOTHER
I wanted to keep the leaves red for you.

GIRL
I don't want you to do it for me.

GRANDMOTHER
What am I supposed to do?

GIRL
Find someone else to share your silence with.

―――――――

GIRL
I was thinking we could have gone for a drive in my old truck.

GRANDMOTHER
I thought we did.

―――――――

GRANDMOTHER

Ahw'uste's still living. Up there on the hill, straight through (*indicating*) near Asuwosg' Precinct. A long time ago, I was walking by there hunting horses. There was a trail that went down the hill. Now there's a highway on that hill up there, but then, the old road divided. Beyond that, in the valley near Ayohli Amayi I was hunting horses when I saw them walking and I stopped.

They were this high (*indicating*) and had horns. They were going that direction (*indicating*). It was in the forest and I wondered where they were going. They were all walking. She was going first, just this high (*indicating*), and she had little horns. Her horns were just as my hands are shaped— Five points, they call them five points. That's the way it was. Just this high (*indicating*). And there was a second one, a third one, and a fourth one. The fifth one was huge, and it also had horns with five points. They stopped a while and they watched me. I was afraid of the large one! They were turning back, looking at me. They were pawing with their feet and I was afraid. They were showing their anger then. First they'd go (*paw*) with the right hoof and then with the left and they'd go: *Ti! Ti! Ti! Ti!* They kept looking at me and pawing and I just stood still.

They started walking again and disappeared away off and I wondered where they went. I heard my horses over there and I went as fast as I could. I caught a horse to ride and took the others home.

There was a man named Tseg' Ahl'tadeg and when I got there [at his house] he asked me, what did you see?

I saw something down there, I told him.

What was it?

A deer. She was just this (*indicating*) high and she had horns like this (*indicating*) and she was walking in front. The second one was this (*indicating*) high and the third one was this (*indicating*) high and the fourth one (*indicating*)— then the rest were large.

It was *Ahw'uste*, he said.

GIRL

I thought you said *Ahw'uste* lived in a house in Deer Creek.

GRANDMOTHER

Well, she did, but these were her tribe. She was with them some-times.

GIRL

She's the only one who lived in a house?

GRANDMOTHER

Yes.

GIRL

In Deer Creek?

GRANDMOTHER

Yes, in Deer Creek.

GIRL

Your deer dress is the way you felt when you saw the deer?

GRANDMOTHER

When I saw *Ahw'uste*, yes. My deer dress is the way I felt, transformed by the power of ceremony. The idea of it in the forest of my head.

———————

GIRL

Speak without your stories. Just once. What are you without your deer dress? What are you without your story of *Ahw'uste*?

GRANDMOTHER

We're carriers of our stories and histories. We're nothing without them.

GIRL

We carry ourselves. Who are you besides your stories?

GRANDMOTHER

I don't know— No one ever asked.

———————

GIRL

OK Bucko. I find out you're married. But not living with her. *You aren't married in your heart,* you say. *It's the same as not being married.* And you got kids too? Yeah, several, I'm sure. Probably left more of them behind to take care of themselves than you admit. You think you can dance me backwards around the floor, Bucko?

GRANDMOTHER

Why would I want to be like you?

GRANDMOTHER

Why can't my granddaughter wait on the spirit? Why is she impatient? It takes a while sometimes. She says— *Hey spirit, what's wrong? Your wings broke down? You need a jumper cable to get them started?*

My granddaughter wants to do what she wants. Anything that rubs against her, well, she bucks. Runs the other way. I'm not going to give her my deer dress to leave in a heap on some dude's floor. It comes from long years from my grandmother—

I have to live so far away from you. Take me where you are— I feel the pull of the string. (*She touches her breastbone.*) Reel me in. Just pull. I want out of here. I want to see you ancestors. Not hear the tacky world. No more.

GIRL

You always got your eye on the next world.

GRANDMOTHER

I sit by the television watch those stupid programs.

GIRL

What do you want? Weed the garden. Do some beans for supper. Set a trap for the next spirit to pass along the road.

GRANDMOTHER

The spirits push us out so we'll know what it's like to be without them. So we'll struggle all our lives to get back in—

GIRL

Is that what life is for you? No— for me —I get busy with day-to-day stuff until it's over.

I told 'em at church I didn't take the commodities— well not all those boxes— I told 'em— shit— what did it matter?

Have you ever lost one job after another?

GRANDMOTHER

Have you eaten turnips for a week? Because that was all you had in your garden. In your cupboard. Knowing your commodities won't last because you gave them to the next family on the road? They got kids and you can hear them crying.

GIRL

Well just step right off the earth. That's where you belong. With your four deer feet.

GRANDMOTHER

Better than your two human ones.
All you do is walk into trouble.

GIRL

Because I pick up someone now and then?
Didn't you know what is was like to want love?

GRANDMOTHER

Love— Ha! I didn't think of that. We had children one after another. We were cooking supper or picking up some crying child or brushing the men away. Maybe we did what we didn't want to do. And we did it everyday.

GIRL

Well I want something more for my life.

GRANDMOTHER

A trucker dude or two to sleep with 'til they move on? Nights in a bar. The juke box and cowboys rolling you over.

GIRL

(*She slaps her.*) What did I do? Slap my grandmother?

You deserved it. Sitting there with your smug spirits. I don't curl up with stories. I live in the world I see.
I've got to work.
Christ— where am I going to find another job?

GRANDMOTHER

You can't live on commodities alone.

GIRL

You can't drive around all day in your spirit-mobile.

———————

GIRL

I been paying ten years on my truck, Bub. You think I need a new transmission? 'Cause I got 180,000 miles on the truck and it's in the garage? You think you can sell me a new one, Bubby? My truck-'ll run another hundred thousand. I don't have it paid for yet. You think you can sell me a used truck? You couldn't sell me mudflaps. Just get it running— Try something else and my grandma'll stomp you with her hooves. My truck takes me in a vision. You got a truck that has visions? I don't see it on the list of options.

———————

GRANDMOTHER

Gu'-s-di i-da-da-dv-hni My relatives—
I'm making medicine from your songs. Sometimes I feel it. But mostly I have to know it's there without seeing. I go there from the hurts he left me with all those kids and no way to feed them but by the spirit. Sometimes I think the birds brought us food. Or somehow we weren't always hungry. That's not true. Mostly we were on our own. Damned spirits. Didn't always help out. Let us have it rough sometimes. All my kids are gone. Run off. One of my daughters calls from Little Falls sometimes. Drunk. Drugged. They all have accidents. One got shot.

What was that? *E-li'-sin*— Grandmother?

—No, just the bluejay. The finch.

Maybe the ancestors— I hear them sometimes— Out there raking leaves —Or I hear them if I think I do.

Hey— quiet out there, my granddaughter would say.

Just reel me in, grandmother, I say.

GIRL

So I told 'em at my first job interview— no, I hadn't worked that kind of machine— but I could learn.

I told 'em at my second interview the same thing—

I told 'em at the third—

At the fourth I told 'em—
My grandmother was a deer. I could see her change before my eyes. She caused stories to happen. That's how I knew she could be a deer.

At the fifth I continued— I'm sewing my own red deer dress. It's different than my grandma's. Mine is a dress of words.
I see *Ahw'uste* also.

At the rest of the interviews I started right in— Let me talk for you— that's what I can do.

My grandma covered her trail. Left me without knowing how to make a deer dress. Left me without covering.
But I make a covering she could have left me if only she knew how.

I think I hear her sometimes— That crevice you see through into the next world. You look again it's gone.

My heart has red trees.
The afterworld must be filling up with leaves.

You know I've learned she told me more without speaking than she did with her words.

END

Urban Tattoo

Marie Clements

Artist's Statement

I believe each play, like each human, has different characteristics, different structures, bones, in which the words of the story can flesh out and breathe an undeniable force that takes its own unique shape and place in time. Rhythms, images, technology, text, movement are all integrated to respond to the flight of the story.

Urban Tattoo came quite naturally in two parts; first flowing like the Mackenzie Delta landscape, and then fragmented like the rhythm of the city. The impulse came from blood memories, the place of dreams and hope, the knowledge of transformation as a form of survival, and our own deep rhythm that propels us forward despite the gravity of past scars.

Urban Tattoo is the raising of these scars to the surface of the skin. Scars that have defined us can only be redefined by us. In this way, in this tattooing, we wear the markings of a warrior of our own design, our own making.

Urban Tattoo

Characters

ROSEMARIE, a young Metis girl in her teens. Beginning the play at the end, Rosemarie appears as an older version of her city self in the prologue of the play. As she flies back to her younger self, she becomes younger and rediscovers her story, gathering tattoos and strength through to the end.

Although *Urban Tattoo* is a one-woman show, all other characters are presented through storytelling, or are represented by sound or projected images generated by slides and video.

Setting

The prologue is set in the present. Rosemarie takes flight and her story begins in the 1940s in a small northern town called Ft. Good Hope, in the Northwest Territories. It begins where she came from, and where her dreams began. As the story progresses she leaves her land and moves to the city where she ends up living on the streets. Rosemarie transforms through decades to reclaim her beginning and her tattoos of survival.

Playwright's Note

Urban Tattoo is a play that is best realized when it transforms ideas of traditional storytelling, theatrical magic in performance, and spoken word into one. At best, a live performer is layered visually, textually, and musically toward achieving a visceral experience for the audience that includes both myth and the universal human. The interaction of imagistic technology, sound, and performer all play their respective roles as characters in the same play communicating with each other, relying on each other for the telling. Although the play doesn't have set scenes and acts, I believe it does have a series of rhythms and beats that underscore the action of her environment and are true to Rosemarie's flight and gravity.

Production History

Urban Tattoo is a new performance work that presents a radical approach to storytelling, incorporating multimedia and music. It takes the themes of identity, displacement, and survival and redesigns them into an urban context. *Urban Tattoo* was workshopped at the Native Earth's Performing Arts Weesageechuck Festival in Toronto with dramaturge and director Margo Kane in 1995. It was given a work-in-progress performance with Maenad Theatre in Calgary in early 1996 and a staged reading at the Native Voices Festival in New York, directed by Randy Reinholz, at the American Indian Community House. In the summer of 1997, *Urban Tattoo* was presented at the University of Leeds, in England, and went on to be workshopped with Peter Hinton and Chapelle Jaffe at the Playwright's Theatre Centre in Vancouver. *Urban Tattoo* premiered a workshop production at the 1998 Women In View Festival in Vancouver, in collaboration with Lynda Hill, Terri Snelgrove, and D.B. Boyko. *Urban Tattoo* has since toured an American production, directed by Randy Reinholz and produced by Native Voices at the Theatre of the World Festival in San Diego, the Autry Museum Wells Fargo Theatre in Los Angeles, the Aboriginal Arts Festival in Toronto, the Glenbow Museum in Calgary, the University of Miami in Oxford, Ohio, Illinois State University in Normal, and the New World Theatre in Amherst, Massachusetts. The Canadian production, directed by Teri Snelgrove, premiered at the Belfry Theatre's Festival '99 in Victoria, and was selected to represent one of two Canadian works at the 2001 international Festival de Theatre des Ameriques, in Montreal.

It is dark. It is quiet. Still. The conversation of the city slowly filters in. ROSEMARIE *climbs to the highest level of the stage. Standing, she looks down on the space and is silhouhetted by a back screen that is a sky and then a raven. She breathes and prepares herself to jump down and through the building, down toward the pavement. The city street conversation mixes and increases, and wings flap, and a voice calls out like a raven and flies down as* ROSEMARIE'*s body jumps slightly upward, and begins to spin slowly in a circle, as images on the front scrim fall with her, over her, and on her, memories and buildings twirling, and finally the sky descends and then ascends to the beyond.*

It is grey. The sound of wings flapping softly whisper. The sound of time going backward, yawning, faint images and sounds flying past, images of other ghostly wings moving. ROSEMARIE *interacts with the image journey.*

ROSEMARIE (*Voiceover*)

> A grey mist washes my face with its ghost's hands and the whisper-
> ing of a thousand ancestors yawn past my ears.

(ROSMARIE *falls bird-like down and perches as if sitting on a white cross and looking down on a small town.*)

ROSEMARIE (*Voiceover*)

> I fall into a layer of blue and hit the tip of a white cross that
> stretches its hand so far up to try and shake its God's hand. I
> perch here for an eternity and take a deep chalk thought and let
> the shit fall proud how it blots the landscape. I think some more
> on this and descend down black and blue from my experience.

(ROSEMARIE *moves to a land level, wings outstretched to overshadow images on the back screen. A combination of Native and Celtic music flies down with her. As she lands, flying backward, moving on land, a black-and-white aerial view of the town of Ft. Good Hope, Northwest Territories, comes into clear view.*)

ROSEMARIE

> Flying back you can reclaim your bones from your landscape,
> reclaim your skin from the earth, the water, the stars—the story of
> dreams that made you original—the journey that makes you
> remember your place.

(*Images of Ft. Good Hope appear on the back screen—small white buildings, the Mackenzie River, a small white church with a graveyard to its side.* ROSEMARIE *walks.*)

ROSEMARIE

Walking in the past I walk past the Mackenzie River. I walk past the high cross that pierces the land. I walk past a garden of small mounds and white crosses.

(She looks back at the white church and begins to go toward it.)

I walk towards the only building with a white cross on it. Walking past but towards everything I open the door and I reclaim the sky that used to be mine.

*(*ROSEMARIE *turns and motions to open the door. She reaches up toward the sky of the church. The inside of the church is small but has been beautifully painted. Stars cover the ceiling and walls of the church. Pews file down with bibles pocketed into each seat of every row. Everything is black and white. She moves toward the audience.)*

It is a starry sky. It's always a starry sky here in my memory. No matter how grey or muddy it gets out there, it is always starry in here. Stars that are so blue and yellow and white rimmed all over the ceiling. Perfect. Set apart from each other perfect.

I used to call them Baby Jesus stars. Baby Jesus stars painted by an ancient French priest. And I mean ancient. Dead. An ancient French priest surrounded by Indians. This must have been his haven from us. His place to come when the brown faces engulfed him on the land. Here it was just Him and his God and His painting Hand and He controlled the stars here and the front door and the Good Indians could come and go as they liked as long as He was holding the door.

I used to sneak in here when there weren't any Good Indians around, or the Good priest. I used to sneak in here and close the door.

*(*ROSEMARIE *lies down on the stage box and looks up toward her starry sky.)*

I'd lay here between the pews when I needed a haven from all the goodness and greyness. I lay here.... ... between the pews and trace my future from star to star ... from ... I wishes ...

(She closes her eyes in a wish and a white bra appears on the back screen.)

Marie as Rosemarie. Photo by Teri Snelgrove, 1999.

to I wishes ...

(*She wishes on another grey star—a handsome man leans in to kiss her from the back screen.* ROSEMARIE *goes to him and then reaches upwards toward the stars.*)

... or sometimes, I climb real close and dig my fingernail into the star itself and chip off a bit of blue, or sometimes I just stand tall and trace the painted stars as if I am the painter ...

as if those stars had come from me....

(*She walks forward and motions painting a star on her stomach. The lights go to black and the image of a star tattoos itself on her stomach.*)

… As if we had an understanding.

(*The Mackenzie River washes and swirls over the front scrim. A montage of black-and-white historical photos submerge in and out of the water. She watches, hesitates, and then goes with it.*)

I'm going down the river. I'm going down the river.

My Grandpa took me down the river to Norman Wells and all these guys in army uniforms were supposed to be building a road to somewhere.

(*On the back screen a historical photo of a long line-up of U.S. Army men. She looks back at them, looking down the line at each soldier.*)

Even saw myself a couple of black guys. Real dark. I asked my Grandpa "Where those men come from with the black skin?" He said "Africa." Africa. That's a long way to come to build a road I thought. Anyways one of those black guys was reading a magazine when I was sitting waiting for my Grandpa to finish at the Hudson's Bay store.

(*The image of a black man slowly turns on the front scrim and looks directly at her. She stares at him.*)

He looked at me because I was staring at him. "Whatcha looking at girl" he said. I didn't really know what I was looking at. I mean I'm not sure if I was looking at him because I had never seen any-body from Africa before or because he had this magazine in his hands that had a real glamorous girl on front. So I said I was looking at the magazine. He just said "Uh-huh" like he didn't believe me.

Finally he said to come over there.

(*Colored and polished Hollywood pinup pictures from a magazine flip on the screens …*)

We looked at a lot of pictures in the magazine.

(*… and stop at a picture of Jane Russell on a haystack.*)

My favorite was a girl sitting on a haystack. He said it was Jane Russell. I said I looked like Jane Russell. He just smiled and after awhile of looking at Jane Russell he tore the page out and handed it to me.

(*She takes the picture. It disappears.*)

That's when I thought I could be just like Jane Russell the movie star and maybe even take the man from Africa's road to somewhere. I put the picture in my pocket.

(*The river swirls on the front scrim. She walks into it. It becomes dark. The black-and-white interior of the church becomes focused.* ROSEMARIE *lights a candle and places it before the altar. Jane Russell takes her place above the altar growing in holiness on the back screen.*)

I take Jane out when I'm in church and nobody's around. I take her out and put her on the altar. Lean her up against the candle stick. Perfect. I light the candle and sit under the stars and ... sit under the stars ... and sit under stars and press my lips together like this, and cross my legs like this and stick my boobs out.... And just sit there all pretty like Jane Russell.

(ROSEMARIE *mirrors Jane Russell's pose on the haystack.*)

She didn't look like she had to do a damn thing. Just sit there all pretty. From where I come from this is called lazy. Good for nothing. I don't know why she was sitting in a barn with hay all around but she sure looked good. My sister says that her Dad is probably rich and that's what rich people do. They sit around all day and do nothing. That doesn't explain why she's in a barn but my sister says rich people can do whatever they want. This doesn't explain why she's in the barn sitting on a haystack, but maybe she just likes animals. Anyways she sure looks good. We have the same color hair and the same color skin don't you think? If you don't think so then just squint your eyes and you'll see what I mean. Almost identical. The man from Africa says she lives in Hollywood, Hollywood. And that they even have stars on the ground in Hollywood. Even stars on the ground.

(A big band sound fades up and ROSEMARIE *begins to sing "I only have stars for you" in the tune of "I only have eyes for you."* ROSEMARIE *waltzes and as she becomes more and more involved in her dream, her dance becomes ultra-Hollywood.)*

(The loud laughter of ROSEMARIE's *sister cuts in loudly ending her dream dance. Jane Russell starts to fade and the face of* ROSEMARIE's *sister appears on the front scrim. Her face is overpowered by her mouth. The mouth watches and then begins to take action mouthing non-stop.* ROSEMARIE *blows out her candle.)*

My sister says I shouldn't want to be a movie star because no one gets out of here except for Mary who got pregnant and wasn't even married. Her parents sent her down South to have it, though nobody's supposed to know about that. But everybody does. And nobody's supposed to feel sorry for her because she made her bed and now she has to lie in it. But I think everyone's just relieved it wasn't them. I'm not going to get married or pregnant for a long time, not until I am a movie star. My sister says how can I even be a movie star when I haven't even seen a movie. I just said I heard about it and I can picture it all in my head. My sister just laughed and said no Indians ever been a movie star. I said "Well, I am part Irish." My sister laughed harder and said "Yeah, with a combination like that all you could hope for is being a good drinker." I don't care what she says. I'm getting out of here.

(The Mackenzie River washes the mouth away.)

My Dad got me this real nice job in Edmonton … don't disappoint me…. My Dad was buying me some real nice Edmonton clothes when I saw that guy again from the store.

(The black man appears and turns slowly to look at her.)

He was sitting in the exact same place I left him last time looking at his magazine. He said "How are you doin Miss Jane Russell" I said "Just fine thank you soldier."

(The black man disappears and she turns.)

When I came out some big white trapper was in the big black guy's face. Called the black man a nigger and no nigger should be reading a magazine with white women in it. No nigger should be looking at any white women. They just stared hate at each other for a real long time. Real quiet.

(ROSEMARIE *hesitates and then stands high on the stage box.*)

So I went over there and told the trapper that it was my magazine thank you very much and that the man from Africa was holding it for me while I went in the store. He finally just walked away.

(*She sits.*)

The black man just sat down all sad sorta. "What's a nigger?" I said. He said "That's what white men call black men back where he comes from in the United States and that's how white men treat Indians in Canada." I said "I guess we are just two niggers then."

(*The sound of the black soldier laughing.*)

He laughed and laughed really hard for a real long time. I didn't get it.

I didn't get it then.

(*The river washes* ROSEMARIE *to the city. She changes adding a white collared shirt to her dress. A house clock strikes.*)

I finally got out of here. I went down to Edmonton. I took my real nice clothes Dad had bought for me and went to work for a real nice job Dad had got for me and worked for a real nice family cleaning up their real nice ... stuff.

Don't disappoint me ... don't disappoint me ... don't disappoint him.

(*Hyper black-and-white domestic images start appearing in front of her. Faucets, and furniture, family pictures of this household, bathtubs, well-made beds, doilies, etc.* ROSEMARIE *appears in the center of all the images. She begins washing them.*)

I stuff my pockets with Jane Russell and the paint from those church stars and clean and clean and clean. I stuff them deep down no see through bulges and clean. I stuff my words deep down with them. I stuff. I clean. I stuff. I clean. I clean. I clean. I clean ... don't disappoint him. I clean. I clean. I stuff I stuff I stuff I stuff until I thought my head was going to explode.

(*She backs away from the images and they disappear. She kneels down and begins scrubbing with renewed determination.*)

They said with nice smiles that Indians don't talk much but really I had no one to talk to. Jane was a way down deep, there was no stars, there was only this tight polite house and tight polite words that meant different things. I was polite until the man touched me.

(ROSEMARIE *freezes. A round bright surface emerges on the front scrim. It becomes the bald head of a man. She keeps her head up high and stares at the head moving and turning to reveal his face.*)

He undid one of my buttons on my clean white Edmonton blouse.... I just knelt there ... he said to be quiet.... I just knelt there ... he put his two hands on my breasts and started milking me like I was a cow or something ... all the time the beads of sweat waltzing down his shiny bald head. I just stared at those beads of water balancing on his skin head till they tumbled down. I just knelt there ... it's like I wasn't even breathing. I just knelt there ... one of his hands undid the zipper of my skirt and one of his milking hands went down there. I started to cry ... he said "Shut up, it wasn't like I was a virgin or something...." I said it wasn't like he was a movie star or something. That hand went down there until it dug into me and until his wife walked in.

(ROSEMARIE *gets up, gathering herself she stands.*)

I just stood there ... she was slapping him so hard I thought that bald head of his was going to roll off and become a bowling bowl. I almost laughed until she looked at me like I was less than nothing. She said she was going to call Dad and tell him what a whore I was.... I said it wasn't my fault. She said I just stood there....

... Don't disappoint me ... don't disappoint me ... don't disappoint him....

... I just stood there.

(*A loud cry erupts from above, wings flap and the rain falls.* ROSEMARIE *turns to the rain. Her body separating. Rain descending.*)

It was raining ... raining hard ... no stars ... nowhere to go but the rain. She just walked hoping maybe the rain would paint her with the stars and she would be clean again.

(*She staggers.*)

But that couldn't happen unless she was naked so she took her blouse off and she took her skirt off and she took her slip off and she took her stockings off....

(ROSEMARIE *takes pieces of her clothing off letting them fly.*)

She took her nice clothes off and she just walked all the while the rain soaking into her more and more ... little streams becoming big streams flowing down her taking away that burning where his hands had touched her ... taking away. She just walked ... it was just raining.

(*A lamppost appears on the back screen. A bright light floods white from above.* ROSEMARIE *gravitates to the light.*)

She walked until she saw this lamppost with a big beautiful light way up in the sky and water crystals floating down to her ... touching her softy ... talking to her softly ... talking to me.

(*An ambulance light begins to circle red, flashing over everything.*)

She just turned in circles there for hours. They picked her up there. Not that she remembers.... She remembers a high cross straight and stiff upwards which the ravens perch shitting flying white chalk, stars so blue and yellow and white rimmed perfect, Jane Russell. She remembers I am a nigger. She remembers someone saying crazy Indians ... circles ... someone asking her if she had family anywhere ... circles. She remembered Indians don't talk much....

... She remembers don't disappoint me.

(*Blackout.*)

(A light is turned on. A lightbulb swings past a crucifix forever moving. ROSEMARIE *is caught behind as overwhelming bright surges of light electrocute her and the space. Each surge of light leaves splinters of a visit—the sound. Each jolt causes a flutter as if something is being shifted, wings ruffled and flapping viciously. The sound of a raven screaming. Bright light. The soldier whistles and then speaks—voiceover.)*

THE SOLDIER
How you doin Miss Jane Russell?

ROSEMARIE
Just fine, thank you soldier.

THE SOLDIER
Just fine.

ROSEMARIE
Perfect.

THE SOLDIER
Look them in the eye.

ROSEMARIE
Why?

THE SOLDIER
So they won't forget.

(A shock of light fills the stage. The raven screams. Wings shifting. The sister laughs— voiceover.)

ROSEMARIE
Shut up.

SISTER
I haven't even said anything yet.

ROSEMARIE
Perfect.

(It is quiet.)

ROSEMARIE
My sister didn't say anything. Where am I ?

(*Silence.*)

ROSEMARIE

Whatever happened to Mary?

SISTER

Well, she got pregnant and had a baby with Joseph.

ROSEMARIE

Not that Mary. The Mary that went down south.

SISTER

When are you coming home?

ROSEMARIE

It's not like I just had a baby.

SISTER

So when you coming home. When are you coming home?

(*A shock of light fills the stage. The raven screams. Wings shifting. Jane Russell speaks—voiceover.*)

ROSEMARIE

You look pretty. Do you think we look alike? Really ... truly. Do you think you could tell me where to find my haystack. Hey ... what do you think Jane ... I like animals too ... Jane?

(*Jane starts to fade.*)

ROSEMARIE

Don't disappear Jane. I didn't say you were lazy or anything. I just said....

(*A shock of light. The raven screams. Wings shifting. Her Dad's voice—voiceover.*)

DAD

Don't disappoint me. Don't disappoint me. Don't disappoint me.

ROSEMARIE

Dad ... I just want to come home.... Dad, I'm sorry ... I'm....

DAD
Don't disappoint me … don't disappoint me … don't disappoint me.

(*A shock of light. The raven screams. Wings shifting. Baby Jesus gagas—voiceover.*)

ROSEMARIE
Hello Baby Jesus.…

BABY JESUS
Googoogaga

ROSEMARIE
You sure are cute? But people always say you are cute when you are a baby. After that you just get uglier and uglier. So enjoy it I'd say.

BABY JESUS
Googoogaga

ROSEMARIE
I have one of your stars. Or I think it's one of your stars. I know the ancient Father painted them for you … so I guess it means it's yours. I hope you don't mind.

BABY JESUS
Googoogaga

ROSEMARIE
I put it in my pocket so nobody would get it. I put it in my pocket so I wouldn't lose it. I think it's melted though. I can't feel the points. Oh … baby it used to be so pretty. So pretty.

BABY JESUS
Googoogaga

(*A shock of light. The raven screams. Wings shifting. Her Grandad laughs—voiceover.*)

ROSEMARIE
Hey Grandad.

GRANDAD
Hey Girlie.

ROSEMARIE
Take me up the river Grandad. Take me up the river. Please.

GRANDAD
Close you eyes.

(*The sound of a violin takes over, a Native drum plays in. The Mackenzie River swirls through and over the projected image of her as she shuts her eyes. A shock of light bombs the image. A shock of light. A shock of light. White out.*)

(ROSEMARIE *rises up to the image of herself behind bars. Blackout.*)

(ROSEMARIE *is found standing under a bright light.*)

I must of fell from the sky on a rainy night. Drizzle down and just sat here for what seemed like an eternity.

(*She turns into the city landscape. A soundscape of car streams, traffic, and rain beat out a rhythm, splintering each other and fragmenting the sound. A traffic light flashes its colors, rainy city streets, and reflections hit the back screen.*)

Red light—stop, yellow light—think about it, green light. Green lights. Go. Let's go.

Streets so wet you could slip on them, towards them downstream dead. Traffic noises, sounds of exhaustion, lights fishing for a reflection, my face upturned sky craned. Give me a piece of the blue, so I can stuff it in my pockets … so I can stuff it in my pockets when things have gone all hopeless, when things have gone all over the place and all I have is this one blue thing between me and the spiral.

(ROSEMARIE *reaches up and snatches a blue star from the screen. She looks at the front scrim trying to catch a reflection.*)

Puddles a small tear of the streets. I look for my reflection I see no relation just myself. A dark half. Mudded and blurred splashing everywhere in puddles.
I must of fell from the sky on a rainy night. Drizzle down and just sat here for what seemed like an eternity.

(*The trinity visits. Each character she encounters is musically represented by an instrumental sound and the text acts as an addition to the composition to the city beat. Urban*

street images start to race by her. Graffiti, and signs, etc.... A heavy set sound of Christian music sits down!!!!!)

!!!!!! Woman sits down next to me she says she's not my cousin. I understand, I say. *!!!!!* But she says she could save me. Great I say. *!!!!!!!* Actually her and Jehovah could save me. Do a real good job. Save me from what I say? *Hell. Hell. Hell.* She hands me a pamphlet. It looks like Hell alright. She is selling Jehovah. Today, next week is the last day. The very last day. *!!!!* Would I like to buy in before it's too late. Too late for what I ask? *Hell. Hell. Hell.* I shouldn't have asked the second time. *Dumb. Dumb. Dumb. Dumb. Dumb.*

(Car streams !!! An obese blob of a sound waddles in OOOOOOO.)

Despair... *!!!!!* pizza *OOOO* Despair *!!!!* pizza. *OOOO* It works. Tonight I am desperate therefore I am pizza. An extra cheese please. *OOO* A 12-inch after 11-o'clock when you know you're not going anywhere. When you know the wedges will transform them-selves to extra globs on your hips sticking
out in huge configurations from your jeans. *OOOO*
You are just a glob. *OOOOO* A pizza woman. *OOOOOO.*
A pizza woman with amazing hips. *OOOOOOO*
A   pizza   woman.   *OOOOOOO*   A   pizza   woman
OOOOOOOOOOOOOOOOO
What? Walk on-walk in nothing to see here. *OOOOooooo*

(Car streams—oooooo. The obese sound deflates————A sexy but slimy male sound $$$$$$.)

$$$$$$* Man says honey you belong on a cruise ship with that body. I think you obviously didn't see how many pizza slices I just ate. *$$$$$* Man says honey you belong on a cruise ship with that body, again. I think, no shit? Actually I just laughed. *$$$$$$$$$ Man says My name is Jackal because I come alive at night. (*Sound of wings.*) I say, no shit? I'm no shitting out of here.

*(*ROSEMARIE *points to the back screen depicting a seedy nightclub.)*

Sometimes I feel like I could of been born on a planet and tossed down. Tossed down still. Wind stop. Stop. Breath. Fell a long way's down past myself to get here.

(*A neon sign "Ladies" appears.* ROSEMARIE *walks toward it. A 1940s nightclub. She begins her dream transformation. She puts on a jacket.*)

Gotta smoke ... gotta light ... gotta money ... gotta sense of humor ... gotta dress ... gotta shoes ... gotta hair ... gotta lipstick ... gotta boobs ... you gotta look good.

(*She has arrived. A beautifully dressed and manicured Hollywood persona à la Jane Russell. She opens the door. Detailed images from the bar place themselves in detail.*)

(*A great Hollywood dream scene emerges. The Hollywood grand band warms up and plays. She descends upon her audience in full color as interior pictures of a 1940s upscale bar transform and the sound of bar business rises in clanks and laughable chatter. She works the room.*)

Since I have become rain. It rains here inside and out.

(*A soft drizzle of bar sounds descends. A smoky mist ascends. Detailed pictures of hip patrons enjoying themselves.*)

A Noah rain of endless days and nights of the pitter patter. This chitter chatter language makes me tired. Noah's Ark is dark and smoky ... body heat rising in sweat and the puff of a hot word rising to taste. You see a sheep or two, sitting two by two at the bar their fluffy rumps upturned on a red leather stool. Their heads downturned, their eyes upturned here and there to catch a glint of sex if it happen to sparkle. If it happen to sparkle.... It sparkles low this loneliness. It sparkles low below the belt. It catches our eye. It catches the sighs. It leaves us damp. It leaves us thirsty. When all we wanted to do was hold on.

(*She arrives at the stage surrounded by her spotlight. The band awaits. The audience awaits. She motions the band to begin. They start to play "I only have eyes for you." She begins to lip-sync a grand version of "I only have stars for you." It is great until the music starts to distort. She tries to please but is unbalanced and off key. People start to laugh and shout "Take it off." She continues but finally stops ... taking off her dream....*)

Do you want a part of me? Which part do you want?

I could say I love you.
I could say it will be alright, baby.
I could say watch your hands man, or lower.

I could say watch who you step on.

I recognize you I recognize the lament dance.

I will pick out the biggest, the hardest, the loudest monster and caress it, and rise it and think of swallowing it.

I might even feel sorry for it for a minute and think of kissing it full on the mouth. Oh dear.

I will look into your cold eyes dropping dead wishes upon my chest and sharpening them into my groin and say

"Do you want a part of me?" I can devour you, dig it?

I'm getting sexy, I'm feeling sexy. History makes me feel sexy.

(ROSEMARIE *turns a 1950s cool cat look. Black-and-white images of Jack Kerouac and the boys* On the Road *hit the back screen.* ROSEMARIE *takes her place with the guys in her own version of the beat. The band backs her up musically on her road.* "Breathless roles" *on the front scrim.*)

it is a sunny Sunday kinda day when you wish you didn't have to do anything but when nothing happens you wish something would ... a great white car shaves its head and convertibles down the West Coast blaze of spring and on you could drive on if you knew where to go if you didn't have to get up and dance the dance if you didn't have to eat in three quick stares at the table cloth if the world was fairer and greater than your mind imagined in grade three when everything was so fair you didn't know it and the only times things weren't just you just screamed

jack and his buddy sit on the nation and yes they look black and white and handsome and you wish you could sit with them sit on them with them but they are both dead beats and time rolls on and nobody you know writes poetry or at least nobody who will read it on an old couch in the middle of a morning back somewhere when everything was turquoise blue and you weren't even seen and hippies were pacing about before you had time to Howl or go On the Road or wish for justice on a rainy night man—beat beat I'm doing the beat

it is a beat I'm after my beat not a pale fifties beat of sex and drugs and black-and-white pictures of men doing exactly what they wanted how original how beat maybe that is the beat a male beat that repeats itself with self patting hands and the right hand of god's fingers jacking off a revelation to their society Jack Kerouac was French Canadian and not an American so who really knows anything and he was on the road with a bunch of self serving men and their self serving pricks and mouths sucking everything that could not suck back and some that did an unfair judgement perhaps but I'm doing the beat with or without you Jack because I don't have to stop and you don't have to get it

("Breathless" fades to black. She sits and watches the reflections of time stomp by. The sound of hooves approaching, marching feet trample through baaing. Images and sound impressions of the 1960s march on, on both the scrim and screen.)

The animals here file past me in a steady blow. From where I am sitting I watch the shuffle of their shoed feet hit the pavement in clacks. Nick nack patty wacks....
I know they are being herded but I see no great herd-er.
I smell their fear of going the wrong way.
I smell their softness. A pinkness.
A cuddly white fluffiness that presses against each other into a convenient sleep.

(1970s images and sound impressions. Close-up of welfare offices, government hand-shakes, religious leaders march on.)

This animal whispers yeses I hear it under their marching breaths.
Even when they are saying yes they are pushing no.
Even when they are praying yes they are giving no.
Even when they are nodding yes they are all knowing no.
Smiling YES meaning NO....

(1980s images and sound impressions. Food line-ups and booze line-ups and drug line-ups and welfare line-ups elongate and march on.)

In the food line, the booze line, the welfare line.
Follow that line, follow that design.
Smiling yes everything will be fine ... just fine.
In the food line, the booze line, the welfare line.
Follow that line, follow that design.
Smiling yes ... meaning NO....

No parking, no barking, no shitting, no smoking, no joking.
No men, no women, no children, no minors.
No dogs, no Indians, no family.
No clothes, no shoes, no service.
No entrance.
No exit. Enjoy your stay.
Little Bo Peep sits in her corner losing her way.
Little Jack Horner sits in his corner jacking humanity away.

Don't stare at me sheep.

(*The images wind down.*)

I will not run with you. Little hooves. I will not try to keep up with your pathetic rhythm.

(*Tall business towers emerge on the front scrim. They begin to move slowly and then accelerate in speed.*)

I will not enter your house. I will not enter your two-faced doors. I will not be bought or brought down.

(*A sound of wings flutter and the sound of breathing builds under.*)

I had wanted to run with the buffalo … too late. I had wanted to run with the bulls since I had read about it. I had wanted to run through the thin streets of Barcelona—wild eyed, hair flowing, panting laughing mad though the streets of Barcelona hooves behind gaining ground … I wanted to swill a gulp or two of tequila, taste the salt, and head out head strong through the bodies of macho men clad in white shirts and the stained brains of real men. I had wanted to run. Feel the breath surge up in fear, paralyzing fear that could motivate one to run to live. I had wanted to run from the beasts and with the beasts. I did not want to run with the sheep that file through these wide streets the sheer number of them a fearful rhythm. I did not want to run with them. I did not choose to run with them. So I just stopped.

(*Large dead buffalo mounds replace the buildings. She stops in all directions. The landscape of Ft. Good Hope surrounds her. Whisperings and a montage of memory sounds and through….*)

So I just stopped.

So I just stopped.
So I just stopped.

(ROSEMARIE *falls to her knees.*)

So I just knelt down
So I just knelt down.

Heavy.
I just knelt down
and began to dig.

Sharp points,
memories getting caught on my skin.
Sharp points.
I knelt down to myself ... and began to dig deeper.
unearthing the burden,
unearthing the dead weight,
Heavy baby,
like birds hitting glass,
beaks breaking,
wings whispering,
lips promising they will remember,

(*The landscape of Ft. Good Hope appears in black and white and then washes itself with brilliant color.* ROSEMARIE *stands up as the voice encourages her to remember.*)

remember me the earth said,
remember me the river said,
remember me the stars said,
remember me she said.
You cannot walk anywhere and hope to summon yourself you have to find the exact spot the exact time and say I remember you.... I remember when ... oh remember the time ... oh remember the time. You bury everything. And slowly it grows from your earth. The perfect being.

(ROSEMARIE *turns and moves toward the audience. She stands in front of the scrim, in front of the audience.*)

So I just stand

So I just stand
So I just stand tall
And trace the painted stars
And trace the tainted scars
Digesting them between worlds
As if I was the painter.
As if those tattoos had come from me.
As if we had an understanding that in going past I know my place
and in going forward I have I become bigger than you can
imagine.
Amen.
Ho.

(ROSEMARIE *leaves and a raven perches on the back screen and flies toward the front scrim where wings fly forward and beyond.*)

ROSEMARIE VOICEOVER
   I am with you remembering everything and flying tattooed.

(*Blackout.*)

END

Winnetou's Snake Oil Show from Wigwam City

Spiderwoman Theater

Lisa Mayo
Gloria Miguel
Muriel Miguel
with Hortensia Colorado

Artists' Statement

As personal chords are sung, whispered, screamed, or muttered by the performers, they strike up resonant reactions with the audience who become part of Spiderwoman's web...

Spiderwoman Theater, composed of three Kuna/Rappahannock sisters, Lisa Mayo, Gloria Miguel, and Muriel Miguel, is the oldest continually running women's theater company in North America. They take their name from the Hopi goddess Spiderwoman, who taught the people to weave and said, "You must make a mistake in every tapestry so that my spirit may come and go at will." Spiderwoman has prophetic insight into the future, speaks all languages, and by nature of being a spider is ever present to give and to guide. The women call their technique of working "story-weaving," in which they create designs and weave stories with words and movement, creating an overlay of interlocking stories, where fantasy and power are comically intertwined.

Spiderwoman Theater's work commands a plain, humorous, no-frills style, like agitprop street theater. Their capacity for comedy, ritual, impersonation, and satire creates a powerful medium for social change. With great flair and tongue-in-cheek whimsy they translate the images of their dreams and the stories of their lives into movement and narrative. The essential threads of human existence are woven into a tapestry that covers all they see. Whether exposing racism or espousing women's rights, contemporary topics are placed in historical context and examined—often with a vengeance—through the techniques of Native storytelling and theatrical conventions. The audience often wonders whether they're being put on or set up. They're entertained, but they're also being slipped a little awareness. Spiderwoman Theater drives their point home by spitting back the stereotypes with a vengeance and a wink, with a nudge and a chuckle.

Their powerful, deeply felt work addresses issues of the differences and the complexity of the factors that form their ethnic heritage. Spiderwoman Theater has a proven ability to speak with depth and complexity about the intersections of race, ethnicity, sexuality, and community. Their work dispels forming conclusions on the basis of preconceived notions. They have performed their work on reservations and in mainstream American society and in so doing have helped other Native Americans to have more respect for their culture and themselves. Thay also enlighten, educate, and entertain a wide and diverse general public.

Cast/Characters

HORTENSIA COLORADO: WILD-EYED SAM, WITCH #1, MOTHER MOON FACE, DEMON #2, HORDES #1, HORTENSIA

WILD-EYED SAM: A true American. I was inspired by Gabby Hayes; a cantankerous know-it-all, he is a racist who appears to be a funny old man. He would burn the woods and not think twice about it. He spits all over creation and kills four-legged creatures, fish, and winged animals for sport. Knows more than any foreigner that comes to these shores. Tolerates Indians and makes sure they keep their place.

WITCH #1: Evolves from WILD-EYED SAM, the dark side becomes the flamboyant. With her power, she will put in motion history in its most ridiculous vein.

MOTHER MOON FACE: Prances out of the WITCH. She was given her name by Grandfather in a workshop. She was inspired to become a horsewoman when, as a child, she put a nickel in the gyrating horse in front of the K-Mart. She wants to be loved by men and women. She's nearsighted. The Wild West Show is her life.

DEMON #2: One of three witches who create Winnetou Snake Oil.

HORDES #1: Evolves from MOTHER MOON FACE as all the stereo-types there ever were of Indians. So steeped in stereotypes is she that she goes off into impersonations of various stereotypical Indians. Like worms in your skin.

HORTENSIA: Comes out of the HORDES of Indians; out of being put down by her family and other Indians. Reclaiming her ancestors, her blood, she stands in her circle—a woman of power celebrating her ancestors and looking to the future in an ongoing struggle.

LISA MAYO: GUNTHER, WITCH #2, PRINCESS PISSY WILLOW, DEMON # 3, LISA MAYO

GUNTHER: A German tutor who becomes a brave man of the West.

WITCH #2: One of three witches who create the Winnetou Snake Oil.

PRINCESS PISSY WILLOW: A sharpshooter in the Wild West Show. In the Plastic Pop-Wow Workshop, I reveal myself as a plastic shaman, willing to sell shamanistic secrets to people for a fee.

DEMON #3: A dung beetle who is a facet of who LISA MAYO is: a voracious eater, one who gorges herself.

LISA: At certain moments, during the serious times of the play, I am LISA MAYO, Kuna/Rappahannock.

GLORIA MIGUEL: BEAR, KLEKEPETRA, WITCH #3, MINNIE HALLRUNNER, DEMON #1, HORDES #2, GLORIA

BEAR: Is a happy bear. He represents the last vestiges of life that the greedy white person was killing, the killing of the last animal. It isn't enough just to kill him and be over with it, it is overkill that is used, as was used on this country.

KLEKEPETRA: An elder and WINNETOU's dumb sidekick.

WITCH #3: An evil character who mixes potions.

MINNIE HALLRUNNER: A copy of an Indian princess who does nice sweet things but she's all show business. She is a fake.

DEMON #1: Not only the dark side that is a part of us all, it also represents the spirituality within Native tradition that our people believe in.

HORDES #2: Indians in the forest.

As GLORIA, I voice my political feelings toward plastic shamans and people who want to steal spirituality for their own gain. This is my reaction to spirituality being stolen; how we've grown from being Indian princesses to women possessing political awareness using our deep spiritual commitment.

MURIEL MIGUEL: WINNETOU, ETHEL CHRISTIAN CHRISTIANSEN, MURIEL

WINNETOU: A noble savage as seen from an outsider's viewpoint. He is a noble savage of the forest, plains, or anywhere in North America. He is smarter, faster, stronger than anyone. WINNETOU is willing to befriend GUNTHER and teach him everything he knows. WINNETOU is then surprised when GUNTHER thinks he knows more and is better than WINNETOU and then leaves WINNETOU to die.

ETHEL CHRISTIAN CHRISTIANSEN: The golden darling. She is a mixture of Ethel Kennedy and Lynn Andrews. She thinks she can see the future but makes sure she leaves nothing to chance in the present. Underneath her shyness and gold lamé lies a heart of steel.

MURIEL: I think at the age of nine, I was politicized. Social studies in school insisted that we were a dying culture and that there were very few Indians alive. I could not comprehend how a teacher, who was supposed to know, could tell such lies. I would look around at the faces of my family and my family's friends and know we were not dying.

Setting

There is no set of which to speak, except for Spiderwoman's signature backdrop made of many different pieces of cloth to form a hodge-podge patchwork quilt, and a projection screen made of old sheets. The stage is bare. All props that are used are brought on by the cast.

The film footage used in the play was shot by the Miguel sisters' Uncle Joe and consists of "home movies" of old powwows dating from the early 1940s into the 1970s. The more recent footage was filmed in the 1980s by Bob Rosen, in the same style as Uncle Joe. The idea is to juxtapose the real powwow imagery against the Snake Oil Show.

Playwrights' Note

The legend of Winnetou was written at the turn of the century by Karl May, a German novelist who never came to America and never met an American Indian. It tells the story of a German man, Gunther, who comes to America to seek his fortune. While everybody he meets is inferior to the German race, Gunther befriends Winnetou—a noble savage, as handsome and smart as a white man— and the two become blood brothers. They save each others' lives many times, but in the end Winnetou dies ... he and the entire Indian race, pagan savages all, are doomed. Although Winnetou is a fictional character, Germans and most Europeans take the character as a true representative of an American Indian.

Winnetou's Snake Oil Show is a result of the culmination of all these feelings over all these years, the feelings of our culture being taken away from us. Years ago, hobbyists (non-Indian people who take up Native cultures as a hobby) were content to don the outward manifes-tations of our culture (clothes, jewelry, dancing, etc.). They didn't give a damn about what was really happening inside of us. We had some-thing to hold onto for the time being. As years went on, though, they started to be interested in the spiritual part of us. They suddenly knew more about Indians than the Indian people themselves. The question, as a result, becomes for us, How do we approach this steal-ing of spirituality? Do we confront each incident of theft or do we ignore it, let it slide, and then feel like we are sellouts?

Production History

Winnetou's Snake Oil Show was first performed at Holland's Stage Door Festival in 1988. In 1989, *Winnetou's Snake Oil Show*, partially funded by the New York State Council of the Arts, had its United States premiere at the Theater for the New City in New York City. The director was Muriel Miguel, the costume designer was Jane Zipp, and the lighting designer was Zdenek Kriz. Uncle Joe, Bob Rosen, and Jane Zipp did the film. The piece then toured during Spiderwoman Theater's 1990 US tour. Additional performances include:

1990   The Group Theatre, Seattle, Washington
1990   Festival of the Larch, Cranbrook, British Columbia
1990   Festival 2000, San Francisco, California
1990   Highway's Performance Space, Santa Monica, California
1991   Evergreen State College, Olympia, Washington
1992   Buffalo State College, Buffalo, New York
1993   Native Earth Performing Arts, Toronto, Ontario
1994   Montana Indian Contempory Arts, Bozeman, Montana
1994   Myrna Loy Theatre, Helena, Montana
1994   TOUR: The Great West Consortium, Santa Fe, New Mexico; Telluride, Colorado; Aspen, Colorado
1996   North Carolina State University, Raleigh, North Carolina
1996   Nazareth College, Rochester, New York
1996   University of Wisconsin, Madison, Wisconsin
1998   The American Indian Community House, New York, New York
1999   Miami University, Oxford, Ohio
2001   Tennessee Technological University, Cookeville, Tennessee

Music Note

For use of all copyrighted music in a performance of *Winnetou's Snake Oil Show from Wigwam City*, music rights must be obtained.

As the house lights go out, the theme to the Magnificent Seven *begins. The movie then comes on. Lights up on* WILD-EYED SAM. *As he begins to speak, the music goes out.*

WILD-EYED SAM

First time out West? Hey! I say, first time out West? Gunther, come on! (*The movie goes out, full stage light bumps up,* GUNTHER *enters.*) I'm going to show you how we hunt out West.

GUNTHER

(*In a German accent.*) Yah, Wild-Eyed Sam, I am willing to learn. I will follow you. (GUNTHER *mimics* WILD-EYED SAM *as he walks around the stage.*)

WILD-EYED SAM

Did you tether your horse? Horses have been known to run away on such an occasion.

GUNTHER

What occasion? ... BEARS!!!!

WILD-EYED SAM

Are you scared? Hey, hey, sometimes the bears out here are nine feet tall, weigh as much as a thousand pounds or more.

GUNTHER

Yah?

WILD-EYED SAM

Makes the ground shake when they walk. Teeth are this long.

GUNTHER

Yah?

WILD-EYED SAM

There are rules to follow. Do you have a knife and a rifle?

GUNTHER

I have one knife, two revolvers, and your hammer.

WILD-EYED SAM

Good. Don't use them 'til I tell you. Follow me. (*They walk another circuit of the stage.*)

GUNTHER

Are there any Indians around here?

WILD-EYED SAM

If there was, you'd smell them.

(*We hear a bear roar. The* BEAR *enters. It attacks* WILD-EYED SAM. GUNTHER *shoots the* BEAR. *It releases* WILD-EYED SAM, *who exits, and stalks* GUNTHER. GUNTHER *shoots the* BEAR, *hits the* BEAR *with a hammer, then stabs it. The* BEAR *dies in an elaborate death scene as in an opera dying scene.*)

WILD-EYED SAM

The Bear is dead, thanks to my quick thinking and agility. You foolish greenhorn, you broke my hatchet!

GUNTHER

What! I saved your life! I killed that Bear with a hit on the head, a shot in the eye, a stab in the chest.

WILD-EYED SAM

That ain't true! Are you gonna stand there flat-footed with your bare face hanging out and tell me that you killed that there Bear?

GUNTHER

It is an indisputable fact that I killed that Bear with a hit on the head, a shot in the eye, a stab in the chest.

(WILD-EYED SAM *and* GUNTHER *fight. As the fight is happening, the* BEAR *is quietly crawling off, leaving the costume in the center of the stage. The fight continues.* KLEKEPETRA *enters.*)

KLEKEPETRA

Stop! Have you gone mad, gents? What reason could there be for white people breaking each others' necks?

WILD-EYED SAM

Klekepetra! Ugly ... UGLY! Did a horse walk on your face?

KLEKEPETRA
> Well you can't judge a frog by its croak. (*Spots the* BEAR.) Oh, oh, there's that fellow we've been after. He is dead. What a shame. (*He yells offstage.*) EYAH! EYAH! EYAH!

WINNETOU
> (*From offstage.*) UFF! UFF!

KLEKEPETRA
> EYAH! EYAH!

WINNETOU
> UFF!

KLEKEPETRA
> (*Screaming.*) EEEEYAHHHHHHHHH!

WINNETOU
> UFF!

(WINNETOU *enters. The following sequence is sung in an operatic style.*)

KLEKEPETRA
> Winnetou!

WINNETOU
> (*Dances fake Indian style, banging drum tied around her waist around bear costume.*)
> I am Winnetou ... a grizzly bear. Boom, boom, boom, boom. This Bear has been hit on the head, shot in the eye, stabbed in the chest. Who did this deed?

GUNTHER
> I did.

WINNETOU
> He killed the grizzly bear with a hit on the head, shot in the eye, stab in the chest. I shall call him Old Shatterhand.

ALL
> (*Sung in harmony.*) Shatterhand ... Shatterhand ... Shatterhand.

WINNETOU
He shall become my blood brother.

GUNTHER
Blood brother.

(*We return to a normal manner of speaking.*)

KLEKEPETRA
Let the ceremony begin. First we will smoke our peace pipe, then we will cut our wrists and become blood brothers. (*They do a choreographed, fake ceremonial dance which quickly disintegrates into confusion, à la West Side Story.*)

GUNTHER
Hough, hey, hey, hey. Hough, hey, hey, hey. Hough, hey, hey, hey.

KLEKEPETRA
Her?

WILD-EYED SAM
Who?

WINNETOU
Him.

GUNTHER
Me.

(*Lights fade to center special, demon light. All exit except* WILD-EYED SAM. *He crosses to garbage can which is offstage right and drags it to center stage. He then does an interpretive dance in the style of Martha Graham while turning into the* WITCH.)

WITCH #1
What shall this concoction be? Pure white cat, daughter of a pure white mother. Porcupine piss, boiled 'til the hair falls off. Velvet antlers of a well-hung moose. Find the left hind leg and suck the marrow out. Bull turd.

(WITCH #2 *and* WITCH #3 *enter.*)

WITCH #2
Bat shit.

WITCH #3
Yum, yum from a bum. Cockeyed sheep eyes.

WITCH #1
Toe nails of a lounge lizard.

WITCH #3
Vomit sauce.

WITCH #2
Skunk cum.

WITCH #3
Putrid liver from a dead cat.

WITCH #1
What shall this concoction cure?

WITCH #3
Running asshole.

WITCH #1
Constipation.

WITCH #2
Half-breeditus.

WITCH #3
And the name ...

ALL
YATAHOLAY INDIAN SNAKE OIL.

(*Lightning and thunder begin. The movie begins. The cast moves stage right to change* HORTENSIA *from the* WITCH *to* MOTHER MOON FACE *and to put on their jackets. They pick up coconut shells.* MOTHER MOON FACE *picks up her mop* [*horse*] *and rides into the film followed by the rest of the cast playing their coconuts as horses' hoofbeats.*)

ALL

> (*Singing.*) Rollin', rollin', rollin.
> Keep them doggies rollin', RAWHIDE!

(*They make a spectacular configuration onstage and all gallop off except for* PRINCESS PISSY WILLOW. *As they leave, the lights bump up to full and the movie goes off and* PRINCESS PISSY WILLOW, *in a circus ringmaster's voice announces:*)

PRINCESS PISSY WILLOW

> Ladies and gentlemen, welcome to the Winnetou Snake Oil Show from Wigwam City. Now for our Grand Entry, I would like to introduce to you three genuine Indian princesses. Princess Mother Moon Face (*she gallops around in a circle and gallops off*), Princess Ethel Christian Christiansen (*she does some odd choreography in a circular motion and then goes off*), Princess Minnie Hallrunner (*she walks around in a circle and then goes off*), and your mistress of ceremonies tonight, I am Princess Pissy Willow. As your first entertainment, I present a magnificent act, a woman all the way from New Mexico, whose mother was a full-blooded Apache and whose father was German, which is why she likes eating fry bread with her sauerkraut.

ALL

> (*Offstage.*) HA! HA!

PRINCESS PISSY WILLOW

> Not only is she an expert bullwhipper, she is also a famous opera singer. Ladies and gentlemen, I present, Minnie Hallrunner!

(MINNIE HALLRUNNER *enters with her imaginary whip, singing in an operatic voice.*)

MINNIE HALLRUNNER

> Snap! Crackle! Pop! (*From stage right trots in her two assistants.*)

PRINCESS PISSY WILLOW

> As her two assistants we have Mother Moon Face and Ethel Christian Christiansen, ladies and gentlemen. (ETHEL CHRISTIAN CHRISTIANSEN *and* MOTHER MOON FACE *go to a box onstage with their props in it. For the first trick, they each pull out a tube of rolled up newspaper about one foot in length,* ETHEL CHRISTIAN CHRISTIANSEN *holding it in her right hand,* MOTHER MOON FACE *in her left. They face* MINNIE HALLRUNNER.)

PRINCESS PISSY WILLOW

Each of our Indian princesses is holding a rolled-up tube of newspaper in her hand. Watch, ladies and gentlemen, as Princess Minnie Hallrunner snaps the end off each side until the newspaper tubes are both gone. (MINNIE HALLRUNNER, *facing* ETHEL CHRISTIAN CHRISTIANSEN *and* MOTHER MOON FACE, *snaps each side as they alternatively crunch the tubes into their hands as they disappear. There is applause.* MINNIE HALLRUNNER *bows.*) Yes, ladies and gentlemen, wasn't that terrific? (ETHEL CHRISTIAN CHRISTIANSEN *and* MOTHER MOON FACE *next pick up a rolled-up newspaper about two feet in length and hold it between them in their mouths.*) Princess Ethel Christian Christiansen and Mother Moon Face are holding a larger tube of the *New York Times* in their mouths. Princess Minnie Hallrunner will cut the tube in half without touching their noses. (MINNIE HALLRUNNER, *facing them, snaps the tube in half,* ETHEL CHRISTIAN CHRISTIANSEN *actually cutting it with a pair of scissors. Applause.* MINNIE HALLRUNNER *bows.*) Let's hear it for her, ladies and gentlemen. (ETHEL CHRISTIAN CHRISTIANSEN *and* MOTHER MOON FACE *next hold an open sheet of newspaper between them, holding it at the top corners.*) Princess Ethel Christian Christiansen and Princess Mother Moon Face are holding a sheet of the *New York Times* between them. Princess Minnie Hallrunner will snap the sheet in two from behind her back. Watch her now as she takes a bead on her object. Are you ready, Minnie?

MINNIE HALLRUNNER

(*Singing.*) Yes. (*She snaps the whip.* ETHEL CHRISTIAN CHRISTIANSEN *and* MOTHER MOON FACE *carefully tear the newspaper in half by pulling at her corner. There is applause and* MINNIE HALLRUNNER *bows.*)

PRINCESS PISSY WILLOW

Isn't she wonderful? (MOTHER MOON FACE *next blindfolds* MINNIE HALLRUNNER, *then goes back to stage left where* ETHEL CHRISTIAN CHRISTIANSEN *places a red cowboy hat on* MOTHER MOON FACE'S *head.*) Now ladies and gentlemen, a most dangerous trick. As you can see, Mother Moon Face has blindfolded Minnie Hallrunner. Ethel has placed a cowboy hat on Mother Moon Face's head. Minnie Hallrunner will knock the hat from Mother Moon Face's head. One false move and she could be decapitated. Watch her now as she feels her space. Are you ready, Minnie?

MINNIE HALLRUNNER

Yes. (MINNIE HALLRUNNER *snaps the whip.* ETHEL CHRISTIAN CHRISTIANSEN *knocks the hat from* MOTHER MOON FACE'S *head.*)

PRINCESS PISSY WILLOW

Ladies and gentlemen, Princess Minnie Hallrunner! Let's give her a big hand. (*There is incredible applause;* MINNIE HALLRUNNER *removes the blindfold, bows, takes her props offstage, and returns.* ETHEL CHRISTIAN CHRISTIANSEN *goes into the audience to pick a contestant for later, and* PRINCESS PISSY WILLOW *introduces* MOTHER MOON FACE.)

We now present to you a magnificent act. All the way from the Ponderosas of Colorado, an equestrian par excellence. She has been around horses most of her life, in fact she was born on a horse. I now present to you, the one, the only, Mother Moon Face! (*Applause.* MOTHER MOON FACE *comes onstage riding her horses [two string mops]. She canters, trying to control the animals.* PRINCESS PISSY WILLOW *tries to get her to stop moving.*) I now present to you two magnificent animals, Silver Turkey and Pinto Bean. These animals are highly educated in mathematics, Pinto Bean give me the sum of two plus two.

MOTHER MOON FACE

Two plus two, two plus two. (*She stamps her left foot, counting. When she reaches four,* PRINCESS PISSY WILLOW *starts the applause.*)

PRINCESS PISSY WILLOW

Yes, ladies and gentlemen, what an intelligent animal. Now, Silver Turkey, not to be outdone, I give him the sum of nine divided by three.

MOTHER MOON FACE

Nine divided by three, nine divided by three.

PRINCESS PISSY WILLOW

Not you the horse.

MOTHER MOON FACE

(*She stamps her right foot, counting. When she reaches three,* PRINCESS PISSY WILLOW *starts the applause. They all acknowledge it.*)

PRINCESS PISSY WILLOW
>   Amazing, amazing. Now ladies and gentlemen, these animals will
>   play dead.

(MOTHER MOON FACE *throws the two mops on the floor in front of her.*) Yes,
ladies and gentlemen, let's give them a big hand. Now, ladies and
gentlemen, for your edification and pleasure, Mother Moon Face
will now ride around this ring with two horses, jumping from horse
to horse.

(MOTHER MOON FACE *rides around the stage, jumping from mop to mop, with
great applause. At this point,* ETHEL CHRISTIAN CHRISTIANSEN *has found a contestant and has brought her onstage and is instructing her.*)

>   The next trick, the next trick is so difficult, that it can only be
>   executed with one horse. Minnie Hall Runner, will you lead one
>   of the horses away?

(MINNIE HALLRUNNER *leads one of the horses off with some difficulty.*)

>   Mother Moon Face will now ride backward on one foot, with her
>   eyes closed with this fluffy feather in her mouth. (MOTHER MOON
>   FACE *does this after having had difficulty in keeping the instructions straight. There
>   is thunderous applause. She bows.*)
>   Ladies and gentlemen, Mother Moon Face!

(*She bows again. Exits with her horse.* PRINCESS PISSY WILLOW *then picks up her
rifle and moves to stage right.*)

ETHEL CHRISTIAN CHRISTIANSEN
>   (*Crosses stage left and in a circus ring master voice announces:*) Ladies and gen-
>   tlemen, Princess Pissy Willow is not only a marvelous mistress of
>   ceremonies, she is also a crack shot. She is known from Brooklyn
>   to Tierra del Fuego. (ETHEL CHRISTIAN CHRISTIANSEN *asks the con-
>   testant her name.* PRINCESS PISSY WILLOW *gets ready to shoot.* MOTHER
>   MOON FACE *gives the contestant two balloons. She is put into position, holding a
>   balloon in each hand above her head.*) Princess Pissy Willow will now
>   attempt to shoot the balloons out of (name)'s hands.

PRINCESS PISSY WILLOW
>   Are you ready, (name)?

NAME
> Yes.

PRINCESS PISSY WILLOW
> I am going to shoot the balloon out of your right hand. (*Everyone points to the correct hand.*) One, two, three. (PRINCESS PISSY WILLOW *shoots the balloon in the right hand, it pops. Applause.*) Now, I am going to shoot the balloon out of your left hand. (*Everyone points to the correct hand.*) One, two, three. (PRINCESS PISSY WILLOW *shoots the balloon in the left hand, it pops. Applause.*)

ETHEL CHRISTIAN CHRISTIANSEN
> Minnie Hallrunner will now rotate Princess Pissy Willow around three times. One, two, three. Now bend over.

(PRINCESS PISSY WILLOW *is turned around three times. She bends over, the rifle is pointing in the wrong direction. She is turned so that the rifle is pointed in the correct direction. The contestant holds one balloon over her head with both hands.*)

ETHEL CHRISTIAN CHRISTIANSEN
> Ladies and gentlemen, Princess Pissy Willow will now attempt to shoot the balloon out of (name)'s hands from between her legs.

PRINCESS PISSY WILLOW
> Are you ready, (name)?

NAME
> Yes.

PRINCESS PISSY WILLOW
> One, two, three. (PRINCESS PISSY WILLOW *shoots the balloon, it pops. Applause.* PRINCESS PISSY WILLOW *bows. The contestant is thanked and escorted off the stage by* MINNIE HALLRUNNER.)

PRINCESS PISSY WILLOW
> Thank you, ladies and gentlemen. Last but not least, we have a trick roper. And now we present Princess Ethel Christian Christiansen. She uses a rope so fine it cannot be seen by the naked eye. Watch her, ladies and gentlemen. (ETHEL CHRISTIAN CHRISTIANSEN *takes the invisible rope and using it as a lariat, makes a very large circle. She keeps twirling it until it becomes a very tiny circle.*)

PRINCESS PISSY WILLOW
Wonderful, ladies and gentlemen. (*There is applause.* ETHEL CHRISTIAN CHRISTIANSEN's *second trick is to make another very big circle and to insert her very graceful foot into and out of the circle formed by the rope.*) Ladies and gentlemen, Walking My Baby Back Home. (*There is applause.* ETHEL CHRISTIAN CHRISTIANSEN's *third trick is to form a very large circle again, a vertical one this time. She jumps back and forth through the circle.*) Ladies and gentlemen, isn't she terrific? (*Great applause.* ETHEL CHRISTIAN CHRISTIANSEN *goes to get two ropes.*)

PRINCESS PISSY WILLOW
Ladies and gentlemen, she now has two ropes of a finer denier than the first. Watch her now as she begins twirling one, and now the other.

(MOTHER MOON FACE *and* MINNIE HALLRUNNER *are on either side of her.* ETHEL CHRISTIAN CHRISTIANSEN *snags each of them with a rope and pulls them toward her at center. Applause. She releases the two princesses.*)

Now ladies and gentlemen, this next trick is known as the psychic rope trick. This particular trick has never before been performed in public. (MINNIE HALLRUNNER *gets a rope.* MOTHER MOON FACE *gets a stool.* ETHEL CHRISTIAN CHRISTIANSEN *sits on the stool. She goes into a trance.*) Now, we take a rope and tie her up.

(MINNIE HALLRUNNER *and* MOTHER MOON FACE *tie her up.*)

Ethel, can you hear me?

ETHEL CHRISTIAN CHRISTIANSEN
Yes.

PRINCESS PISSY WILLOW
Ethel, do you have a message from the other side?

ETHEL CHRISTIAN CHRISTIANSEN
Yes ...

PRINCESS PISSY WILLOW
Your message.

ETHEL CHRISTIAN CHRISTIANSEN
I have hemorrhoids.

PRINCESS PISSY WILLOW
This ties in with our sale of Yataholay Indian Snake Oil. Our snake oil comes in three different varieties. (MINNIE HALLRUNNER *demonstrates with her plastic hammer.*) We have a liquid, a salve, and tonight, we have the aerosol can. Minnie Hallrunner will now administer this to Ethel Christian Christiansen. (MINNIE HALLRUNNER *taps the back of the stool with the hammer.*) Ethel, can you hear me?

ETHEL CHRISTIAN CHRISTIANSEN
Yes.

PRINCESS PISSY WILLOW
Do you have a message from the other side?

ETHEL CHRISTIAN CHRISTIANSEN
Yes.

PRINCESS PISSY WILLOW
What is it?

ETHEL CHRISTIAN CHRISTIANSEN
I HAD hemorrhoids. (ETHEL CHRISTIAN CHRISTIANSEN *is untied, she stands up unsteadily.*) Where am I? Movie, please. (*The lights fade and the movie comes on.* DEMON #1 *appears stage right.*)

DEMON #1
EEEEEEEEEE. (*Two other demons appear center stage with the first demon joining them.*) Sulubevia, Oloindalgina, Matchahapipi. My father believed in demons. Listened to Chief Ncle and captured tortoise. At the age of thirteen, his body was covered with blue dye from the Poli Wala tree. And he slept three nights and three days alone in the rain forest. EEEEE. He left Nargana on the San Blas islands and became an able-bodied seaman. EEEEEEEE.

DEMON #2
My father worked the fields, he washed dishes, he swept floors.

DEMON #1

He traveled to Marseilles. (DEMON #3 *exits.*)

DEMON #2

He paid his way.

DEMON #1

Cologne, Monte Carlo, Paris, New York City. He still believed in demons. To chase away the demons, he gulped down a bottle of whiskey.

DEMON #2

He followed the demon serpent, winding his way North. He followed the feathered serpent, Quetzalcoatl.

DEMON #1

He never returned to Nargana. He still believed in demons. He believed in demons until the day he died.

DEMON #2

He crossed to the other side. (DEMON #1 *exits.*)

(HORTENSIA *walks downstage right, picks up conch.*)
Digging, digging, digging bones.
This is the bone of our ancestors.
This is the bone of our relations. (*Crosses to upstage center.*)
Digging, digging, digging for bones.
He went down to the land below.
Down to the land of the dead.
To bring back the bones
(*Sits downstage left. Film is projected onto her.*)
The boy knew it was time to leave.
He left San Luis Potosi.
Hills of gold.
Hills, mountains, rivers, deserts.
Down to the land of the dead.
To bring back the bones.
The boy grew into manhood.
After years of traveling

he arrived at the border
and crossed to the other side.

(Lights bump up to full. WINNETOU *and* GUNTHER *enter. There are animal noises from offstage.)*

(Noises: owl, coyote, crow, pig, donkey, dog, lion, duck. We then hear "Polly want a cracker.")

WINNETOU

Hear that? That is Indians talking to each other. We must be very careful.

GUNTHER

Yes, but they are not ready to attack yet. Among Indians, the leader gives the signal with a scream, then the rest join in. (WINNETOU *is making faces because* GUNTHER *really is a know-it-all.*) The screaming is intended to scare the shit out of people.

WINNETOU

I can make that sound. (WINNETOU *woo-woos.*) Like that.

GUNTHER

I hear no birds, I hear no animals. (*The theme from* The Good, The Bad, and The Ugly *plays. We hear the sounds of Indians offstage. The* HORDES *of Indians enter.*) We are surrounded by hordes of Indians!

(As GUNTHER *is being captured.)*

HORDES #1

You gettum' that one, me gettum' this one.

HORDES #2

Him me gettum' good.

WINNETOU

Winnetou is captured! (GUNTHER *and* WINNETOU *are herded to the center of the stage by the* HORDES *of Indians and tied to each other.*)

HORDES #1

You mangy cur, cheeky bugger, toilet bowl, you diarrhea lips.

HORDES #2

(*Operatically à la Gilbert and Sullivan.*) Yes, Mr. Winnetou. You are going to be shot, stabbed, poisoned, impaled, put to the wheel, hanged, tortured in front of your wives and your children. Ha, ha, ha, ha!

GUNTHER/WINNETOU

No, no, no, no!

ALL

(*Operatically.*) Tortured in front of your / our wives and your / our children.

HORDES #1

Ha, ha, ha, ha!

GUNTHER/WINNETOU

No, no, no, no!

GUNTHER

Halt! You cannot kill him. He is my blood brother. I beg you not to kill him. (WINNETOU *crawls offstage right.*)

HORDES #1

You shall have your wish, if you fight a duel.

GUNTHER

With whom and with what?

HORDES #1

With a huge Indian with a real sharp knife.

GUNTHER

Bring him on!

(HORDES #2 *removes her blanket. She returns to downstage left and begins to assume various bodybuilding positions.*)

HORDES #1

First we will make a large circle. (*She outlines it on the floor.*) You will not be allowed to step outside of the circle. A fight to the finish.

(HORDES #2 *walks forward into the circle, egging* GUNTHER *on.* HORDES #1 *exits stage left.*)

GUNTHER
Braggart!

HORDES #1
(*Enters stage left.*) Braggart, braggart. (*Exits stage left.*)

HORDES #2
You dare insult me! I shall have the vultures devour your entrails!

GUNTHER
Entrails!

HORDES #1
(*Enters stage left.*) Entrails, entrails! (*Exits stage left.*)

GUNTHER
(*During the following speech,* HORDES #2 *continuously changes the position of the knife in her hand, to conform to what* GUNTHER *is saying at any particular moment.*) So he is not going to run his knife through my heart, he is going to slit my stomach. Aha! His right arm is hanging straight down. He is holding his knife so that its handle is resting against his small finger and the blade is sticking out between thumb and index finger, cutting edge turned up. If he was going to strike downward, he must hold the knife so that the edge of the handle rests against the thumb and the blade protrudes alongside the little finger.

HORDES #2
Attack, white coward! (*Thunder and lightning. They fight.* HORDES #2 *is wounded.*) Mangy cur!

(GUNTHER *and* HORDES #2 *exit as lights go down.* HORTENSIA *enters, blowing a conch.*)

HORTENSIA
Tlatzoteotl in her jardin. Sweatbeads on her forehead. Mama smell.

(LISA *enters.*)

LISA

You have a lovely mother.

(GLORIA *enters.*)

GLORIA

Six times seven is forty-two. Sit on the stove. Scratch your head and blow your nose.

(MURIEL *enters.*)

MURIEL

I would have liked, I would have liked her to have been taller. I would have liked her to be like every other mother in the neighborhood.

HORTENSIA

Hummingbird, mama Metiza.

LISA

You have a lovely mother.

GLORIA

I thought she was so pretty.

MURIEL

I would have liked, I would have liked.

LISA

She came into the world with an extra piece of skin covering her head. It was a caul. C-A-U-L. And Grandma said that she saved the caul and that one day she was going to give it back to Mama. Grandma kept the caul all wrapped up in tissue paper in a special box. And one day she showed it to me. She let me hold it. It looked like a piece of wrinkled brown paper bag. And then she wrapped it up again and she put it away. Grandma said "Your mother was born with a caul, so she has strong psychic powers. She can tell the future. She can see through anybody." And Mama could tell the meanings of the symbols left by coffee grounds and tea leaves in the bottom of cups. Mama would go into a trance and she said everybody changed in the world. All sound stopped and it became so quiet that you could hear sounds that had been there before. And people who had been there before. She could actually see them and then thoughts would come into her body and she would tell you what she had received. But no one paid Mama any money. They brought crackers, buns, and tea and all her friends came to her. And those friends told other friends. And so it continued. And Mama became a wise woman.

HORTENSIA
And Grandma said ...

GLORIA
Be a good girl.

MURIEL
And Grandmother said ...

HORTENSIA
You should be thankful....

GLORIA
You have a gifted mother.

LISA
And Grandma had that gift, too. And all of my grandmother's children have that gift. And all their children's children have that gift, too. (*There is a continuous repetition of these lines as they all move together and upstage and then to exit. The lights bump up.* ETHEL CHRISTIAN CHRISTIANSEN *enters.*)

ETHEL CHRISTIAN CHRISTIANSEN
I used to be a white woman. It's true. I was Irish ..., German ..., Norwegian...? Then one day, my skin turned bronze and I became a shamaness. I must share with you this vision I had. I was in the subway, waiting for the F train and there was this noise and I looked up and a white light was coming towards me. No, it wasn't the F train. It was a white buffalo. And seated on that white buffalo was a noble savage, naked ... except for his loin cloth. His skin was the color

of bronze, with just a touch of gold. His hair was the color of Lady Clairol No. 154, midnight blue. He wore it in long braids, intertwined with rattlesnake skins. And growing out of his skull was an eagle feather, signifying he was a chief. He is a chief, I am a shamaness. His eyes were as black as coals and energy came at me like flick, flick, flick ... and his eyes pierced my skin and seared my heart. His lips moved, what were they saying?

(*She stares as he moves closer. She starts channeling, her body contorts, she begins to sing.*)

Your cheatin' heart will tell on you
You cry and cry, the whole day through ...

(PRINCESS PISSY WILLOW *enters carrying a large plastic watercooler bottle on her shoulder.* MINNIE HALLRUNNER *enters with a large placard. Both these items are emblazoned with the words* Yataholay Indian Snake Oil.)

PRINCESS PISSY WILLOW
Ladies and gentlemen, two weeks ago this woman was nothing but a plain old white woman but after taking one swig of out Yataholay Indian Snake Oil, she now has a Cherokee grandmother with black braids down to here.

(*She indicates her waist.* MOTHER MOON FACE *then enters with two large placards.*)

Ladies and gentlemen, welcome to our Plastic Pop-Wow Workshop.

(*She indicates first placard.*)

MOTHER MOON FACE
A package deal. Two days, three nights plus a coupon worth $100 towards the purchase of ...

PRINCESS PISSY WILLOW
Yataholay Indian Snake Oil! (*She indicates second placard.*) Three meals a day ...

MOTHER MOON FACE
For breakfast, nuts, berries in season gathered at dawn; for lunch, corn soup, and

ALL
FRY BREAD!!!

MOTHER MOON FACE

And for dinner, anything you can catch, with a choice of vegetable: corn, beans, squash, and

ALL

FRY BREAD!!!

MOTHER MOON FACE

And all the spring water you can drink.

PRINCESS PISSY WILLOW

And all for the low, low price of $3,000 for the weekend. And now, Princess Minnie Hallrunner will walk among you and bring back our first client.

(*As* MINNIE HALLRUNNER *is walking through the audience,* PRINCESS PISSY WILLOW *holds up the photocopy of the face of an Indian man and the photocopy of the face of an Indian woman.*) If you are a man, you will look like this (*indicating man*). If you are a woman, you will look like this (*indicating woman*). (MINNIE HALLRUNNER *has found someone, brings him up on stage. He is very blond and very fair-skinned.*)

PRINCESS PISSY WILLOW

(*To client.*) What is your name?

(*He tells her.* PRINCESS PISSY WILLOW, MOTHER MOON FACE, *and* MINNIE HALLRUNNER *chat him up for a while. As this is going on,* ETHEL CHRISTIAN CHRISTIANSEN *is preparing the stage for the transformation ceremony. She places three bath mats across the stage. The stage right one is by itself. The center stage one is placed with a plant spritzer, and toilet bowl plunger, the stage left one is placed with a paper medicine bag and the photocopy of the man.*)

MOTHER MOON FACE

Now, (name). We will begin. (MOTHER MOON FACE *and* MINNIE HALLRUNNER *walk him to the stage right bath mat.*) You will now enter your first space. Bend over, now step forward into the space and stand up. (*He does so.*) Good, good. Now we will perform a spontaneous dance of rejuvenation. (*All perform an Indian dance complete with vocal sound effects.*) OK, (name). That was very good. You are now ready to proceed. Bend over, step backward, and stand. Good.

Now we will go to our second space. (*They walk to the second space.* ETHEL CHRISTIAN CHRISTIANSEN *throws the stage right bath mat offstage left. As the whole process is happening, there are constant comments about the transformation, i.e. higher cheekbones, skin browner. There is also a subplot of* MOTHER MOON FACE *having the hots for the client.*) Good (name). Now bend over and step forward into your second space. Now you can stand. I will now treat you with essence of sweatlodge. (MOTHER MOON FACE *picks up the plant spritzer and spritzes him with water.*) Now, Princess Pissy Willow will suck the evil juices out of you. (PRINCESS PISSY WILLOW *picks up the toilet plunger and sucks the floor stage left, upstage, and stage right of him. She then places the plunger on his behind and makes a sucking noise.*) That was wonderful, (name). Now bend over, step back, and we will move on to your third and final space.

(ETHEL CHRISTIAN CHRISTIANSEN *gets rid of center stage props and then moves downstage with the two final large placards. They move to the final space.*) Now (name). Bend over, step forward and stand up.

PRINCESS PISSY WILLOW

How are you feeling (name)? Now a very important decision. You must choose the name of your Indian tribe.

(ETHEL CHRISTIAN CHRISTIANSEN *holds up the placard with the Indian tribes written on it.*)

Your choices are: #1 Condaho, #2 Mescalotex, #3 Washamakokie, #4 Rappa Hamburg, #5 Wishee Washee, #6 Gelderfoot, #7 Wanahoho. (*He thinks about it briefly and chooses an Indian tribe. The cast applauds him.*) Now, (name), you are about to make the most important decision of your life, your choice of Indian name. (ETHEL CHRISTIAN CHRISTIANSEN *holds up the placard with the choice of Indian names on it.*)

(ETHEL CHRISTIAN CHRISTIANSEN *with* MOTHER MOON FACE *and* MINNIE HALLRUNNER *do a fake ceremony.* ETHEL CHRISTIAN CHRISTIANSEN *has audience repeat after her "umm" then "ahh." Gets audience to repeat "umm" "ahh" over and over. Then all three with the bone and placard go to the four directions; when they reach the west they collide with each other.*)

Your choices are: #1 Long Gone Lillie, #2 Cross to the Other Side, #3 Old Dead Eye Dick, #4 Old Drop by the Wayside, #5 End of the Trail, #6 Down the River, #7 Old Rocking Chair, #8 Two Dogs Fucking. (ETHEL CHRISTIAN CHRISTIANSEN *has been vigorously pointing to the last one.*) This is not a decision to be taken lightly. Think about it. (*Everyone is now trying to get him to choose the last name. He finally chooses.*) (Indian name) of the (Indian tribe). You may bend over step back and leave the final space. (*Everyone is congratulating him, shaking his hand, kissing him on the cheek.* ETHEL CHRISTIAN CHRISTIANSEN *clears the final props.*) Now (Indian name) of the (Indian tribe), may you go in peace. On your journey, you must take this medicine bag and you must wear this in front of your face for the rest of your life.

(PRINCESS PISSY WILLOW *gives him the photocopy of the Indian man.* MOTHER MOON FACE *escorts him off the stage; they all line up and wave goodbye as he goes back to his seat. The lights fade, and* MOTHER MOON FACE *exits.* GLORIA *and* LISA *stand stage left.*)

LISA AND GLORIA
(*Singing.*)
Out of my lodge at eventide
Among the sobbing pines
Footsteps echo by my side
My Indian brave, Pale Moon
Speak to thy love forsaken
Thy spirit mantle throw

(MURIEL *does sign language to the words of the song.*)

Ere thou the great white dawn awaken
And to the East thou swingest low, swingest low.

(HORTENSIA *enters from between them.*)

HORTENSIA
MEXICAN, MEXICAN, MEXICAN! A surge of heat would rise through my body and my face would begin to burn. All those Mexicans playing Indian parts. She ain't no Indian, she's Mexican. She speaks all

that Spanish stuff. I wanted to say something, but I just stood there, my face getting redder and redder, looking out into space. Mexican, Mexican, Mexican. I am an Indian woman. I speak Spanish and I am learning Nahuatl. Before the invaders, there were no borders.

My grandmother married a man whose people came from Spain and when they came to visit, they would lock her in the back room, so they wouldn't have to look at her. Mexican, Mexican, Mexican. And there is no going back to anywhere. I'll stay here with this Indian face. (*Walks stage right and gestures in sign language.*)

MURIEL

(*Walks dowstage.*) She looked at me and smiled and said "I'm an Indian, too." Too! (*Walks upstage, turns, continues sign language. Everyone signs through the rest of the dialogue in this scene.*)

LISA

(*Walks dowstage.*) Sell out. Am I? White man lost in make believe at the powwow. Craftsman, woodcarver. I like him but ...

GLORIA

(*Crosses center.*) Thank you, thank you, thank you. For discovering me, for recognizing me, for saving me. Thank you for giving me the opportunity to exist. For knowing more about me than I do. Thank you for giving me spirituality. Thank you.

LISA

Leave me alone. Don't take your fantasies out on me. Have the decency to have your fantasies in private.

GLORIA

For only through your eyes am I remembered.

MURIEL

Sell out, sell out, sell out.

GLORIA

I am no more.

LISA

Inside, outside, I always say, if I hold my breath, they'll go away.

GLORIA

Remember me, earth mother, princess, handsome brave, warrior.

LISA

Or think of something nice to say.

MURIEL

(*Walks dowstage.*) That's nice. I smile. My rubbery lips stretch over my teeth. My eyes go blank. My shoulders go up. Sell out, sell out, sell out, sell out. (*Upstage back to audience.*)

GLORIA

Thank me, thank me, thank me. My spirit, my body, my wisdom. You feed on me, create on me, enjoy my remains. Thank me, thank me, thank me.

(*Thunder and lightning begin. They walk around in a circle,* MURIEL *with the thunder sheet,* GLORIA *with the rattle,* LISA *with the bone, and* HORTENSIA *with the conch. All exit. Lights bump up.* WINNETOU *enters.*)

WINNETOU

(*Announces.*) The death of Winnetou!

(*Discovers she is not wearing her fringed outfit, goes offstage to put it on, comes onstage, and announces again.*)

(*Singing.*) The death of Winnetou!
They'll be coming round the mountain
when they come. Toot, toot.
They'll be coming round the mountain
when they come. Toot, toot.
They'll be shooting Winnetou when they
come. Bang, bang.
They'll be shooting Winnetou when they
come. Bang, bang.
(*She falls to the ground.*)
Winnetou is dying.

GUNTHER

Winnetou is dying.

HORDES #2
(*Offstage.*) Dying, dying, dying.

HORDES #1
(*Offstage.*) Dead.

GUNTHER
Where has my brother been hit?

WINNETOU
Right here (*pointing to heart*).

GUNTHER
Here Winnetou lies, an Indian and a great man. He who once had strength now creeps about in corners like a mangy cur.

WINNETOU
Mangy cur?

GUNTHER
The Indian did not become great because he was not permitted to. Here lies the Indian, a sick and dying race. (HORDES #1 *and* HORDES #2 *enter.*)

WINNETOU
Don't you think that's a little hard?

HORDES #1
Who died and left you, Indian?

HORDES #2
Hey, Mr. Shatterhand, knock, knock. (GUNTHER *looks confused.* WINNETOU *prompts him.*)

GUNTHER
Who's there?

HORDES #2
Winnetou.

GUNTHER
Winnetou who?

HORDES #2

Winnetou, lose a few. (*Blackout. All laugh in the dark. The movie comes on.* HORTENSIA *stands in the movie.*)

HORTENSIA

He went down to the land to bring back the bones. (*Lights begin to come up.*)

MURIEL

On his days off, he went to his patch of land. He planted corn, cilantro, string beans, carrots, rhubarb.

LISA

Father would sit at the window and look out at the sky. A mist would cover his eyes and the child knew he had left.

GLORIA

(*Singing.*)
I wish I had wings of an angel.
Over these prison walls I would fly.
(*She continues to hum the tune.*)

(MURIEL *joins her.*)

LISA

Daddy, don't go. Daddy take me.

GLORIA

Some day.

MURIEL

Some day.

LISA

The father would say "One of these days, I'm going to go back home."

HORTENSIA

One day his walk got slower and slower. He went out in the back-yard, sat down, and died. (*They all repeat "sat down and died" as* GLORIA *speaks.*)

GLORIA

See me. I'm talking, loving, hating, drinking too much, creating, performing, my stories, my songs, my dances, my ideas. Now, I telling you, step back, move aside, sit down, hold your breath, save your own culture. Discover your own spirituality.

ALL

(*In overlapping chorus.*) Now I telling you. Watch me. I'm alive. I'm not defeated. I begin. Now I telling you. (*They continue in an overlapping chorus as they exit.* HORTENSIA *is last, blowing the conch. Lights fade out. The movie plays to the end of the reel.*)

HORTENSIA

(*In Spanish same words.*) Now I telling you.

MURIEL

My stories my songs.
My culture.

LISA

Our homes are not in museums. We are not defeated. We are still here.

END

Takeover of the Andrew Jackson Reading Room

A PLAY

Sierra Adare

Artist's Statement

Writing, like the imagination that feeds it, is limitless. I cannot remember a time when I did not want to be a writer. Through words I could travel to any place in time, explore the universe, and experience the lives of historic or fictional characters. While a Visiting Fellow with Cornell University's American Indian Program, I began experimenting with teaching techniques. I wanted to make the history of the Indigenous Peoples of North America come alive for students who found history, in any form, extremely boring. The result was this play.

Theater, when performed by students in the classroom, becomes an interactive teaching tool. The students are not just reading about individuals' lives or deeds, they are taking on the persona of those individuals, experiencing aspects of history, ideas, lifestyles. What evolves are questions, comments, and a sense of understanding that exceed the standard classroom learning experience.

Takeover of the Andrew Jackson Reading Room

Characters

The Writers:

CATLIN BENGE, Cherokee
ANNA MORSE, Muscogee Creek
BEN WATERMAN, Onondaga
GINNY OAKES, Mohawk
LISA SOUTHERLAND, the white voice
MARIAM HARDGATE, the wannabe Indian

The Writers' Characters:

HANDSOME LAKE
FREEDANT
ASSEM
WOLF-WAITING-IN-THE-TREES
REBECCA BALLARD
CANASTEGO
RICHARD VAN DERMARK
GOING SNAKE WALKER
ANDREW JACKSON
JUNALUSKA
SHOEBOOTS
RED STICK
TWO OR THREE INDIAN CHILDREN, non-speaking
STRONG MEDICINE WOMAN
DEER MOTHER
LITTLE DEER

Setting

Upstage is a reading room in any library in any town or city with a large oblong table and folding chairs around it. A large picture of President Andrew Jackson hangs on the wall. Outside the reading room is a bulletin board for posting notices. Downstage is where the scenes the writers have written will be acted out. These vignettes are an alien landscape setting, a Mohawk village on the edge of the forest, a Haudenosaunee council grounds, a forest setting, and a roadside. These can be surreal or very incomplete backdrops.

Scenes

Scene 1.   If They Don't Get the Joke, They Shouldn't Show Up
Scene 2.   Those Who Are, the Wannabe Princess, and the White
               Voice for Indians
Scene 3.   Handsome Lake in 2407
Scene 4.   Nights of Savage Love
Scene 5.   Indian History in Their Own Words—Ha Ha
Scene 6.   Shoeboots Delivers a Swift Kick to Andrew Jackson
Scene 7.   How I Found My Indianness at a Powwow and Other
               Exploratory Essays of Indian Spirituality
Scene 8.   Death to the Deer
Scene 9.   They Did It to Us Again!

Playwright's Note

While this is a rather sarcastic and irreverent play, there is a serious undertone. I wrote this play to be a bridge between Native and American cultural perceptions. Through it, one culture can hold up Takaki's "different mirror" in order to see things through the other culture's reflection. I also wanted to create a vehicle for teaching American Indian history and its connection to current issues facing indigenous people today that would turn the learning experience into something more enjoyable and entertaining than reading textbooks and listening to lectures.

As writers begin to read their work, it is then acted out downstage. Indian drumming can be heard offstage before Scene I and between scenes. It should be war drumming before Scene I, welcoming/ friendship before Scene 2, fast traditional Haudenosaunee before Scene 3, romantic traditional Haudenosaunee before Scene 4, Hollywood stereotypical before Scene 5, Cherokee war drumming and rattles before Scene 6, New Age Indian with flutes and synthe-sizer before Scene 7, poignant drumming with flutes and rattles before Scene 8, and war drumming before Scene 9.

If the production is short on cast members, a total of six men and six women can make up the cast—five women and one man for the parts of the writers and a total of five men and one woman for the parts of the writers' characters, reusing the same cast for each scene. In Scene 6, the actors who portray the women characters in other scenes could replace the children to whom Going Snake tells his story.

Production History

During 1999 and 2000, *Takeover of the Andrew Jackson Reading Room* had staged readings at Cornell University and the Telluride House in Ithaca, New York, as well as at SUNY Cortland in Cortland, New York, and Thompkin County Community College in Dryden, New York. The play has also been taught as part of Cornell University's "North American Indian History to 1890"course in Fall 1999, and SUNY Cortland's and Thompkin County Community College's American Indian literature courses in Spring 2000.

Scene 1

ANNA *and* CATLIN, *two young Indian women dressed in jeans and blouses and wearing Indian jewelry (not overdone), are standing in front of a bulletin board outside the door of the library's Andrew Jackson Reading Room, where general interest and library announcements are posted.*

ANNA
> (*She reads the notice as she posts it on the bulletin board.*) "Indian Writers Critique Group forming this Thursday evening 7 P.M. in the library's Andrew Jackson Reading Room. Any interested Indian writers are welcome to attend." (*She looks at* CATLIN.) Don't you just love the irony? Jackson … the jerk who tried to annihilate all the Indians east of the Mississippi. Hopefully we'll fill the room with Jackson's worst nightmare … educated Indians with pens and computers.

CATLIN
> (*She laughs.*) If they don't get the joke, they shouldn't show up.

ANNA
> Yeah, I love the irony. I hope we get a few takers.

CATLIN
> Me too.

Scene 2

The scene takes place in the Andrew Jackson Reading Room, located upstage. There is an oblong table with folding chairs around it. Centered on the wall behind the long side of the table is a portrait of Andrew Jackson. He appears to be scowling down like Big Brother at those seated at the table. CATLIN *and* ANNA, *wearing clothing similar to those in Scene 1, are seated at the far end of the table away from the open doorway,* CATLIN *at the head.* BEN *walks in, an Indian man in his late twenties to mid-thirties wearing jeans, a shirt open at the neck, and a turtle necklace (a carving of a turtle suspended on a thin leather strip). He looks from the portrait to the two Indian women and grins.*

BEN
> Oh, yeah, this is definitely the right spot.

(BEN *takes a seat next to* CATLIN *and across the table from* ANNA. LISA, *a middle-aged white woman, conservatively dressed, shoulder bag, glasses, and graying brown hair tucked into a bun, steps just inside the doorway. She holds a spiral notebook with several photocopy pages stuffed into it in front of her like a shield.* MARIAM, *hard on* LISA's *heals, practically runs into her.* MARIAM *is close to middle-age, with dishwater blonde hair in braids and very pale skin. She is wearing one of those fake buckskin skirts and blouse, Apache boots, a huge squash blossom necklace, silver belt, big silver and turquoise bracelets on both arms, earrings, rings, bone and bead choker, and feathers tied in her braids—basically New Age "Indian" overdone.*)

LISA

(*Adjusting her glasses.*) Can any writers join this group or is it just for Indians?

(MARIAM *sails past* LISA *and into the room.*)

MARIAM

Speak for yourself, sister. I'm one of them.

(CATLIN, ANNA, *and* BEN *exchange a look.* MARIAM *takes a seat next to* BEN, *scooting her chair closer to him, almost touching him. She smiles at him. He bares his teeth at her.*)

CATLIN

(*Speaking to* LISA.) No, we don't discriminate against race.

BEN

(*In an amused tone.*) That's because Indians are such good runners.

(CATLIN *and* ANNA *giggle.* LISA *and* MARIAM *look a bit confused.* LISA *takes a seat, sitting a little away from the others. She sets the notebook on the table and reaches into her purse for a pen before placing the purse in her lap, resting her arm across it to keep it safe.* GINNY *breezes through the door.* GINNY *wears tight jeans and a t-shirt with an Indian slogan on it. With a mischievous smile on her lips, she raises her hand in the classic Hollywood Indian greeting.*)

GINNY

(*In a chant.*) Hi, how are ya? Hi, how are ya? (*The Indians laugh. The two white women look even more confused.*) I'm Ginny Oakes. But since my parents are forever claiming I will one day drive them to drink, everybody calls me Gin.

(GINNY *takes a seat at the end of the table opposite* CATLIN *and next to* LISA. LISA *immediately scoots her chair away from* GINNY. CATLIN *looks at her watch.*)

CATLIN

Well, it's 7 P.M. Indian time, or 7:30 standard time. Let's get started. I'm Catlin Benge. I'm collecting Cherokee families' oral histories, my own family's histories included, of course. I'm writing them down and backing them up with quote "historical facts" unquote in hopes that people will realize what my people remember really *did* happen ... regardless of what the history books say.

(CATLIN *looks at* ANNA.)

ANNA

And I'm Anna Morse. I'm afraid I exemplify the stereotype of the Indian writer. I'm a poet.

BEN

(*Grinning.*) Isn't it amazing how people, some Indians included, just assume all Native writers write Indian myths and poetry? With oral history falling under the myth category.

CATLIN

Too true! (*Looking at* ANNA.) But I don't think your poetry is stereotypical.

ANNA

Well, maybe my subject matter isn't. But, regardless, I feel poetry is the best form through which I can express the horrors of the holocaust my people faced.

LISA

(*Readjusting her glasses on her nose and looking at* ANNA.) Oh, you're Jewish?

MARIAM

(*Sizing* ANNA *up.*) I'd say Mexican-looking rather than Jewish.

ANNA

(*Looking angrily at* MARIAM *first, then at* LISA.) For your information, the Jews are not the only people to survive a terrible holocaust. I'm

Muscogee Creek and Cherokee. The centuries of genocide began when the Spanish came in search of gold in the 1500s. They took us captive, enslaved us, tortured us, mutilated us, brought us their diseases, destroyed our villages ... all in their quest for gold and fame. Then the French and the English came, and they treated us no better. They plundered and murdered their way across our lands. After them, it was the Americans. They took everything we had. They forced us beyond the Mississippi River, then took everything we had there, too. All the Indigenous people in this country have had similar holocaust experiences.

LISA

(*Snippy.*) Well, I know that. In fact, that's what I want to write about. (*She sits up straighter in her chair.*) My name is Lisa Southerland. And I've discovered some wonderful old documents in the library here that present Indian history from an Indian perspective. Just look at these. (*She opens the notebook and holds up several photocopies.*) I got photocopies made of all the documents. I am so excited about finding them. You see, they have never been written up before. So I can finally set the record straight about the Indians. I'm going to tell everything ... *everything* from an Indian's perspective. I'm so excited to be the one to tell the Indian's story. Goodness knows *somebody* needs to tell it for them.

CATLIN

(*Through gritted teeth.*) Like we're not capable of telling our stories ourselves.

LISA

(*Looking innocently at* CATLIN *as she lays the photocopies on the table.*) Well, so far you haven't.

(CATLIN *starts to say something, but* BEN *interrupts before she can say anything.*)

BEN

(*In a deceptively mild tone.*) Why from an Indian's perspective? Why not from your own point of view?

LISA

(*Tucking a stray strand of hair into her bun.*) Well, really! Isn't it perfectly obvious? (*She taps a finger on the pages in front of her and stares at* BEN.) These documents are from an Indian's perspective. So ... of course, I'm writing my book from an Indian viewpoint. Besides, the only way to write the Indian's story *is* from the Indian's perspective. You should know that!

CATLIN

Really? It seems to me that (*fingers making quote marks in the air*) "the Indian's story" as you call it has rarely been written from the Indian's POV.

MARIAM

POV?

ANNA

Point of view.

LISA

(*Gathering up her copies and closing them in her notebook with an air of finality.*) But that's my point. Books about Indians haven't been written from the poor Indian's perspective. I intend to rectify that.

ANNA

(*Clearing her throat to hide her anger.*) Well, which Indians are you talking about anyway? Which Indian nation was written up in those documents of yours?

LISA

(*She smiles.*) Oh, I'm going to write about the Iroquois.

BEN

Which one?

LISA

(*Frowning.*) What do you mean which one?

BEN

(*Looking skyward a second before looking at* LISA.) There is no such thing as one tribe named the Iroquois. The Iroquois, or

Haudenosaunee as we call ourselves, are a confederation of six nations ... the Onondagas, like myself, the Mohawks....

GINNY

(*Interrupting with a perky smile.*) Like me.

BEN

(*Continuing.*) The Oneidas, the Cayugas, the Senecas, and the Tuscaroras. All of our nations make up the Iroquois.

GINNY

Iroquois also refers to a linguistic family that not only includes the Haudenosaunees but the Cherokees, as well. (*She gestures toward* CATLIN *and* ANNA.)

LISA

(*She shifts uncomfortably in her seat and clears her throat.*) Uh, I will have to check my notes at home for the exact tribe.

CATLIN

Good idea.

(*There is a moment of silence.*)

MARIAM

Well, I'm Mariam Hardgate. (*She brushes a feather away from her face.*) I went to this powwow last year in some dinky little berg in Oklahoma. I think it was called Tall-ee-que-hah.

CATLIN

(*Rubbing her forehead as if she has a headache developing.*) You mean Tahlequah, the capitol of the Western Band of Cherokees.

MARIAM

Something like that. Anyway ... (*she becomes very animated, waving her hands around as she describes things*) they had dancing and drumming and chanting and these great Indian tacos, ohoo ... and fry bread. And anyway, that's when I realized ... when I just knew I had an affinity with *all* Indian people. Well, naturally there had to be a reason for this instant and intense connection. So, you know what I did? I started digging up the old family tree ... and guess what I found? Some Indian ancestors! (*She wiggles excitedly in her chair, rubbing up against* BEN *in the process. He shifts slightly away.*) So it naturally follows that I want to write about my experiences discovering my Indian roots and my Indian spirituality.

GINNY

(*Very innocent tone.*) How do you propose to do that?

MARIAM

I'm going to write it all up in a collection of inspirational essays, of course.

LISA

(*Readjusting her glasses.*) At the risk of sounding unenlightened, what exactly are inspirational essays?

MARIAM

Oh, you know ... gut-wrenching emotion, deep introspection, discovering the ultimate epiphany of life while sitting on a rock one day, listening to the tide roll in from the ocean at Newport Beach. That kind of thing.

GINNY

Ugh. I don't go for all that highbrow stuff. The whole point is to get people to read what you've written, and I don't think people actually read that nose-in-the-air stuff. That's why I'm going to write a historical romance novel.

(ANNA *and* CATLIN *groan.*)

MARIAM

(*Sounding shocked.*) A romance novel! Well, really!

ANNA

Please tell me your romance novel is not going to be one of those wretchedly stereotypical poor little rich girl blonde bombshell falls hot and heavy for the savage hunk in a loincloth.

CATLIN

Hey, that wouldn't be so bad ... if the savage hunk looks like Charlton Heston did chained to the oar on that Roman slave ship in *Ben-Hur*. Now *that's* how a guy in a loincloth should look! Hubba hubba, baby!

GINNY

(*Winking at the silent* BEN.) Maybe I won't have my savage hunk wear a loincloth. Maybe I'll just have him standing there in just his standing manhood.

(*Everybody but* LISA *laughs.*)

ANNA

You wouldn't!

GINNY

Wanna bet? I'm going to play that white woman-savage hunk stuff for all it's worth in my book. And you know why? Because amongst all those heaving bosoms and that bronzed manhood, (GINNY *dramatically places the back of her hand against her forehead*) and the oh-so-white blonde bombshell having to decide if she can forever turn her back on her *civilized* society and take up the *lustful* ways of the pagan children of the forest, I plan to slip in some accounts of how the Mohawks really lived in colonial times.

(*Even* LISA *giggles this time. The others roar with laughter.*)

ANNA

Hey, I got news. Don't forget the great-great-grandmother story with the white guy marrying the proverbial (*she elbows* CATLIN) Indian p—

CATLIN

(*Adamantly interrupting, pointing a finger at* ANNA *and shaking her head.*) Don't you dare say it! You know how much I hate it when people tell me how their great-great-great-umpteen great grandfather married a Cherokee Princess.

MARIAM

(*Innocently.*) But what's wrong with saying that? My aunt told me my grandfather's ancestor *did* marry a Cherokee Princess.

CATLIN

(*Speaking each word succinctly.*) There is no such thing. We Cherokees had two leadership positions which women held ... the Beloved Woman and the War Woman, neither were hereditary. Nor were they necessarily held by the daughters of chiefs.

MARIAM

I've read about Beloved Women and War Women. They're just myths ... legends.

CATLIN

(*Bracing her hands flat against the table top to keep from pounding fists.*) No, that's just ethnocentric historian speak. Women in Cherokee society, as well as all the other Indian societies I know of, could and did go to war. They didn't just sit home and knit socks, you know. Furthermore, the women who distinguished themselves in battle became War Women, and a War Woman sat on the war-time council. You see, during war, the Cherokee government consisted of the Red War Chief, the War Chief's second, seven War Counselors, a War Woman, the Chief War Speaker, messengers, ceremonial officers, and a War Scout. Only the seven war counselors, who were elders, could declare war, and the War Woman decided the fate of captives and prisoners. No one, not even the War Chief, could countermand her decisions. The retired War Woman became a Beloved Woman whose advice was sought and taken at council meetings. War Women earned their titles by their deeds and were voted into a position of power by the entire tribe. Or they were until the United States government illegally outlawed our sovereign right to govern ourselves.

(*The other Indians lean back in their chairs and applaud* CATLIN.)

LISA

(*Adjusting her glasses again.*) Well, maybe that's so, but Cherokee history books mention Cherokee Princesses in them all the time.

CATLIN

(*Bitterly.*) Yeah, and they're written by white people, too, aren't they? Europeans couldn't wrap their brains around the concept of leaders governing by consent. Instead, they overthrew their rulers or assassinated them. And they had the gall to call us savages!

MARIAM

(*Waving feathers away from her eyes.*) But the Cherokee were one of the Five Civilized Tribes, weren't they? I've read that they were a cut above the average Indian. People don't think of the Cherokee as being savages. Being one of the Five Civilized Tribes, that made it acceptable for white people to marry a Cherokee.

CATLIN

(*She buries her head in her arms.*) Everybody and their brother who thinks they are Indian or wants to be Indian claims to be Cherokee. (*She lifts her head and glances around the room.*) Do you have any idea how hard that makes it for *real* Cherokees? Three generations of my family are on the Dawes Rolls, for godsake.

MARIAM

What is the Dawes Rolls?

CATLIN

(*Looking skyward.*) Oh, only the government's way of taking our land ... guaranteed by several treaties ... and our Indianness away from us *yet again.* (*She looks at* MARIAM.) You see, during the Trail of Tears the United States government forced our people to leave our ancestral homelands in the southeastern part of the country and herded us to Indian Territory, now Oklahoma, like so much cattle. We were supposed to be allowed to live there in peace for "as long as the grass grows and the water is blue" crap. That's what the treaties said. But, in 1887, Congress passed the General Allotment Act, commonly called the Dawes Act. What that act meant was that the Cherokees got to keep less than one-third of one percent of the original seven million acres granted to them by the United States government in the bogus New Echota Treaty that traded our lands in the East for land in Indian Territory. But you see, that was all a lie. It was all in preparation for dissolving the Indian nations in Indian Territory and setting up the state of Oklahoma. So, in order for the Cherokees to keep even that tiny scrap of land when statehood rolled around, the government forced us to register on the Dawes Rolls ... with a catch. If any of us said we were full-blood, we instantly lost our land.

LISA

(*Snippy.*) That's impossible. The federal government would never do anything like that.

BEN

(*Deadpan.*) Read the official federal government records on microfilm. They not only could behave dishonorably, they did ... repeatedly ... and still do when it comes to Indian policies.

CATLIN

The government forced all the so-called "Oklahoma Indians" to list their blood quantum on the Dawes Rolls, and anyone who said they were a full-blood instantly became a ward of the state with no rights to land ownership. You see, the government, in its infinite wisdom, decided full-blood Indians were too incompetent to manage their own lives. So us supposedly dumb Indians lied. I have relatives on the rolls who were siblings ... with the same parents, mind you ... who listed their blood quantum as everything from three-quarters Cherokee down to an eighth. Those same parents both listed themselves as two-thirds, and *their* parents, who were deceased, were listed as full-bloods. Do the math.

ANNA

(*Sighing.*) What's worse is that we're still being penalized based on blood quantum. My family lied, too. In reality, I'm actually a quarter Muscogee Creek on my mother's side and a quarter Cherokee on my father's. But my father's family refused to register on the rolls ... and my mother's side lied. As a result, I'm one-eighth Creek and not Cherokee at all according to the federal government. Now, I could care less what the government thinks I am, only I want to go back to college and get a Ph.D. So I applied for some of those governmental scholarships for Native American students. But that's when I found out that I had to *prove* I'm Indian. And they weren't happy with just that. I have to prove I have a blood quantum of at least one-fourth, too. And thanks to the Dawes records where my family was damned if they did list their correct blood quantum, I'm screwed because the government forced my ancestors to lie. Needless to say, I'm not eligible for a scholarship. I'm supposedly *not Indian enough*! Then to top it all off, I have this friend who is one-eighth Chinese. She received all sorts of Asian-American funding for college, and she didn't have to prove a thing. Not a thing!

BEN

(*Leaning forward.*) I heard that. Double jeopardy is against the law unless it's one dealing with Indian treaties. (*He glances around the room.*) I'm Benjamin Franklin Waterman and—

LISA

(*Interrupting.*) I thought Benjamin Franklin was a savage-hating colonial. Why did your parents name you after him?

BEN

(*Laughing harshly.*) I believe Franklin was the most enlightened white thinker of his time. Granted ... he was a product of his day in referring to the Haudenosaunees as savages, but he qualified that by saying, and I quote, "Savages we call them, because their manners differ from ours, which we think the *perfection* of *civility*; they think the same of theirs," unquote. Franklin worked closely with his Indian neighbors, observing our ways of politics and government. Even today, most Americans have no idea just how much the early documents of the United States mimic Haudenosaunee models. The Iroquois Confederacy had a built-in system of checks and balances centuries before the Founding Fathers drafted theirs. Each of the nations in the Confederacy maintained their own independence and still do, yet they are part of the greater union. Benjamin Franklin even borrowed our terms for aspects of government in his Albany Plan of Union.

LISA

What on earth was that?

BEN

The Albany Plan of Union was Franklin's attempt to organize the thirteen colonies into one confederated unit. In the same breath he used to call us savages, he conceded that we had forged an enviable federation. He also said that we had created an agricultural system that was productive and efficient, and that we had exhibited more civility, his word, Lisa, than either the British Parliament or American clergymen had shown. That was well over 200 years ago.

CATLIN

So, Ben, are you writing about Franklin's wonderfully humanizing essays concerning the Indians? One of my favorites is "The Paxton Boys of Pennsylvania" in Franklin's *A Narrative of the Late Massacres in Lancaster County*. His sarcasm aimed at the white good guys is right on target.

BEN

(*Leaning back in his chair and smiling.*) Ah, the Paxton boys. (*Quoting Franklin from the Paxton essay from memory in a lofty tone.*) "Unhappy People! to have lived in such times, and by such neighbors! We have seen, that they—(*in* BEN's *normal tone*) meaning the Indians—(*back in lofty tone*) would have been safer among the ancient *Heathens*, with whom the rites of hospitality were *sacred*. They would have been considered as *guests* of the public, and the religion of the country would have operated in their favor. But our frontier people call themselves *Christians*! They—(*in* BEN's *normal tone*) again meaning the Indians—(*back in lofty tone*) would have been safer, if they had submitted to the *Turks*; for ever since *Mohammed's* reproof to *Khaled*, even the cruel *Turks* never kill prisoners in cold blood. These were not even prisoners. But what is the example of the *Turks* to scripture *Christians*?" (*In* BEN's *normal tone.*) Now *that's* writing! But in answer to your question, Catlin, no, I'm not writing about Franklin. I'm writing science fiction. It's about time we got some *real* Indians in outer space.

(GINNY *giggles.* BEN *winks at her.*)

CATLIN

Well, it sounds like we have quite a mix of writing projects. If it's agreeable with everybody, (*scanning the room*) let's meet here next week at the same time. And everybody bring something you've written this week.

Scene 3

It's a week later. The writers' group again assembles in the reading room, manuscript pages in hand. Everybody wears clothing similar to what they wore the previous week and sits in the same chairs as last week. CATLIN *and* BEN *have insulated mugs of hot tea.* ANNA, LISA, GINNY, *and* MARIAM *have bottled water.*

CATLIN

Who wants to go first?

(No one immediately volunteers.)

BEN

(Taking a sip of his tea.) Ahhh. If nobody else will, I'll go first. *(He shuffles his pages around.)* As I said last week, I'm writing a science fiction novel about an Indian explorer ... only he doesn't go around doing things to the cultures he encounters the same way Columbus did when he so-called "discovered" us.

GINNY

Do you have a working title?

BEN

For now, I am calling it "Handsome Lake in 2407." Handsome Lake is an Onondaga who—

GINNY

(Interrupting.) But Handsome Lake was a Seneca.

BEN

(Frowning at her.) I *know* that! But that's *the* Handsome Lake. My character in 2407 can be named in honor of *the* Handsome Lake, if I want to. It's my universe and I can do what I please with it. Can't I?

GINNY

Well, of course, you can. It's just that.... *(She waves a hand in a dismissing gesture.)* Oh, nevermind.

BEN

You mean that part about Handsome Lake's teachings that said the Creator would only let the world continue until around the year 2100?

GINNY
 Yeah.

MARIAM
 (*Looking worried.*) What!

LISA
 (*Taking her glasses off and wiping them on a tissue she pulls out of her sleeve.*) Who
 is this Handsome Lake? (*She puts her glasses back on and stuffs the tissue up
 her sleeve again.*) I gather he was a real person.

BEN
 The real Handsome Lake was a Seneca man who had a near-death
 experience followed by receiving visions from the Creator in the
 form of four messengers. The messengers gave Handsome Lake a
 new code for living for the people.

MARIAM
 (*Perking up.*) Like Moses and the Ten Commandments?

BEN
 Handsome Lake received 130 messages, stories, songs, cere-
 monies, and addresses. So his teachings were more like those of
 Jesus.

LISA
 (*Shocked.*) That's sacrilege!

BEN
 (*He gives her a look.*) Depends on your point of view, doesn't it?

CATLIN
 (*Holding up her hand like a traffic cop.*) Hold it. Just hold everything.
 This is not a theological discussion group. We're here as writers,
 remember? I think now would be a good time to read what you've
 written, Ben.

BEN
 Right. (*He looks at* GINNY *who is taking a drink of her water.*) How many
 worlds did the original Handsome Lake mention in his teachings?

GINNY

(*Putting the cap back on the bottle.*) Mmm. Let me think. (*Counting them on her fingers.*) Well, there was the Earth, of course ... and the world under the Earth ... and the New World he was going to after he died.

BEN

(*Nodding.*) That's right. Well, I got to thinking. What if Handsome Lake's teachings actually meant that planet Earth would be so overrun with corruption and decadence by 2100 that the Real People would leave it to travel elsewhere.

MARIAM

Who are the real people?

GINNY

(*Cheeky.*) Indians, of course.

BEN

Handsome Lake also taught that the Real People need not fear extermination at the hands of the white race because Creator will take care of them. Well, we've lasted this long. Why not have all the Indians going into outer space to live in peace and practice their own ways and religions ... (*tongue-in-cheek*) sort of like the colonists did when they came to America? First the Real People colonize the Earth's moon, but that's too close to the corruption, so they go to Mars. That gets too close, too, so they keep going. My character Handsome Lake is the captain of a spaceship full of people, animals, and plants in search of a new world. They think they have found the perfect spot, an uninhabited moon that orbits a planet named Ashmole. The Ashmoleans are divided into two groups ... the Freedants and the Assems. The two groups are on the brink of war and both claim ownership of the moon. In this scene, Handsome Lake goes down to the planet to meet with a Freedant and an Assem representative.

(The spotlight fades from the reading room upstage. Downstage, the spotlight, with some purple and blue lights sweeping back and forth, focuses on an alien outdoor setting. HANDSOME LAKE *wears a khaki-colored jumpsuit reminiscent of traditional Haudenosaunee dress.* FREEDANT *wears a purple robe and gaudy apparel and jewelry similar to the King Henry VIII period and has a bluish tint to his skin and hair.* ASSEM *wears a plain gray suit of some sort and has orange hair and skin.)*

FREEDANT

> *(In a grand manner with sweeping hand gestures.)* Only we are masters over the orbital Villein. We Freedants have no objection to your people settling there so long as you pledge your duty to us and become our bondserfs.

ASSEM

> *(Stamping his feet and clicking his tongue.)* Don't listen to this *quintain!* They have no right to Villein. *We* planted our banners there first. *We* mapped it. The orbital belongs to *us*. Side with us and we will allow you to settle Villein as liege allies.

HANDSOME LAKE

> *(Hands open in a calming manner.)* Many, many hundreds of our years ago a people called the English came into our country. They extended their hand in friendship to us as your peoples have done. Like you, the English wished to forge a strong union with our people ... to become our brothers. Their leader, the Governor, came to our people at the land which we called Beyond the Openings to hold council with our leaders. The Governor was concerned that the rope we had used to tie their ship to the great mountain would perish in the course of years as it was only fastened with wampum. The Governor promised us he would give us a silver chain, which would be much stronger ... one that would last forever. We accepted the English silver chain and fastened their ship to our land with it. But it did not last. The English took their silver chain and wrapped it around our feet and forced us into bondage. They took all that was ours. So, I thank you both for your kind offers. But we have learned the teachings of our ancient ones well. We are taught from many years past not to take sides in matters of other races ... no matter how

noble or just their cause may be. It is not our way. The Creator will lead us to a new tree of peace and life. There we will sit beneath it, enjoy its shade and watch our children's children grow. Until then, we will continue our journey.... Maybe one day your peoples will come together to plant your own tree of peace.

(*The scene downstage fades and the spotlight again focuses on the writers upstage at the table.*)

GINNY

Wow! Sign me up for outer space. I want to go.

BEN

And I'll be more than happy to take you to any heights you want to go to.

(GINNY *giggles.* ANNA *and* CATLIN *exchange a look.*)

Scene 4

BEN

I want to hear this Indian romance of Ginny's. She should read next.

GINNY

Sure. Why not. I'm calling my book "Nights of Savage Love."

(*Everybody giggles.* CATLIN *drinks some of her tea.*)

GINNY

Anyway, Rebecca Ballard, a Pennsylvania colonist, gets abducted by Shawnee warriors during a raid in 1754, at the beginning of what is commonly called the French and Indian War. The following year, she is formally adopted into the Mohawk Nation by a family who lost a son in the war.

BEN

(*Leaning back in his seat and crossing arms over his chest.*) Shades of Mary Jemison and the Senecas?

GINNY

Why not? She led a better life as a Seneca woman than she would have had she remained with the whites. And she knew it. Otherwise she wouldn't have run away and hid from the whites who tried to take her back.

LISA

But I thought you ... (*she waves her hand from* GINNY *to the other Indian women*) or one of you said something about it was usually the other way around and white men married Indian women.

ANNA

(*Nodding.*) Historical statistics suggest that. However, that was not the case 100 percent of the time, any more than 100 percent of the women who were captured by Indians chose to remain with them. Many did stay. Some didn't.

BEN

Yeah, like Mary Rowlandson. What a piece of work she was!

GINNY

And what a hatchet job she did on the Wampanoags who—

MARIAM

The Wampawhose?

GINNY

The Wampanoags.... You know, the Indians who threw the Thanksgiving dinner for the Pilgrims. *Those* Indians were the Wampanoags. And not long afterward they found themselves having to fight to preserve their land and their way of life from the British invasion ... and I'm not talking about the Beatles. Did you know that archaeologists have proven that the Wampanoags were living on what is now Martha's Vineyard 10,000 years ago? But today, the Wampanoags barely have a toehold on that ritzy island, let alone in quote "New England" unquote. It really burns me that Rowlandson's captivity narrative was a colonial bestseller.

BEN

Yeah. I especially like the part where she, (*dramatically placing a hand on his heart in a swearing gesture*) the good, God-fearing wife of a minister and the picture of superior Christian motherhood that she portrayed herself to be, stole the food right out of a captive English child's mouth and didn't even express the slightest remorse for making the child starve.

GINNY

(*Also dramatically placing a hand on her heart in a swearing gesture and speaking in a lofty tone.*) "And savory it was to my taste" (GINNY's *regular tone*) is how I believe she put it. What was her justification for it? Oh, yeah. (*Lofty tone.*) "Thus the Lord made that pleasant and refreshing which another time would have been an abomination." (GINNY's *regular tone.*) I love that. She used the Lord as the perfect justification for behavior which her so-called "barbarous heathen" Indian captor was thoroughly disgraced by. Had I been her captor, I would have hit the old witch (*she pounds a fist on the table for emphasis*) instead of just threatening to if she did such an outrageous thing again.

BEN

(*Playfully sarcastic.*) You barbarous heathen you!

GINNY

You betcha. But to get back to my story, Rebecca, whom the Mohawks named Flower-beside-the-Water, falls in love at first sight with a handsome hunk of a warrior named Wolf-Waiting-in-the-Trees.

ANNA

Why are you using an English translation? Why not just use their Mohawk names?

GINNY

Because that's the first thing the editor will toss out. I know an Indian romance writer. She has a major battle on her hands every time she turns in a manuscript. Her idiot New York editor who has never been west of the Holy Hudson ... let alone seen an honest-to-goodness Indian in person ... is constantly trying to rewrite history and tribal traditions to make every tribe match Hollywood's idea of Indians. So, in hopes of getting my story published, I plan to give 'em exactly what they want.

BEN
God, you really are a barbarian!

GINNY
(*Giving him a look.*) Stick it, Ben.

BEN
(*Grinning.*) Mmmm. I love forceful women.

GINNY
(*She glares at* BEN, *then looks at the others, continuing.*) The scene I've written takes place somewhere toward the end of the beginning of the book. It's what came readily to mind, and it fleshes out the two main characters ... so to speak. Anyway, here's what I've got so far. (*Reading from her manuscript.*) Rebecca stood outside the longhouse. She stretched, experiencing the unaccustomed weight and feel of buckskin against her flesh. Sunrise blazed orange across the sky, awakening the chatter of birds. Her indigo blue eyes scanned the forest, attempting to pinpoint the birds' location. That was when she saw him. He stood at the edge of the woods, a tall, broad-chested, virile male, with an overcast brow and black eyes as wild as the wilderness he emerged from. His bronzed, half-naked body glistened with—

BEN
(*Interrupting in a deadpan voice.*) Which half is naked?

ANNA
Who cares! I'll take him regardless of which half is naked.

CATLIN
No way! You can't have him. He's mine. I want him!

ANNA
(*Patting a hand over her heart.*) Be still my *savage* breast!

GINNY
Excuse me, but can I get on with my scene? Uninterrupted this time, please.

BEN, ANNA, AND CATLIN
(*In unison.*) Sorry.

GINNY

Now where was I? Oh, yeah. They called him Wolf-Waiting-in-the-Trees.

CATLIN

Wait a minute. What happened to his half-naked body?

ANNA

(*Swallowing some water quickly.*) Yeah!

GINNY

(*Glowering.*) Okay. His bronzed, half-naked body glistened with a sheen of sweat. They called him Wolf-Waiting-in-the-Trees. The name fit. Every time he came near her, which was often, she felt his power ... that of a wolf waiting to spring on her and carry her off. Her heart raced ... but in fear or anticipation, she knew not which. All she knew for certain was that he was coming straight toward her.

(*The spotlight fades upstage on the writers group. The spotlight focuses downstage on* WOLF, *dressed in a buckskin loincloth, leggings, and moccasins, walking out of the forest toward* REBECCA, *dressed in a buckskin dress, leggings, and moccasins, who is standing next to a longhouse pounding corn in a hollow log. The lighting suggests early morning. A few birdcalls sound offstage, coming from the direction of the forest.*)

WOLF-WAITING-IN-THE TREES

Flower-beside-the-Water, I knew you would be waiting for me. (*He takes the pounding pestle from her hands and wraps her in his arms, crushing her against his chest.*) Soon the Mohawk warriors will leave the valley. The English have called on us to war against the French and their Indian allies. Sir William Johnson is gathering Yankee militia to take a place they call Lake George from the French. He has asked that his Mohawk brothers join him in this worthy battle. Many whites may come to our valley. They will want to take you away from us. They will want to take you back to live among your people. You must decide whether you want to go with them or stay with your Mohawk family.

REBECCA

    (*Running her hands over his muscled arms and chest, she looks into his eyes.*) I want to stay ... with you. But I want to see my family again, too. How can I decide? My father or my older brother made all the decisions at home. I don't know how to decide ... what to decide. You must help me. You must decide for me.

WOLF-WAITING-IN-THE TREES

    (*Looking scandalized, holding her at arm's length.*) I cannot. You are now the daughter of a strong clan mother. No man has the right or would even dare to suggest what a clan mother or her daughters should do. Only you can decide your fate ... your future.

REBECCA

    (*Turning away from him toward the audience and wringing her hands.*) But I tell you I don't know how to decide.

WOLF-WAITING-IN-THE TREES

    (*Standing behind her, wrapping his arms around her waist.*) Take council with your mother. Place-of-Sunshine will advise you well. Her wisdom is great and known throughout the Mohawk Valley.

(*The scene fades and the spotlight again focuses upstage on the writers at the table.*)

BEN

    Aren't you getting a bit obsessive with "Mohawk" this and "Mohawk" that?

GINNY

    Obviously you have not read many (*fingers making quote marks in the air*) "Indian" romance novels.

BEN

    (*Chuckling.*) No. Can't say that I have.

GINNY

    Obviously not, otherwise you'd know they constantly label the Indians by tribe.

CATLIN

    I guess that's so the white readers can keep all us straight in their heads.

ANNA

(*Winking.*) Yeah, because everybody knows we all look so much alike!

LISA

(*Adjusting her glasses.*) It isn't that way at all. We've been sitting here for two weeks now, and I still have trouble trying to figure out which one of you belongs to what tribe.

ANNA

Don't get me wrong.... We're all very proud of who we are and which Indigenous nation we come from ... but white people are so hung up on categorizing us and asking for proof of who we are, that I feel I'm supposed to get my tribal affiliation tattooed across my forehead.

GINNY

(*Waving a dismissing hand.*) Oh, girl, don't do anything so permanent. The government is libel to change your tribal designation at any moment or declare you an extinct tribe. Then where will you be? It'd be a little tricky trying to change (*drawing the letters across her own forehead with a finger*) "Creek" into "Other" like the option on some forms that don't even have a Native American option box. (*She stands up and dramatizes what she says.*) Personally, I'd go for those peel and stick labels and slap it right on my butt.

BEN

And you've certainly got a cute one.

GINNY

(*She curtsies before sitting down again.*) Why thank you, kind sir!

Scene 5

LISA

I want to go next.

CATLIN

Go for it.

LISA

As I mentioned previously, there is this excellent collection of papers in the library by this man named Richard Van Dermark. He traded with the Indians and lived among them during the 1700s, and he left several diaries and official documents of his translations of Indians' treaty talks, daily transactions, and travels, as well as accounts of Indian massacres and other bloodthirsty cruelties carried out against the poor colonists.

(ANNA *covers the groans of the other Indians by coughing.*)

ANNA

So, Lisa, where did these events take place? Which Indians are you writing about?

LISA

I haven't decided yet.

CATLIN

(*Choking on the drink she was sipping.*) What do you mean you haven't decided? I thought you were supposed to be writing a nonfiction book.

LISA

I am. But, you see, Mr. Van Dermark always referred to them generically as Indians. He never named an actual tribe.

BEN

How typical. The guy supposedly lives with a group of people for years and never bothers to find out who they are. Don't you love it? (*He looks directly at* LISA.) But you, as the historian, should be able to pinpoint the Indian nation or nations Van-what's-his-name dealt with from the locations he mentioned in his accounts.

LISA

(*She waves it away as unimportant.*) Oh, I'll get to that later. The important things are to clean up the spelling and punctuation of the documents and arrange the syntax so that readers today can understand what the Indians were saying. But mainly, I plan to just let the Indians speak for themselves.

GINNY

(*Muttering.*) It's *How*-dee-duty time.

BEN

Emphasis on *how*.

(CATLIN *and* ANNA *chuckle.* LISA *ignores them.*)

LISA

The piece I'm going to read now is the one I first came across and the one that got me interested in this project. (LISA *clears her throat, takes a sip of water, and begins reading from her manuscript.*) The following speech was given by an Indian Mr. Van Dermark identified as Cainaswayga. He delivered this speech at an Indian treaty talk with the colonists. Mr. Van Dermark described Cainaswayga as an elderly man of at least sixty years or more, worn in features and stature. Cainaswayga, speaking for all his tribesmen, came before the colonists to plead for a more civilized way of life for his pitiful people. He said: "In the year of our Lord seventeen hundred and forty-four, I come before you, our older, wiser brethren to beg a union and pleasing agreement between us and you our masters. We will never disagree, but safeguard a strict friendship for you, and thereby, we will become stronger."

BEN

Wait a minute. Wait just one minute! That sounds like a very poor interpretation of Canastego's speech delivered at the Lancaster negotiations which had nothing to do with the Onondagas asking to become more civilized. On the contrary, Canastego's speech very clearly indicates that the Onondaga people considered themselves a sovereign people who had the rightful claim to the land and who did not consider themselves subject to the English Crown. Canastego was an eloquent and forceful orator. This interpreter Mr. Van-what's-his-name you are quoting is incredibly ethnocentric and quite inaccurate. If you want a decent interpretation of that same speech, and an accurate description of the man who was tall and vigorous, read Conrad Weiser. He was considered Pennsylvania's most reliable interpreter of the timeframe.

LISA

(*Pointing to her papers.*) But Richard Van Dermark is not inaccurate. He couldn't be. He was there. He wrote down the Indian's speech *word for word*.

BEN

(*Deadpan.*) Then Van Dermark wrote the speech in Onondaga?

LISA

Of course not, silly. Indians have no written language.

CATLIN

(*Almost screeching.*) Excuse me, but the Cherokees certainly do have a written language.

LISA

Well, not until the Americans gave you one.

CATLIN

What! I'll have you know Sequoya, who developed the Cherokee syllabary, never learned to speak, read, or write English. Furthermore, we were the first Indian nation to have our own newspaper, written in *our* own language, as well as in English ... until United States citizens illegally entered our nation from Georgia and destroyed the paper's printing press and the newspaper office. So much for Freedom of Speech and Freedom of the Press!

GINNY

You Cherokees are lucky. The missionaries did give my people, the Mohawks, some letters of the alphabet from which to create a written language. But they only gave us twelve letters, feeling that we weren't intelligent enough to handle the complete English alphabet.

(BEN *stands up.*)

BEN

Your Mr. Richard Van Dermark must have been drunk on rum when he interpreted that speech. I'm going to show you real Indian oratory. I'll be right back.

(*Exit* BEN. *He enters the reading room a moment later with a library book in hand. Standing just inside the door, he opens the book, checks to index and turns to a page in the middle.*)

BEN

> This is Conrad Weiser's interpretation of Canastego's speech. The section your Mr. Van Dermark so poorly reported is from Canastego's concluding remarks, made ironically on July fourth, 1744. He was representing all of the Haudenosaunee people, and his speech was actually advocating the colonial subjects of King George II to consider the example of the Haudenosaunees' ability and methods of forging a strong, workable union. What he actually said versus what your Mr. Van Dermark wrote is:

(From this point, the speech that BEN *begins reading is acted out downstage. The spotlight fades from the reading room upstage and focuses downstage on a council grounds scene.* CANASTEGO, *dressed in buckskin breeches, leggings, and moccasins, presents his speech at a treaty gathering. According to Weiser's description,* CANASTEGO *was sixty years old, tall, strong, vigorous, and broad-chested when he gave his Lancaster speech.* RICHARD, *a young white man, dressed in colonial fashion circa mid-1700s, sits on the ground near* CANASTEGO, *writing down the Indian's words between taking sips from a pewter mug.)*

CANASTEGO

> We heartily recommend union and a good agreement between you our brethren.

RICHARD

> (*Reading aloud his interpretation as he writes it.*) In the year of our Lord seventeen hundred and forty-four, I come before you, our older, wiser brethren to beg a union and pleasing agreement between us and you our masters.

CANASTEGO

> Never disagree, but preserve a strict friendship for one another, and thereby you, as well as we, will become stronger.

RICHARD

> We will never disagree, but safeguard a strict friendship for you, and thereby, we will become stronger.

CANASTEGO

> Our wise forefathers established union and amity between the Five Nations.

RICHARD
>   (*Taking another sip of rum.*) *Your* wise forefathers established commu-
>   nion and amity between the three ... (*scratching the word out*) no, five
>   nations?

CANASTEGO
>   This has made us formidable; this has given us great weight and
>   authority with our neighboring nations.

RICHARD
>   This union.... (*Scratching out what he has written.*) No ... your union
>   has made you formidable; this has given you great weight and
>   authority over our neighboring nations.

CANASTEGO
>   *We* are a powerful Confederacy; and, by your observing the same meth-
>   ods our wise forefathers have taken, you will acquire fresh strength and
>   power; therefore whatever befalls you, never fall out one with another.

RICHARD
>   (*Writing in a grand manner.*) *You* are a powerful confederacy and, if we
>   observe the same methods your wise forefathers have taken, we
>   will acquire some strength and power, therefore whatever
>   becomes of us, never forsake us.

(*This scene fades and the spotlight focuses on the writers upstage at the table.*)

BEN
>   See the difference?

LISA
>   (*Folding her arms over her chest unconvinced.*) I have faithfully copied Mr.
>   Van Dermark's documentation of an Indian's speech. He was
>   there. We weren't. I don't believe Mr. Van Dermark was inter-
>   preting that whoever-you-called-him's speech. My version, Mr.
>   Van Dermark's version, stands as is in my book.

(BEN *snaps the book shut and, walking toward* LISA, *sets the book down on the table in front of her. Then he walks to his chair and sits down in his seat again.*)

Scene 6

ANNA

Catlin, why don't you read yours next.

CATLIN

All right. Like I said last week, my book is based on family oral histories told generation after generation after generation. At the start of each chapter, I will give readers some historical background, then present the oral history. Since we're meeting in the Andrew Jackson Reading Room, I thought it would be appropriate to begin with a part of my own family's oral history that deals with the infamous Mr. Jackson before he became president. In this chapter, the year is 1814. The British and the United States have been at war again for two years. The Americans called it the War of 1812. To my people, it was the Red Stick War, as it was the Red Stick warriors of the Muscogee Creeks who used the whites' war as a reason for attacking my people when we refused to join them and Tecumseh's Shawnees in fighting the Americans. My ancestor, Going Snake Walker, gave the following account of what the whites called the Battle of Horseshoe Bend. Going Snake, who married my multiple-great-grandmother's sister, was the nephew of the Cherokee warrior Shoeboots. It was Shoeboots' battle plan that won the day for Jackson.

(*The spotlight fades from the reading room upstage and focuses downstage on* RED STICK *who is dressed in buckskin and moccasins, wearing feathers in his hair and a tomahawk tucked in a belt around his waist. The background is dark behind him, as he is narrating this portion.*)

RED STICK

On the Americans' date of March 27, 1814, Andrew Jackson and his mountain militia launched an attack on the Red Sticks who were in a horseshoe-shaped bend in the Tallapoosa River in current-day Alabama. Jackson, or Old Hickory as he was called, decided the battle would be an easy victory because the Red Sticks were, and I quote the American press, "penned for slaughter." And Jackson needed a victory. Two months earlier his men attacked the Red Sticks at a river bend and had to retreat. But the Red Sticks then attacked Jackson's rear company. According to American historical accounts of that battle, the militiamen scattered in panic without even firing at the advancing Red Sticks. One of the officers, Colonel Stump, was last seen running away from the battle. So Jackson was desperate for a decisive win. But even using their artillery, Jackson's force can't dislodge the Red Stick warriors from Horseshoe Bend, as the Red Sticks have constructed a strongly resistant breastwork five to eight feet high of pine logs across the narrowest portion of the bend. The Cherokees, whom historians so generically call the "friendly Indians," had, before the battle had begun, been ordered to defend the rear and cut off any Creek retreat or reinforcement attempts. The Cherokees quickly sized up the situation and an old warrior named Shoeboots went to Jackson with the Cherokees' plan.

(*The spotlight fades from* RED STICK *and focuses further downstage on* GOING SNAKE *and two or three* CHILDREN *sitting at his feet as he retells his story.* GOING SNAKE *is dressed in homespun circa early 1800s white-style clothing, but also wearing white feathers in his hair, deer tails on his shirt, carrying a war club. He has a tomahawk and knife tucked into his belt. He also has a sliver-mounted rifle which he will pick up at the end of his story. The* CHILDREN *are also dressed in circa early 1800s homespun in white style. Downstage from* GOING SNAKE *will appear* SHOEBOOTS *and* JUNALUSKA, *wearing clothing similar to* GOING SNAKE. JACKSON *is wearing circa early 1800s Tennessee militiaman clothing—knee-length black boots, pants, and jacket with gold braids on the shoulders. As* GOING SNAKE *tells his story, a spotlight will also appear on* SHOEBOOTS *and* JACKSON, *then later* JACKSON *and* RED STICK, *acting out what* GOING SNAKE *says.*)

GOING SNAKE

My children ... in the time of the Red Stick War, the warriors of the *Tsalagi* fought with the Americans against the Red Stick Creeks and their allies the British. Shoeboots, a wise war leader, walked up to the white leader called General Andrew Jackson and outlined a plan, which Jackson ignored. Shoeboots pounded his fist on his breast, saying....

(*Spotlight focuses on* SHOEBOOTS *and* JACKSON *downstage from* GOING SNAKE. *But a spotlight also remains on* GOING SNAKE *and the* CHILDREN.)

SHOEBOOTS

We warriors of the *Tsalagi* will break the hold of the Red Sticks. We do not have the heart of chickens.

GOING SNAKE

Then, to add force to his words, Shoeboots leaped onto a tree stump, and, amongst a firestorm of bullets and arrows, he flapped his arms about and crowed like a rooster.

SHOEBOOTS

(*Leaping on a tree stump, flapping his arms, and crowing like a rooster. The sound of gunfire comes from offstage.*) I defy the one called Jackson to call the *Tsalagi* cowards.

JACKSON

(*Waving his hand as if to rid himself of a fly.*) Although I doubt your ability to seriously affect the outcome of this standoff, carry out whatever plan your warriors have devised.

(*The spotlight fades from* SHOEBOOTS *and* JACKSON. *It focuses solely on* GOING SNAKE *and* CHILDREN *again.*)

GOING SNAKE

(*Using hand and body motion throughout the monologue to act out what he is saying.*) Which we did. Charlie Reese, Tenkiller, and I dove into the cold, muddy river. Amid constant fire from the Red Sticks, we swam to where they had beached their canoes on the bank behind their fortification. As we approached their shore, the Red Sticks shot arrows and bullets at us. Tenkiller received a wound in his shoulder. He motioned for us to keep going. Charlie and I had almost made it to the shore when some Red Sticks lunged at us, their war clubs slicing the air. (*Putting a hand on the knife tucked in his belt and shaking his war club.*) But my knife and war club served me well. The Red Sticks fought and died well. Charlie and I each slid a canoe into the water before more Red Sticks could reach us. As we paddled back across the river, I stopped long enough to pull Tenkiller into my canoe. We reached the far shore and our waiting warriors, the Red Sticks shooting at us the whole time. By the time we had helped Tenkiller out of the canoe, both canoes had filled with warriors. We recrossed the river ... again as the Red Sticks tried to kill us ... and returned to our shore with more canoes. Bullets and arrows whizzed all around, killing some brave warriors, wounding others, still we kept recrossing the river until we had enough canoes for all the *Tsalagi* warriors ... five hundred strong ... to cross the river and face the enemy on his own ground. The Red Sticks fought a fierce battle with guns and swords and war clubs and tomahawks and knives. We killed many Red Sticks and weakened their hold enough for Jackson's force nearly ... 3,000 strong ... to finally join in the battle.

(*Spotlight switches to* JACKSON, RED STICK, *and* JUNALUSKA *fighting downstage from* GOING SNAKE. GOING SNAKE *narrates fight scene from the dark.*)

GOING SNAKE

When Jackson himself came over the barricade of trees, a Red Stick attacked him and wrestled him to the ground. The warrior raised his knife ready to scalp the white leader when Junaluska, a fierce *Tsalagi* warrior, grabbed the Red Stick's hand and forced the knife into the Red Stick's own chest.

(*Spotlight fades from fight scene and focuses on* GOING SNAKE *and* CHILDREN *again.*)

GOING SNAKE

Still the Red Sticks fought. The battle continued until nightfall as the Red Sticks bravely defended their ground and their village of women and children. Nine hundred or more Red Sticks lay dead that night on the land and in the water. Eighteen of our warriors also died bravely. At the end of the day, my friend Tenkiller lived, as did many of the thirty-six *Tsalagi* who lay wounded that day. But something strange happened that very next sunrise. Jackson's men, who thought of us as savages, did, under his orders, cut off and keep the noses of the slain Red Sticks ... warriors, women, and children. He also had his men kill sixteen Red Stick warriors who had lain injured among the dead throughout the night. (GOING SNAKE *picks up the rifle.*) Three years later, their President of the United States, James

Monroe, presented me with this fancy rifle. Charlie and Tenkiller also got rifles. Their president told us he was giving us these rifles because of our valor in battle. (*He runs a hand down the barrel, then lays it aside.*) But it was small compensation for what the American militiamen did to our families after the Red Stick War. For when the *Tsalagi* warriors returned home in 1814 from that war, we found our homes raided, our livestock slaughtered, our clothing pilfered, and our wives and daughters violated by *American* soldiers whom we, (*pounding a fist on his chest*) the *Tsalagi*, had freely and generously shared our corn and our livestock with since the outbreak of the war. All the while the Americans had hoarded their food and treated us worse than they treated *gitli* ... dogs. My own daughter suffered and died at the soldiers' hands. (*He extends a hand and it curls into a fist which he shakes in the air.*) And I was not there to protect her ... to take the blood of her murderer. Instead ... I had just helped to save her murderer's worthless life. I feel what Junaluska feels. I know his anger. For when that very same Jackson became *their* president, and he pushed the Indian Removal Act through *their* Congress, then he refused to uphold *their* Supreme Court's ruling reaffirming our rights, the *Tsalagi* right to our ancestral homelands, Junaluska said:

(*Spotlight shifts to* JUNALUSKA, *going dark on* GOING SNAKE *and the* CHILDREN.)

JUNALUSKA

If I had known that Jackson would drive us from our homes, I would have killed him that day at the Horseshoe.

(*Spotlight shifts back to* GOING SNAKE *and* CHILDREN.)

GOING SNAKE

That is all.

(*The scene fades and the spotlight focuses upstage on the writers at the table.*)

CATLIN

(*Taking a sip of tea.*) The Battle of Horseshoe Bend proved the turning point in the war for the Americans, and it was all thanks to the Cherokees. But Jackson took all the credit. Furthermore, he didn't care that his men looted, pillaged, and destroyed their *allies'* towns on the way home. Critics of his day called his systematic slaughter of Indians quote "cold-blooded cruelty" unquote, adding that his actions had not been quote "exceeded in the annals of the most relentless and savage warfare" unquote. And the real irony is that historians have claimed the Cherokees did everything from disregarding orders and acting on their own that day at Horseshoe Bend to carrying out Jackson's orders to being directed to storm the Muscogee Creek defenses by officers under Jackson's command to Jackson's officers actually leading the canoe raid.

LISA

If these Red Sticks were the Cherokees' enemy, why did you repeatedly say how bravely they fought? And why are you so down on Jackson for killing both the Americans' and the Cherokees' enemy in a time of war?

CATLIN

The words are not mine. They are Going Snake's, and why shouldn't he respect or even admire his enemy? Going Snake believed, as we still do today, that Creator put the Cherokees, (*directing a hand at herself, then toward* ANNA, BEN, GINNY, MARIAM, *and* LISA *in turn as* CATLIN *mentions them*) the Muscogee Creeks, the Haudenosaunees, the whites, the animals, the plants, the rocks, the soil, the wind ... in other words, all forms of life on Earth are here for a reason. We have no right to eradicate or even try to eradicate any form of life which Creator put here. Instead, it is our responsibility ... (*waving a hand around in a loose circle to encompass the room of people*) all of us, to make it all work. Of course, Jackson had other ideas.

GINNY

I hope you're going to call that chapter "Shoeboots Delivers a Swift Kick to Andrew Jackson."

BEN

A well-placed kick.

Scene 7

LISA

(*Folding her hands in front of her on the table.*) I don't know about the rest of you, but I'd like to hear what Mariam has written.

ANNA

(*Shrugging.*) That's fine with me.

MARIAM

Okay.

BEN

Did you know that is a Choctaw word?

MARIAM

What? Okay? (*She take a drink from her bottle of water.*)

LISA

(*Snapping.*) No, it's not.

BEN

Yes, it is. Okay is the Americanized version of *hoke* ... Choctaw for basically "everything's fine." Good Old Hickory (BEN *points to the portrait of Andrew Jackson hanging on the wall*) used to signify his approval on U.S. government documents when he was president with the abbreviation O.K. How's that for irony?

LISA

You are wrong. And I'm going to prove it.

(LISA *stands up and exits the room. She enters a moment later with an unabridged dictionary in her arms. She drops it on the table and opens it, turning through the pages.*)

LISA

(*Reading words on pages as she flips through them.*) Offensive, officiate, off-the-record, often times, ogre, ohm, oink, Ojibway. (*Once she finds the right page her finger runs down the columns.*) OJT on-the-job-training, okay. Here it is. The dictionary says that okay is an abbreviation for "all correct." It came into usage in 1919 when *Woodrow Wilson* used it on governmental documents. (*She nods her head briskly.*) Not Andrew Jackson.

BEN

(*In a quiet, calm tone.*) Your dictionary is incorrect.

LISA

(*Slamming it shut.*) No. You just can't be wrong, can you? About Indian speeches or about American words. Or about anything else for that matter.

CATLIN

(*Also rising to her feet, she plants her hands flat on the table and leans forward.*) Look, guys. This is a writers' group, not a debate team. If you want to continue this, by all means, please do so. (*Punctuating each word.*) But take it out in the hall.

BEN

My apologies, Mariam. Please continue.

(CATLIN *stares at* LISA *until she sits down again. Then* CATLIN *resumes her seat, nodding to* MARIAM.)

MARIAM

Apology accepted, Ben. Well, I'm writing spiritual essays. The one I brought tonight details my thoughts upon learning of my Indianness after the powwow I went to in (*she looks at* CATLIN) whatever you called that town.

CATLIN

Tahlequah.

MARIAM

Yeah, whatever. Anyway, while I was watching the dancers in their jingley dresses and their fancy feathers and their fringed capes stamp around the dance ring, my Indian name came to me. In my Indian soul, I'm called Strong Medicine Woman. In my Indian soul, I shed that part of me which was white, and I no longer identify with it. This essay is my Indian soul speaking.

(*The spotlight fades from the writers and focuses downstage on an Indian woman—* MARIAM's *alter ego,* STRONG MEDICINE WOMAN, *who is wearing a mixture of tribal powwow costumes such as a Plains Indian buckskin dress, Apache boots, a feather*

headdress usually worn by men, and Navajo jewelry. She is carrying a Haudenosaunee fan and a shawl with Cherokee symbols on it. Totally overdo all gestures. STRONG MEDICINE WOMAN *stands alone in the spotlight with no background.*)

STRONG MEDICINE WOMAN

(*Arms outstretched, waving the fan.*) Oh, lost tribe of Israel. At last I have found thee. I am one with thee. We are like the stand of aspens, growing on the side of the mountain ... different offshoots of the same tree ... now ... and forever united ... bonded together in our blood. The beat of the drum courses through my heart ... like life. It becomes the trail that leads me to my Indianness. I hear my ancestors singing. Faintly at first. Then growing stronger ... and stronger in my soul ... until their cascade of voices washes over me like waves pounding the shores of New England. "We came out of a wilderness of sand and forsaken desert to this wilderness of trees and water and fierce beasts that we might live as wild and free as Nature intended," they chant to my Indian soul. "Come, daughter," they call to my Indian soul. "Come, join us. Live among us ... as we have lived." "Yes," my Indian soul replies. "Yes, I will ... so at last, I can understand the things I have so long searched for." "Rest, easy," my ancestors intone to my Indian soul. "We will share with your heart all that we know ... all that we have learned these many centuries past. Go among our children's children. Take them by the hand. Embrace them. Show them that you and they are as one. Go to the sacred festivals. Learn the magical incantations. Remake the sacred tobacco. Perform the magical rituals. Then you will be ready ... when the time comes ... to take your place among us." My Indian soul hears my ancestors. I go West and take a Vision Quest. I must spend the night alone in the wilderness ... no food ... no water ... nothing but my thoughts ... to protect me from the wild creatures that prowl among the trees. Thoughts of all those mountain lions and grizzly bears and Creator knows what else with sharp teeth and claws, all roaming loose in that vast emptiness ... devoid of anything human ... frightens me. But I must endure the Vision Quest in order that I can hear my ancestors more clearly.

(*The scene downstage fades and the spotlight again focuses on the writers at the table upstage.*)

MARIAM

That's as far as I got this week. But I'll have more next time.

GINNY

Uh, Mariam, this is no reflection on your experience or what you have written about, but I feel I must point out something fundamental about Indians. I can't speak for all Indian tribes, especially since there are well over 600 Indian nations found within the United States alone ... and some Indigenous groups who were completely eradicated by the Euro-Americans ... but, as far as I know, no Indians have a word for wilderness in their language. That term is a foreign, very Euro-American concept.

CATLIN

We don't think of animals as being "fierce" or something to fear either. That's pretty Euro-American, too.

MARIAM

(*Waving her hands around.*) But don't you see? That's the point I was getting across in my essay. I endured the wilderness. I survived it. I conquered my fear. And that's what it takes to be able to understand the wilderness ... to master it.

BEN

I thought Vision Quests were strictly a Plains Indian sort of thing.

CATLIN

Well, they aren't Cherokee.

MARIAM

I realize that. But my Vision Quest ... which, by the way, was the greatest experience of my life ... scariness aside ... is merely a way of channeling a better connection with my ancestors. After all, we're just one big happy Indian family underneath it all, now aren't we?

ANNA

(*Through gritted teeth.*) Well, we aren't the lost tribe of Israel, you know.

MARIAM

But many historians argue ... and quite convincingly, I might add ... that the Indians *are* descended from the Jews. They had the same tribal system as early Jews.... The Indians didn't eat pork, thinking it filthy and uneatable.... The Cherokees believed in one supreme being who lives in Heaven and presides over the Earth.... All Indian tribes had prophets and high priests of the faith like Black Elk and Ben's Handsome Lake.... The list just goes on and on.... Then what about the Indian language and dialects? They appear very synonymous with the Hebrew language. I should know. I grew up Jewish. Then I converted to Mormonism and they also believe the Indians are the lost tribe of Israel.

LISA

(*Nodding her head.*) Mariam is correct. Many historians have suggested a connection between the Jews and American Indians.

CATLIN

(*Rolling her eyes.*) I got news. All those historians got discredited. And they didn't need DNA testing to prove we aren't misplaced or misguided Jews.

BEN

(*Tongue-in-cheek.*) Actually, we're pretty doggone good at finding our way through the *wilderness* ... which proves we can't be the *lost* tribe.

Scene 8

CATLIN

I think you're on, Anna.

ANNA

Remember last week when we were talking about the irony of blood quantum and that the government only thinks I'm Muscogee Creek because my father's family refused to register on the Dawes Rolls? Well, there's an even greater irony at work here. My mother was killed in a car wreck when I was quite young and my father's mother helped raise me. So, I know very little about the Muscogee Creeks ... their customs ... their language ... their culture. Then my father remarried ... a Lakota-Arapaho mix-blood woman who taught me pieces of her peoples' traditions. So, I guess you could say I'm a fair representation of the modern Indian. We shared our ways of life with the whites. They stole our heritage and murdered as many of our beliefs as they could. I'm the result. My culture ... my customs ... my traditions are piece-meal fragments that I, myself, have strung together like so many broken beads on a string of sinew. The poem I'm going to read reflects these mixed ways that are neither wholly Muscogee Creek or Cherokee.

BEN

Are you going to address the issue of mixed traditions in the introduction to your book of poems?

ANNA

(*Nodding strongly.*) Definitely. Otherwise, the cultural purists and traditionalists will accuse me of being (*she glances as* MARIAM) a New Age Indian wannabe. (ANNA *looks at the manuscript in her hands.*) Anyway, I call the poem I'm going to read tonight "Death to the Deer." (*She scans the faces of the other writers.*) I wrote it yesterday after seeing a dead doe beside the road. The sight of her once lively body now stiff and bloated consolidated some things in my mind.

(*The stage goes dark. Then the spotlight is turned on downstage from where the writers sit at the table in the reading room. The spotlight focuses on the dead doe beside the road which is actually an actor in a deer robe and deer headdress—not a prop.* ANNA *walks into the spotlight and approaches the dead deer, her hands outstretched in a beseeching manner in front of her.*)

ANNA

Oh, Deer Mother, how can I alleviate your pain, your sorrow?
What Prayers can I say?
To you, For you.
What deeds might I do

To replace
This shame
With respect?
Helplessness invades me.
I stand mired in despair.
Did it invade you, too?
To meet this end
Without the freely giving,
Only the forceful taking of
Their shame.
Their contempt.
Their neglect.
Have they no honor?
No reverence?
No.
How could they?

(ANNA *walks closer, her hand reaches out as if to touch the doe, caress her, but* ANNA
is not close enough to actually touch DEER MOTHER *yet.*)

ANNA
You,
We, are some *thing* to be abused,
Used,
Discarded,
Destroyed.
A sporting whim.
A wasteful aggression.
They have no need.
They hunger
Not for the flesh,
But for the senseless
Death to the Spirit.
Why can't they understand?
Deer Mother.
(ANNA *looks skyward.*) Air grows cloudy.
Sky's brow lowers to frown.

(ANNA *finally reaches* DEER MOTHER *and kneels beside the body.* ANNA *gently strokes the doe's side.*)

ANNA

    The Tree of Life grows sickly
    Deer Mother.
    Its roots grow gnarled, stunted,
    Slashed
    In earth too hardened to receive our tears.

(ANNA *bows her head so that it almost touches* DEER MOTHER.)

ANNA

    Oh, Deer Mother,
    What can I do
    To alleviate your pain, your sorrow?
    What Prayers can I say?
    To you,
    For you.

(ANNA *pulls the small leather pouch which she wears around her neck out from under her blouse. Opening the pouch, she shakes some sacred cornmeal into her cupped hand, closes the pouch and offers* DEER MOTHER *the sacred cornmeal.*)

ANNA

    Here, Deer Mother,
    Taste of the sacred *Selu*.
    Draw from her strength.
    Let her whisper to you
    The way
    Home
    Along the Path of White Peace
    Hear *Selu*'s words.
    Take comfort in them
    So that I may also be comforted
    In knowing
    That your journey goes well ...
    That my journey will continue
    Until our passage converges

On the White Path of Peace,
Deer Mother.

(*After a moment of silence,* ANNA *leans over* DEER MOTHER *and angles the doe's head toward the setting sun as symbolized by an orange glowing light shining from off-stage*)

ANNA
    See the Nightland?
    Deer Mother.
    Does not thc Whippoorwill call out a greeting?
    Does not Little Deer await?
    Tell him that you did not die easy
    That you did not give freely
    That those who killed you
    Did with dishonor,
    Disdain.
    Let your heart sing
    The song of vindication.
    Let your tongue
    Speak the words of retribution.
    Answer Little Deer
    With truth,
    For all our sake.

(ANNA *stands up.*)

ANNA
    Let your Spirit rejoice
    The sun sets,
    Deer Mother.
    Let it lead to the White Path of Peace.

(ANNA *backs away from the dead doe and out of the spotlight.* DEER MOTHER *stands in the last rays of sunlight. The deerskin robe falls away, symbolizing* DEER MOTHER'S *spirit rising from the dead body.* DEER MOTHER SPIRIT *is dressed in a buckskin dress with buckskin leggings and moccasins. She still wears the deer headdress.*)

DEER MOTHER SPIRIT
    My journey ends,
    Begins.
    But one duty remains,
    Carried over.

(DEER MOTHER *spreads her arms wide and slowly turns in a full circle.*)

DEER MOTHER SPIRIT
    Little Deer, I call on you.
    Hear me, Little Deer.
    Come to me.

(LITTLE DEER *is dressed in a buckskin, deer robe, deer headdress with antlers. He carries a bow and arrows. He dances up to her, then around her.*)

LITTLE DEER
    I am here,
    Deer Mother Spirit.
    Did you die well?
    Did the taker of your flesh
    Say the proper prayers?
    Did the taker of your flesh
    Treat you with consideration?
    With veneration?

DEER MOTHER SPIRIT
    No, Little Deer.
    They did not.
    They had drunk of the poison
    That has robbed us of our Brothers, our Sisters,
    Our Children.
    They could have turned away,
    But they did not.
    I did not give
    Of myself.
    They took.
    Heedless.
    Needless.

As their kind has
So often
Done.
They laughed.
Then they yelled at me,
Because *I* damaged
Their property.
Then they ran away.
My blood
Drying neglectfully
Beneath their feet.
Poison
Again on their lips.

(DEER MOTHER SPIRIT *pauses a moment.*)

DEER MOTHER SPIRIT
Little Deer,
Draw your bow.
Seek them out.
Spill my vengeance
As they spilled my blood.

LITTLE DEER
Rest, now,
Deer Mother Spirit,
Contented.
All your duties done.
Mine just begun.

(LITTLE DEER *leans over and sniffs the ground for the trail of blood left by* DEER MOTHER SPIRIT's *killers.*)

LITTLE DEER
Your blood
Will guide me.
(*He puts an arrow in his bow and draws it back.*)
They will feel my point.
Punishment will come.

(*The scene fades slowly to darkness.*)

Scene 9

(CATLIN *and* ANNA *are standing outside the Andrew Jackson Reading Room beside the bulletin board. The Indian women wear clothes similar to what they previously wore.*)

ANNA

(*Hugging* CATLIN.) I'm so sorry the publisher rejected your history book. Did they give you any reason?

CATLIN

Yeah, they claimed Indian oral history isn't reliable enough to be considered true history.

ANNA

True history. Now, there's a real laugh. Obviously that editor you sent your manuscript to subscribes to the school of ye old history with the capital "H" and truth with a capital "T" … otherwise known as, and I paraphrase historian E. H. Carr, the "fetishism of facts," which is "justified by a fetishism of documents," which results in the belief that only when you "find it in the documents, it is so." Well, don't you believe them. Oral history may be out of publishers and historians' comfort zone, but it is every bit as valid as musty old documents. More so, even! So, forget the jerk editor. Send your proposal to the next publisher on the list.

CATLIN

Already in the mail.

(GINNY *joins them, almost dancing up to them. She is wearing a dress.*)

GINNY

You'll never guess! New York wants my novel. Can you believe it?

CATLIN

(*Hugging* GINNY.) Gin, that's great!

ANNA

(*Also hugging* GINNY.) Way to go, girl! (*Standing back,* ANNA *looks at* GINNY's *dress.*) Very chic. In honor of selling your novel?

GINNY

(*Laughing.*) Not exactly. Ben and I have a date after the critique session.

(ANNA *and* CATLIN *exchange a look.*)

CATLIN

Definitely way to go, girl!

(LISA *joins them, smiling widely, wearing a business suit.*)

LISA

(*Speaking fast and excited.*) Oh, I'm glad I caught you before the meeting starts. I have exciting news! I won't have time to meet with the group any more. Wisemen Publishing just accepted my history book, and they gave me a generous advance. But you know New York publishers. My editor has suggested some changes in my manuscript I need to get to work on.

CATLIN

(*Sounding wary.*) What sort of changes?

LISA

(*Hand gestures punctuate her words.*) Oh, you know, punch up the action a bit, add a few more Indian massacres and Indian depravations of the colonists, that sort of thing—all historically accurate, of course. So I have lots of research to do to whip my book into shape. Well, got to run. See you.

(*With a wave of her hand* LISA *exits back the way she came.*)

GINNY

(*Looking from the direction that* LISA *disappeared to* ANNA *then* CATLIN.) Just dandy! She's filling her supposed nonfiction book with ethnocentrically biased "facts" such as Columbus *discovered* America, this continent was an unpopulated wilderness awaiting European settlement and exploitation, and the Indians were uncivilized, savage pagans who wandered across a land bridge onto this continent and, therefore, didn't have any ownership claims on the land ... like the British, French, or Spanish did!

CATLIN
  Yeah, all those so-called facts that are still being taught in class-
  rooms all round the country.

ANNA
  (*Nodding at* CATLIN.) And that's exactly why Lisa's book is getting
  published and yours isn't. Mainstream publishers, just like mainstream historians, cannot separate themselves from their own experiences and cultural judgments long enough to allow for the creation
  of an objective historical truth that doesn't fit within their narrow
  boundaries. Well, at least fiction readers will learn some authentic
  Indian history. Ironic that nonfiction readers won't.

CATLIN
  Yup. Kinda like us meeting in the good ole Andrew Jackson
  Reading Room, huh?

GINNY
  And how!

(GINNY, ANNA *and* CATLIN *exchange a look, then raise their hands, turning the
classic Hollywood Indian greeting into a three-way "high five" hand slap.*)

GINNY, ANNA AND CATLIN
  (*In unison.*) And how!

(GINNY, ANNA *and* CATLIN *then disappear into the Andrew Jackson Reading
Room.*)

END

molly has her say

Margaret Bruchac

Artist's Statement

While I was working on this play, an Abenaki friend said to me, "It's a shame our culture wasn't more permanent, like written records," and I burst out, "Written records can rot, and burn, and be rewritten by any fool with a pen in hand! It takes a lot more to move a mountain, to break up every rock, and tree, and river, to silence every creature, and erase every story … as long as one person is alive to hear the songs and stories, our culture is a lot more permanent than paper!"

The pieces of paper that make up this play are an attempt to record only the smallest fraction of the vital and complicated lives of Abenaki people in contact and conflict with Euro-Americans over the last 300 years. This play was not so much written, as driven, by the traditional songs, the teaching stories, and the voices of the old ones whose spirits are still in this land we call Ndakinna, despite the wars that split our communities, the histories that tried to write us out of existence, and the memories that were nearly lost in the struggle to survive.

The play was only half written when I met the embodiment of Molly Marie, the conflicted young woman whose focus on the written word renders her oblivious to the voices of the old ones. I am grateful to Shelly LaValley for offering her skills as an actress as the perfect foil for my dramatic Molly-self, and for allowing me to disrupt her life with this dream-play. Ellen Kaplan and Leonard Berkman offered artful and inspired guidance in shaping this work, and Muriel Miguel wisely forced Shelly and me into a closer confrontation, for a more dramatic rendition. I offer special thanks to my patient husband, Justin Kennick, who has endured years of watching me shape-shift from one Molly to another. And I thank my mother, the late Marion Flora Bowman Bruchac, for the memories she shared, and for listening to me spin the stories she could not tell.

I have been writing plays into existence since I was a young girl, but this particular play has written itself, in a sense, by reweaving the fabric of my personal memories into our regional history. This work is my gift to all the Abenaki who are still searching for a personal connection with the past. Ktsi wlioni, many thanks, to the renowned Indian Doctress Molly Ockett, for her life, for her wisdom, for inspiring so much of my research, and for demonstrating how to survive all attempts at extinction by traveling, by sharing knowledge, and by telling stories. As a traditional storyteller, I imagine the story physically taking shape around me, as a voice that sounds like mine speaks timeless words. As an actress, I offer my blood and bones to give shape to the old ones, in the hope that these lives and stories will be heard and appreciated long after I am gone.

molly has her say

Characters

MOLLY MARIE, is a mixed-blood young woman, in her late twenties, a graduate student who is both absorbed by her work and frustrated at her inability to choose a clear direction. She is vaguely aware of her Abenaki Indian ancestry, but refuses to acknowledge any personal connection to the past. Although highly sensitive, she has carefully developed the habit of ignoring her intuitions and dreams, regarding them as superstitious distractions. While in the midst of a research project, she is visited by a character from the past, who is visible to the audience but invisible to Molly Marie. Another spirit, Old Mali, who is invisible to all, has guarded Molly Marie her entire life. Throughout the play, MOLLY MARIE turns to her books for answers and ideas, and shuffles through papers, searching for things that seem to be lost, looking for key passages, making notes when she finds them. For most of the play, she cannot consciously see or hear Molly Ockett, but she reacts to much of what the older woman says and does. She is particularly affected by music.

MOLLY OCKETT, the "Indian Doctress," is a middle-aged Pequawket Abenaki woman from the late eighteenth century who knows a great deal about herbs and human nature. She is bitter about the past, but also wryly savvy about New England history, having navigated her way through Indian camps and colonial settlements across Abenaki territory. She is a character from the past, brought into the present, in the flesh, to convince Molly Marie to acknowledge how her personal history has been shaped by the past.

Throughout the play, Molly Ockett is determined to reach into Molly Marie's consciousness. To this end she tells stories, sings, moves books and papers, reminisces, and tries to break through Molly Marie's personal space, searching for an opening before her time runs out. Knowing that her time here is limited adds an urgency to her mission. She listens and speaks to the invisible Old Mali as she would to a powerful grandmother. She sometimes addresses the audience directly, knowing they can see her. Her character is solid, powerful, and loving toward Molly Marie, but she is also fierce in her determination.

OLD MALI, never appears in the flesh, only as a voice, a presence, an ancient grandmother who watches over Molly Marie and advises Molly Ockett. The audience hears her singing and perceives her words through Molly Ockett's response to them, but never sees her.

Setting

The set is a room, sparsely furnished with an old oak chair at an old desk, center, piled with books, papers, and notebooks, with other piles on the floor, and a wastebasket beside. An old wooden bench sits angled at stage right, slightly forward of the desk. A small footstool/bench sits rear stage left. The following are additional staging notes:

Lighting

Lights are set to brighten and dim in at least three areas: stage left, the desk at center stage, and a bench at stage right. The light that aims at the bench can also be used for the spotlight that represents Old Mali, a presence invisible to the audience but visible to Molly Ockett. The lamp on the desk is set to a dimmer switch that is remotely controlled. Other lights may be added for effect, e.g., a separate spotlight to represent Old Mali, a small blue light at rear stage left, and a bright circular spotlight in front of the desk at center stage.

Furniture and Props

Desk, chair, wooden bench, wastebasket, small bench or footstool, desk lamp, lots of books and papers, a current newspaper, a small (two-inch) sweetgrass basket, one strawberry, two identical ceramic mugs (one to keep, one to break). Note: some text (see script) can be preprinted and placed in books for reading.

Costumes

Molly Marie wears a cotton jersey dress, or silk shirt and jeans, or any youthful contemporary costume of choice that is neat, bordering on casual, with minimal jewelry, nothing obviously Indian. Molly Ockett wears eighteenth-century Abenaki women's trade clothing: cotton or linen trade shirt and wool or heavy linen petticoat ornamented with silk ribbons, silver broaches, wampum or other bead necklaces and bracelets, silver earrings, finger-woven sash belt, leather leggings and moccasins, leather pipe bag. For scene 3, add a green wool mid-eighteenth-century English soldier's regimental coat.

Songs

The play includes both traditional and original northeastern Indian songs to evoke particular moods and states of being. Audio recordings may be substituted for the songs that open each act of the play. Traditional songs include "Alibajikway," a Maliseet canoeing song, "Yanigawes," an Abenaki Green Corn Thanksgiving song, and "Gwanuday," a Mik'maq greeting and feast song. Original songs, written in a traditional style, include "Indian Hollow Lament," by Marge Bruchac, named for the Mahican settlement of Indian Hollow in Huntington, Massachusetts, and "Hey Yanna Hey," a healing chant, written by Joe Bruchac to accompany the traditional story "The Boy Who Lived with the Bears," used here with permission. "Gawi Squassis" is a lullaby, with words by Joe and tune by Marge, based on Wampanoag and Abenaki cradle songs. "Quaboag Rock House," by Marge, is an autumn gathering song, named for an ancient Nipmuc winter hunting camp in Brookfield, Massachusetts.

Some of the above songs can be heard on the following recordings: *Zahkiwi Lintow8ganal/Voices in the Woods*, by Marge Bruchac and Justin Kennick, Good Mind Records 1998; *Alnobak*, by the Dawnland Singers, Good Mind Records 1994; and *Boy Who Lived with the Bears*, by Joe Bruchac, Parabola Storytime, 1992.

Abenaki Language and Accents

The western Abenaki dialect is most similar in pronunciation to Penobscot and Passamaquoddy, among northeastern Wabanaki languages. Most words in this script are spelled phonetically, following English language conventions, except for the following: The letter *a*, when it appears in an Abenaki word, is sounded like *ah*, unless paired with a *y*, when it is sounded as *ay*. The letter *i* is sounded as *ee*, and *j* as *dz*. The number *8* represents a nasalized *oh* or *ô* sound. For more information on Abenaki language, see Joseph Laurent's *New Familiar Abenakis & English Dialogues* (Quebec: Leger Brousseau, 1884). For simple spoken phrases as a rough guide to pronunciation, see Gordon Day and Jeanne Brink's recording "Alnôbaôdwa" (1990), available through the Native Authors Catalog, Greenfield Center, New York, or online at http://www.nativeauthors.com.

Please note that Molly Ockett's spoken English in the script is written phonetically, so that her English reflects a strong Abenaki accent, with a little bit of a northern Yankee accent circa 1750–1830— i.e., beginnings and endings of words are often dropped, "your" becomes "yer," "th" is very softly sounded, or replaced by a soft "d," as in "dem" or "de." Please do not mistake her style of speech for a caricature or stereotype, or assume that her lack of attention to grammatical details implies ignorance. Molly Marie, by contrast, speaks in a clear, nearly unaccented, modern American English.

Playwright's Note

The play *molly has her say* focuses on the "hidden histories" of northeastern Algonkian Indian peoples, and the conflict between Anglo-American written histories of disappearance and Native American oral histories of persistence. Two Mollys from the past are trying to speak to young Molly Marie, a Native American graduate student who denies her own Indian identity, even as she researches the details of Abenaki history.

The voices of these Abenaki Indian women speak to the systematic displacement and disruption of Abenaki communities from the colonial period to the present, and their tenacious hold on

Ndakinna—their homeland in present-day northern New England—through personal anecdotes, historical texts, and traditional stories.

Molly Ockett, a late-eighteenth-century Pequawket "Indian Doctress," is trying to reach Molly Marie through her research, asking her to reexamine the texts and myths of extinction, and remember her own family history. Old Mali, the voice of the ancestors, is trying to "sing the world into being," offering strength and connection to a timeless place where the songs and stories live. Molly Marie is just trying to get through her studies with a cynicism and disconnectedness that protect her from having to take any responsibility for these histories or her own Indianness.

Molly Marie complains, "What if I'm not Indian enough? What if nobody believes me ... who's gonna claim me then? Get off me—go find another Indian to kick around! I don't want your stories!" But Molly Ockett reminds her of her responsibility, saying, "The ancestors did the choosin', girl ... ain't your responsibility nohow ... it's jes that now yer th' one holdin' pen an' paper." Through powerful songs, stories, and historical texts, Molly Marie, along with the audience, gains insights into the impact of these tangled histories on her own life.

Production History

In March 1999 *molly has her say* had a public reading as a work in progress at Smith College, directed by Leonard Berkman. In April 1999 rehearsals continued at Smith College, with new directions and text changes inspired by Muriel Miguel. The play premiered May 7 and 8, 1999, with performances at the Mendenhall Center for the Performing Arts, Smith College, Northampton, Massachusetts, with Marge Bruchac and Shelly LaValley, directed by Marge Bruchac. A third performance was held on June 11, 1999, at the Pioneer Valley Performing Arts Charter School, Hadley, Massachusetts. On July 9 and 10, 1999, Marge Bruchac delivered a solo production at the Littleton Opera House, in Littleton, New Hampshire.

Scene I

Stage and audience are in total darkness when the scene starts. As lights slowly come up, MOLLY MARIE *is seen sitting at her desk, center stage, books spread out in front of her.* MOLLY OCKETT *is seated on the bench, stage right foreground. Offstage, a voice can be heard singing.*

Introduction Song: "Indian Hollow Lament"

Mikwalda kagwi, i-oh-dali
Mikwalda kagwi, i-oh-dali
Nizi wal-dam, Mahicaniak wal-dam
Mikwalda kagwi, i-oh-dali
A-loh-sa-da, a-oh-oh mik-wal-da
Mikwalda kagwi, i-oh-dali

Marge Bruchac as Molly Ockett, performance at Smith College. Photo by Kevin Downey, May 8, 1999.

(*Lights. When the song ends, lights fade up on stage right and center. A soft spotlight, representing* OLD MALI, *comes on, aimed from above the audience toward stage right.*)

(MOLLY OCKETT *is holding up a small sweetgrass basket in her right hand, studying it carefully. She gestures and nods in thanks above her, to the unseen presence of* OLD MALI *who has given her the basket. She talks to* OLD MALI, *and glances over her shoulder at* MOLLY MARIE.)

MOLLY OCKETT
> Ktsi wlioni, nokomes. N'dabaznodakabena
> I see yer still makin' baskets fer th' young 'uns.
> Ta utsi wlioni nia skwamiskwa.

(MOLLY OCKETT *smiles, drops the basket into her pouch and draws out a small bag of tobacco. She smells the tobacco reverently, thinking about what she's going to say so intently the audience can almost hear her thoughts. She scatters a little tobacco as she talks.*)

MOLLY OCKETT
> Paakwinogwizian, nokomes ... Tonik'd8nl8nzi?

(*She listens, musing. She gestures confidently toward* MOLLY MARIE, *working at her desk.*)

> Molly? Unh-huh ... I got 'er ... Kizos8o ... th' sun, she's shinin
> ... it's early yet.

(*Lights. Center stage lights up a little more. Desk lamp fades on. Stage right dims a little.* OLD MALI *light fades off.*)

(MOLLY MARIE *is going through a pile of books and papers, thinking of titles. She is speaking in a punctuated, academic style as she writes, with bored, arrogant, or sarcastic comments.*)

MOLLY MARIE
> Let's see ... "Shamanic Intervention in Cases of Neuro-psychological Trauma" ... too New Age-y ... just stick to modern medicine. "Native American Women in Urban Communities" ... nope, city Indians ain't Indians. Hmm, we need a title....

(*As* MOLLY MARIE *is going through this exercise,* MOLLY OCKETT *silently watches, bemused.* MOLLY MARIE *ignores her, continuing reading.*)

"Interweaving Indigenous Knowledge and Academics" ... irrelevant, doesn't fit. "Interdisciplinary Reconfigurations of Multiracial Ethnic Gender-based ... " Oh, man! Too many words and no substance.

What does any of this have to do with ... well, with anything! We need a thesis! What was it, now ... well, let's focus on the idea of written language, the ... uh ....

(She brightens up with an idea, and pronounces it very crisply.)

... the interchange between Native American oral cultures and the discipline of writing....

(Confidently, while writing it down.) Okay, now we've got something.

(MOLLY MARIE searches through a pile of books, opens to a passage, and starts carefully reading. MOLLY OCKETT gets up and gestures at MOLLY MARIE disapprovingly.)

MOLLY OCKETT

Some a' dese young 'uns git ta thinkin' th' stories don' mean nothin'. Jes' words on a page, jes' sounds spoken inta th' air.... Lookit 'er there—prowlin' thru dem papers like dey was life isself in em! Dem scratches got power, girl! Talkin' leaves—akwighigan, we calls 'em—but you be careful whatcha read! Dey kin write ya out, same's dey kin write ya in!

(Shaking her head in resignation.) She knows, but she ain't listenin' ... cain't hear th' voices a' th' old ones ...

(She gestures toward the sky, wistfully.) ... like ol' Mali.

(MOLLY OCKETT is standing behind MOLLY MARIE, speaking scornfully.)

Dese young'uns walkin' 'roun' blind, thinkin' dust 'n' words is jes' dust 'n' words....

(Conspiratorially, she speaks to the audience and then prepares a remark, trying for a reaction.)

Watch this....

(Indulgently, in an old, crackly, motherly voice.) Molly, honey, what'chu be doin'?

MOLLY MARIE

(*Answering reflexively, impatiently, without looking up.*) I'm reading … don't bother me.

(MOLLY MARIE *continues reading for a moment, absorbed, then suddenly stops, putting her hand over the book as if to hide it. She looks up to see where the voice came from.*)

(*Disbelieving.*) What the hell was that?

(*Realizing she is alone,* MOLLY MARIE *shakes her head and goes back to her papers. She opens up an old book, and starts reading.* MOLLY OCKETT *is speaking to the audience, and gesturing toward* MOLLY MARIE.)

MOLLY OCKETT

(*Exasperated.*) Ya see? She hears, but she don' hear. Listenin' ta what suits 'er, an' ignorin' th' sound tha's all 'round 'er…. What be we gon' do wit' you, li' l Squassis?

MOLLY MARIE

(*Reading with pretended awe.*) "Amid all this stillness of Nature, see the Reverend John Eliot place in the hands of an Indian boy the…."

MOLLY OCKETT

(*Interrupting* MOLLY MARIE's *reading.*) An Indin boy, is it?

MOLLY MARIE

"… the Testament, and watch the varying emotions beam across his face, as the tones of …

MOLLY MARIE AND MOLLY OCKETT

(*The two read the words together.* MOLLY OCKETT *is very sarcastic.*)

… the young savage's voice…

MOLLY MARIE

… playing with the rugged words of the unpronounceable language, strike his ear. Eliot's work will greatly further the Indians in learning English law and government."

(MOLLY OCKETT *is disapprovingly looking over* MOLLY MARIE's *shoulder. She is not happy with this choice of reading and makes it very clear, snorting and folding her arms.*)

MOLLY OCKETT

(*Frustrated.*) Well, that ain't no use! Tha's jes' another one a' dem English preachers, goin' roun' prayin' an' convertin' "dumb savages." Dat ain't th' story, Moll!

MOLLY MARIE

(*Closing the book, speaking sarcastically.*) Now isn't that just thrilling? So some Indian kid's reading a book. The brilliant Englishman teaches the ignorant savage to interpret markings ... more sophisticated than scratches on bark....

MOLLY OCKETT

(*Offended at the elite attitude.*) Scratches on bark be a fine way a' communicatin'!

(MOLLY MARIE *shifts gears as an idea strikes her and begins to gesture, thinking it over.*)

MOLLY MARIE

Or maybe it's the whole concept of reading, putting a language of sound, and symbol, and gesture, and emotion ... into anything that makes sense. And imagine, trying to render an alien worldview into an Indian tongue ... it's the effort, the conversation....

(MOLLY OCKETT *shakes her head and nods to the spirit of* OLD MALI.)

MOLLY OCKETT

(*Indulgently.*) Awright, skwamiskwa, you go bury yer head in dem books ... ol' Mali, she's jes' gonna sing you inta bein' ... den yu'll see....

(MOLLY OCKETT *sings the following song in four pieces, starting softly, taking four steps in between each line. Starting at stage left, she circles clockwise, behind* MOLLY MARIE, *and around to the front of the desk where she crouches facing* MOLLY MARIE. MOLLY MARIE *is intently searching for something in her reading—on the first line, she is mildly troubled, and glances warily to one side. On the second and third lines, she gets increasingly disturbed as* MOLLY OCKETT *walks through her space, singing at her.*)

(*The light that represents* OLD MALI *comes on during the singing. Lights are slowly brightening on center stage.*)

(*Song: "Hey Yanna Hey"*)

MOLLY OCKETT

(*Softly at first.*) Hey yanna, hey yanna, hey yanna hey

(*Gradually increasing in volume and intensity.*)

Hey yanna, hey yanna, hey yanna hey
Hey yanna, hey yanna, hey yanna hey

(*Louder.*) Hey, hey yo-o-oh, hey, hey yo!

(*The last line of the song seems to propel* MOLLY MARIE *to get abruptly up and out of her chair as the tune and volume rise.*)

MOLLY MARIE

(*Disgusted, looking around, up.*) What is that?

(MOLLY MARIE *gets increasingly nervous, and it is apparent that she hears something she can't identify or stop, and it's really annoying her. She gets increasingly agitated, walking around the room to get away.* MOLLY OCKETT *doggedly pursues her, still singing. The singing continues simultaneously with* MOLLY MARIE's *words and actions.*)

MOLLY OCKETT

(*Grinning, determined.*)

Hey yanna, hey yanna, hey yanna hey
Hey yanna, hey yanna, hey yanna hey
Hey yanna, hey yanna, hey yanna hey
Hey, hey yo-o-oh, hey, hey yo!

MOLLY MARIE

(*Disgusted, looking around, up.*) What is that? Hey, turn it down! Damn neighbors…. (*Pounding on the wall, insistently.*) I said, "Turn it down!" I'm working here! Damn … this is important!

(*She is seething, muttering, pacing.* MOLLY OCKETT *has now settled herself down into* MOLLY MARIE's *chair, and is still singing, softer. She reaches forward and mischievously brushes some of the paperwork off the desk.* MOLLY MARIE *turns in alarm at the sound of papers falling and kneels down to gather them up.*)

(*Frustrated and angry.*) Hey! What the hell is going on?!

(MOLLY OCKETT *has finally stopped singing. Lightly humming to herself, she selects one book and drops it in the center of the desk.*)

MOLLY OCKETT

(*Soothingly, slightly amused.*) Settle down, li'l one. I left ya somethin' ta chew on.

(MOLLY OCKETT *goes back to her bench and watches carefully as* MOLLY MARIE *settles down at her desk again.*)

(*Lights dim back to previous setting for center stage.* OLD MALI *light turns off.*)

MOLLY MARIE

(*Puzzled, she sees the book* MOLLY OCKETT *set out.*)

Where'd this? ... mm. That was too weird. Now, where was I?

(*She looks around, then opens it determinedly.* MOLLY OCKETT *watches intently.*)

Hmph. What was that passage from Thoreau? Let's see, where was it ... hmm ... Oh! Here we go:

(*Reading from the book.*) "It was a new light when my guide gave me Indian names for things for which I had only scientific ones before. In proportion as I understood the language, I saw from a new point of view. A dictionary of the Indian language reveals another and wholly new life to us.
Look at the word, 'canoe'...

MOLLY OCKETT

(*She speaks clearly, simultaneously with* MOLLY MARIE's *reading.*) Canoe.

MOLLY MARIE

(*She glances up, hesitating as though she heard something.*) ... and see what a story it tells of outdoor life ... or at the word 'wigwam.'

MOLLY OCKETT

(*Simultaneously with* MOLLY MARIE's *reading.*) Wigwam.

(MOLLY MARIE *stops, certain she heard something this time and casts a puzzled look around before she continues.*)

MOLLY MARIE

Wigwam ... and see how close it brings you to the ground. It reveals to me a life, within a life ... threading the woods between our towns still, and yet we can never tread in its trail."

MOLLY OCKETT

(*Approvingly.*) Wlibomkanni, wli squassis ... foller th' track....

(MOLLY MARIE *gets a fresh sheet of paper, and starts writing a list of words, sounding them out, musing over their meaning, and scribbling additional notes.* MOLLY OCKETT *recites the words along with her, and then goes off on a separate track of thinking in relation to each word. Their words and thoughts interweave and overlap, with few pauses. Many of* MOLLY OCKETT's *words and songs are voiced while* MOLLY MARIE *is still talking.*)

MOLLY MARIE AND MOLLY OCKETT

Canoe.

MOLLY MARIE

(*Pedantically.*) "Ca-noe" ... derivation, Carib Indian, or was it Taino ... hmm, they're extinct. West Indies. Also recorded by Harriot in "A Brief and True Report of the New-found Land of Virginia." A primitive watercraft used by the Algonkian and other Indians. Right.

(MOLLY OCKETT, *inspired by the word, is straddling the bench like it's a canoe, singing the "Canoeing Song," "Alibajikway," and miming paddling while* MOLLY MARIE *is talking.*)

MOLLY OCKETT

Canoe! Maskwaiolakw....

(*Song: "Alibajikway"*)

(*Singing lustily.*) Ali baji kway, ya kway yo hey-eh, ali baji kway, ya kway yo hey

(*Speaking.*) Oh, i's spring, sigos, an' the creeks is runnin' wi' th' shad swimmin'

(*Singing.*) Yo, yo winna, yo, yo winna, yo, yo winna yo

(MOLLY OCKETT *leans down as though to dip her hand into water but stops abruptly when Molly recites another word.*)

MOLLY MARIE
"Indian Corn."

MOLLY OCKETT
(*Nodding in agreement.*) Skamon, corn.

MOLLY MARIE
Hmmm, now that's not exactly right. (*She stops writing momentarily, thinking.*)

MOLLY OCKETT
(*Pleadingly, looking off to where she sees* OLD MALI.) Nokomes, she's forgettin' all the songs....

MOLLY MARIE
"Corn" is a European term, any grain, wheat, rye, barley...

MOLLY OCKETT
...green corn, wskamonal ... gatherin' time.
(*Reverently.*) Corn mother. Skamoniskwa.

(*Song: "Yanigawes"*)

(*Singing.*)

Ya nigawes, ya nigawes, ya ha-ah, ni-gawes

(MOLLY MARIE *starts talking while* MOLLY OCKETT *is singing the "Green Corn Song."*)

MOLLY MARIE
Indian corn is rightly "mais" or "maize" ... was that one of those southwestern things?
Well, what's another....
(*Excitedly, as she gets a new thought.*) Wigwam!

MOLLY OCKETT
(*Speaking the word a beat behind, approvingly.*) Wigwam.

MOLLY MARIE
"Wi-ku-waohm," Eastern Abenaki, Wabanaki, dome-like dwelling, primitive....

MOLLY OCKETT
(*Reminiscing.*) 'Member makin' a lodge? Bendin' dem saplin's over, tiein' on th' bark.

MOLLY MARIE
Natick, Narragansett, "We-tu-wo-muk," at the place of dwelling...

MOLLY OCKETT
... spreadin' dem skins by th' fire ... ever'body gathrin' roun', listenin' ta stories in the wintertime ... warm 'n' safe....

MOLLY MARIE
... also Wampanoag "We-tu," ... Mic'maq, "Wee-gu-ohm"—where I dwell....

MOLLY OCKETT
Dat'd be home, Moll. (*Almost whispering.*) Home.

MOLLY MARIE
(*Wistfully, in response.*) Home ... hmmm....

(MOLLY MARIE *starts to visibly soften, putting her chin in her hand, daydreaming a little.* MOLLY OCKETT *watches her carefully and then speaks a word to see if she is listening.*)

MOLLY OCKETT
(*Breathily but insistent.*) Nigawes.

(MOLLY MARIE *excitedly adds the word to her list as though she just thought of it.* MOLLY OCKETT *watches and listens without interrupting, waiting for a pause in thought.*)

MOLLY MARIE
"Nigawes, nee-gah-ways!" ... "Ni" equals "my," "ga-wehs" equals ... hmm, I'm not sure there.... Oh, wait, was that one of those family terms? Gees, the Abenaki, I think it was, had all kinds of terms—your mother, my mother, older sister, younger sister, sister but not sister ... what a strange language....

MOLLY OCKETT
(*Solemnly.*) Gran'mother.

(*During this exchange,* MOLLY MARIE *blurts out similar sounding or completely unrelated to other words, clearly, subconsciously, avoiding* MOLLY OCKETT'*s suggestions.*)

MOLLY MARIE
(*Excitedly.*) "Raccoon!"—Aracun, was it? Another of those Taino words.

MOLLY OCKETT
(*Disgusted at* MOLLY MARIE'*s remarks, insistently.*) Mother.

MOLLY MARIE
"Moose!"—that's a good one—what was it those Micmacs said? A Frenchman's idea of a horse? Oh, actually, I think Eliot tapped that one—"moos-you," "he trims," from the habit of stripping or peeling the lower branches and bark clean off the trees ... like stripping the hide off an animal....

MOLLY OCKETT
(*Encouragingly.*) Good work, girl ... ya 'member how ta do th' skinnin'?

(*This brings up an old association in* MOLLY MARIE'*s memory, and she starts to recall, shuddering.*)

MOLLY MARIE
(*Suddenly serious, remembering.*) God, remember when Dad brought me to that bear carcass, stripped of its hide, looking just like a human lying in that old tub ... (*she holds up her hand, studying it carefully*) ... with hands just the size of mine....

MOLLY OCKETT
(*Lovingly.*) Squassis.

MOLLY MARIE
(*Leaping unconsciously, excited to change the subject.*) "Squash!" Food again! Askutesquash, asquash. Melons, cucumbers, vines, spreading out along the ground, intertwining ... "Succotash!" ... from "Msickquatash," equals "corn boiled whole." Back to corn ... what's another one?

MOLLY OCKETT

(*Solemnly, watching carefully to see what* MOLLY MARIE *does with this one.*)
Squaw.

MOLLY MARIE

(*Exuberantly.*) "Squantum!"—Oh man, that was the name of that
feast!—lobsters, clams, corn, all piled in together on a bed of sea-
weed, steamin' under the ground … mm-mmh.

(MOLLY MARIE *is smacking her lips, remembering.* MOLLY OCKETT *is disappointed. She
gets up and starts pacing around behind* MOLLY MARIE.)

(*Lights off stage right when* MOLLY OCKETT *leaves her bench.*)

MOLLY OCKETT

(*Frustrated, speaking almost harshly now.*) You young'uns don' e'en know
how ta speak ta yer own relatives! "Squaw's" jes' a word, meanin'
"Woman!" … ya don' need ta be runnin' away from it!
(*She steps close to* MOLLY MARIE, *reaching out to her, indulgently.*) An'
"Squassis," tha's what yer gran'mother used ta call ya. How is it ya
can't 'member th' simplest things, with all a' yer fancy book
learnin'?

(MOLLY MARIE, *in her musings, has softened, as she sits at her desk, head in hand,
daydreaming.* MOLLY OCKETT *sees an opportunity, and very slowly, tenderly, steps
behind the young woman, reaching her hands toward* MOLLY MARIE's *shoulders to
embrace her. A moment before she can make contact,* MOLLY MARIE *senses it, and
violently shakes free. Unsettled,* MOLLY OCKETT *stumbles to the side, stage left, and
squats down cross-legged, rebuffed. She seems significantly weaker from the failed effort.
She starts quietly singing a lament to comfort herself.*)

(MOLLY MARIE *shakes like she's getting out of a dirty coat, disgusted. She gets up away
from the desk, and, holding her shoulders, stares back at it, as though something awful is
there.*)

MOLLY MARIE

(*Clearly frustrated.*) How'd I end up reading so damn much?

(*As if answering her own question, she starts to soften as she remembers. She walks toward
the bench, stage right, visibly relaxing as she reminisces.*)

Ya know, Momma used to read to me....

(*Lights slowly up on the other bench, rear stage left.*)

(MOLLY OCKETT *is softly singing a lonesome song, "Indian Hollow Lament," throughout* MOLLY MARIE's *soliloquy.* MOLLY OCKETT's *singing repeats over and over, changing in emphasis to match* MOLLY MARIE's *emotion and the shared sense of loss of the past.*)

MOLLY OCKETT
(*Verse.*) Auu-oh, au, ah-au, auu, au-auu
Auu-oh, au, ah-au, auu, au-auu

(*Chorus.*) Auu-ah-a-auuu, Auu-ah-a-auuu
Auu-oh, au, ah-au, auu, au-auu

(*Refrain, sung with an increase in intensity.*)
Auuu, ah-auuu, a-ah-ah, ah, a-a-ahhh
Auuu, ah-auuu, a-ah-ah, ah, a-a-ahhh

(*Verse.*) Auu-oh, au, ah-au, auu, au-auu
Auu-oh, au, ah-au, auu, au-auu

(*Chorus.*) Auu-ah-auuu, Auu-ah-a-auuu
Auu-oh, au, ah-au, auu, au-auu

(MOLLY MARIE *muses, emotions playing through her as she remembers.*)

MOLLY MARIE
Oh, no, not this kind a' stuff....

(*She gestures at her books dismissively. She settles herself down on the bench, comfortably.*)

Nothing serious, but stories ... there were the family stories, just stupid things from her memory, nothing written down. Then there were the ones in books, she'd kind of act them out—God, I remember that voice....

(MOLLY MARIE *leans her head to one side dreamily. She lets herself get lost in the memory, although she cringes at parts of it.*)

Those blood-red lips parting and closing, and white, white teeth....

(She stares at her hands and makes a clawing motion.)

> And, oh man, those nails! Like talons, sharp and long and red ...
> *(questioning)* or were they red?
> Hmm ... well, those long nails, delicately and deliberately turn-
> ing each page ... I'd study every flower in her housedress just to
> avoid looking at those nails ... I'd hear that strange voice grating
> and crooning, sighing and whispering ... and I'd just melt, melt
> into the sound of a voice reading just for me, just for me ... words
> that no one else could hear, words that brought a whole world to
> life....

(She suddenly laughs heartily, remembering, smiling broadly.)

> You know, the stories she'd tell you, you just wouldn't believe 'em
> if you didn't know our family.

(She sits a little more upright, gesturing as if taking an instrument off the wall.)

> How Gramps would take that fiddle down off the wall and he'd be
> gone—just gone! Weeks at a time! Said he was visitin' family. They
> was chiefs *(Setting her shoulders back proudly, looking fierce.)* Warriors way
> on back, reduced to... *(sarcastically)* lumberjacks and basketmakers.
> Used to think he had a drinking problem.... Didn't find out 'til
> after he died he had another family, one up in the backwoods ...
> the REAL Indians, not half-breeds like us....
>
> *(Questioningly.)* And that uncle who was some kind of a backwoods
> medicine man—what'd they call him?

MOLLY OCKETT
> *(She stops singing and matter-of-factly answers the question, then resumes singing.)*
> A pow-wow.

MOLLY MARIE
> *(With excitement.)* A "pow-wow!" Something like a doctor and holy
> man all mixed into one. An "Indian Doctor." Think of that....

(She remembers for a moment, then abruptly changes to a more serious, melancholy tone.)

> But it's got nothing to do with Momma, really.

(*She suddenly gets up, marches back to her desk, and assumes her work posture.* MOLLY OCKETT *just as suddenly stops singing, as though a spell is broken.*)

(*Light down on both benches. Light up center.*)

Now, where was I?

(*Talking to herself as she flips through a book.*) One of those anthros said those old shamans used to sing the world into being.... What a bizarre concept!

(*She shakes her head sarcastically. A new thought suddenly strikes her.*)

Wait a minute, where was that passage about that "Doctress" who was a storyteller?

MOLLY OCKETT
(*Speaking offstage, up into the lights to* OLD MALI, *surprised.*) Doctress? Nokomes, this be yer doin'? Dat'd be me she's readin' 'bout!

(*She listens for an answer and nods in response. She speaks, then slowly gets up.*)

Well, if ya think she's ready. Seems if it's got 'er on track agin. Le's see what dese words are gonna do ta her way a' thinkin'!

(MOLLY MARIE *flips through a stack of books, finding one. She starts to read, blandly.*)

MOLLY MARIE
Hmph. Where'd this come from? "Story of Molly Ockett and Sabattis. Molly Ockett often boasted of her noble descent, claiming that her father and grandfather were prominent ...

(MOLLY OCKETT *folds her arms and straightens up proudly. She stands near* MOLLY MARIE'S *desk, stage left. They speak the words together.*)

MOLLY MARIE AND MOLLY OCKETT
... chiefs of the tribe."

MOLLY OCKETT
(*Proudly, nodding her head for emphasis.*) ...an dey was proud 'n' fierce folk!

MOLLY MARIE
(*Reading on.*) "... passing through all the exciting scenes of warfare between the French and the English."

MOLLY OCKETT
(*Muttering like a curse.*) Bostoniak ... snakes 'n' butchers....

MOLLY MARIE
(*Continues reading.*) "Molly remembered Lovewell's Fight, which took place in 1725."

(*She makes a written note of the date.*)

> 1725.... "It will be remembered at this time, Chief Paugus and Chamberlin fought a duel on the shores of Lovewell's Pond. The great chief Paugus was killed, and the remaining Indians driven off. This was the beginning of the white man's supremacy over the Indian in this section of Maine...."
> Hmm... I remember seeing something about this at the Historical Society....

(MOLLY OCKETT *is walking slowly, circling counterclockwise behind* MOLLY MARIE. *She stops, angry, pointing at* MOLLY MARIE.)

MOLLY OCKETT
(*Disgusted.*) Don' you trust none a' dem "hee-stor-i-cul" folks! (*Pause.*) Talkin' leaves full a' lies! Ya kin read my story, girl—but git it straight!

(*She calls off toward the lights.*) Old Moll, you there?

(OLD MALI *light bumps on. Light slowly up stage right on the bench.*)

(*Nods in response.*) Good, you jes' keep 'er up, there.

(*She walks over and settles on the bench as* MOLLY MARIE *keeps reading, unresponsive.*)

> Now you jes' lissen up an' ya might learn somethin'. Ya kin' start jes' 'bout anyplace, but I'd be startin' wi' "Lovewell's Massacree." Dem dat didn' kill enuff Indins with guns kep' it up wit' storytellin'. Oh, I know, ya heard a' dem poor Yankee boys goin' out lookin' fer ol' Paugus, an' endin' up gittin' massacred.... But lemme tell ya, from my side a' th' fence, dem English wuz th' savages ta watch out fer...

(MOLLY MARIE *is looking at the book, puzzled. She's not sure what to do with any of this information. She seems to be on the verge of changing her mind again about what to research. Bored, she slams the book shut.*)

MOLLY MARIE

(*Disappointed and sarcastic.*) What's the point? If the Indians are all gone, why bother?!?

(MOLLY OCKETT *continues with her story, a mix of emotions. Her voice is by turns tender, sad, and fierce. She gestures with her hand, as though she is in a canoe, on the river, floating.*)

MOLLY OCKETT

It wuz inna time a' shad runnin', up th' river ... wit' de shadbush bloomin', an' dem canoes paddlin' up an' down, childr'n laugh-in', ever'body workin' ... Nokomes, Old Mali, she wuz young den.... Word went out dem English boys wuz after scalps fer th' bounties, and Paugus wuz out wi' some a' th' menfolk when he run 'cross 'em, lurkin' inna bush... .

(MOLLY MARIE *continues to look questioningly at the book.* MOLLY OCKETT *points to a historical program shelved on the desk, and* MOLLY MARIE *picks it up, opens it, and starts reading. The side facing the audience has a large image of a menacing Indian warrior with tomahawk upraised.*)

You read how dem English wrote 'bout it, girl.

(MOLLY MARIE *starts out solemnly reading, then shifts to a mocking sing-song.*)

MOLLY MARIE

What's this?
Bethel Historical Society, 1881 pageant program, "The Indian Raid." (*Pause.*)
"O, come on ye painted Redskins
From out your hidden nook
The Settlers bold, with muskets old
Wait down by hidden brook
Ah! Many a wife shall rend her hair,
And many a child cry 'woe is me,'
When messengers the news shall bear
Of Lovewell's dear-bought victory...."

(*Disapprovingly.*) Hmmm....

(*Both women shudder as though their skin is crawling with the thought.*)

MOLLY OCKETT
(*Standing up, angrily.*) Dem boys was evil-intention'd, plain an' simple! Dey was after scalp money, tho' the song's not gonna tell ya dat! All full a' noble dis 'n' dat!
(*She spits.*) Ptah!

(MOLLY OCKETT *suddenly starts, and turns, as though being chastised by someone. She hears the voice of* OLD MALI *criticizing her. She explains, bitterly, gesturing at the sky.*)

(*Pleading.*) Nokomes, tha's how it allus begins!
Ni agua pasqueda wakaswak, W8banakiak weskok8gonosa Bostoniak, a few Indins in trouble wit' de English.

(*Emphatically.*) Mziwi wmat8gw8banik—dey coulda all been killed, but fer Paugus ... could a' been all a' dem lost!

(*Pointing at* MOLLY MARIE.) She's got ta hear what's writ inta dem histories!

(MOLLY MARIE *turns the pages, scans down, and continues reading, haltingly, fascinated and appalled at the same time.*)

MOLLY MARIE
"The Ballad of Lovewell's Victory.
Twas Paugus led the Pequawket tribe;
As runs the fox would Paugus run.
As howls the wild wolf, would he howl.
A large bear-skin had Paugus on...."

(MOLLY OCKETT *hovers over* MOLLY MARIE's *right shoulder.*)

MOLLY OCKETT
(*Grimly pleased.*) Now we're talkin', girl, an' Paugus is walkin'—tell 'em 'bout dat snake Lovewell dyin'!

MOLLY MARIE
(*Still reading, unaware of* MOLLY OCKETT's *comments.*)
"'Fight on, fight on,' brave Lovewell said.

'Fight on while Heaven shall give you breath!'
An Indian ball then pierced him through
And Lovewell closed his eyes in death."

(*Disgusted.*) Who writes this stuff? This isn't what I was looking for
at all.

MOLLY OCKETT
(*With vicious insistence.*) Now get his scalp, girl! Turn th' tables!

(MOLLY OCKETT *pulls a crumpled old document out of her pouch and throws it to
the floor.* MOLLY MARIE *shudders involuntarily. She watches the paper fall and looks
up and around her, quizzically, seeing nothing.*)

MOLLY MARIE
(*Muttering.*) Papers falling out of the sky....

(*She picks up the document, starts reading and gasps, covering her mouth in shock. Her
voice and emphasis rise and fall as she realizes what she is reading.*)

(*Light starts to dim center and stage right as she reads.* OLD MALI *light turns off.*)

"Petition to the General Court of Massachusetts.... That your
petitioners, with nearly forty or fifty others, are inclined to keep
out in the woods for several months together, in order to kill and
destroy their enemy Indians, provided they can meet with
encouragement suitable. And your petitioners are employed by
many others ... if such soldiers may be allowed five shillings per
day in case they kill an enemy and possess their scalp, they will
employ themselves in Indian hunting the whole year!" Signed,
John Lovewell, Josiah Farwell, Jonathan Robbins, Dunstable,
November 1724.

(*She keeps reading, horrified, slowly emphasizing the words.*)

"In reply, a bounty of one ... hundred ... pounds was approved
for each Indian scalp taken by Lovewell's company."

(*In a loud whisper.*) Good Lord!

MOLLY OCKETT
(*Nodding her head sadly, bitterly.*) Tha's right, li' l one.
One ... hunnert ... pounds. English sterlin'.

Fer Nokomes, Nigawes, an' her baby girl an' sisters 'n' brother's scalps, like they wuz wild animals. Think on it!

(*Mockingly.*) An' dem settler folk wonder why I set in dem English parlours, sippin' tea an' tellin' 'em stories a' Lovewell 'n' Paugus, chillin' th' blood a' their li'l ones....

(*Gesturing at* MOLLY MARIE, *insistent and bitter.*) Dem words has got power you can' e'en dream of, squassis! Dem pro-cla-ma-shuns near writ yer folks out a' existence!

(*Dismissively.*) You keep up yer readin'! See where it gets ya!

(*Sitting cross-legged on the bench,* MOLLY OCKETT *begins singing the "Indian Hollow Lament" again, but in a minor, off-key, eerie, keening, mournful wail, with eyes closed, nearly crying.*)

(*Lights dim, an eerie blue light comes up on a small bench, rear stage left.*)

MOLLY OCKETT
    Mikwalda kagwi, i-oh-dali
    Mikwalda kagwi, i-oh-dali
    Nizi waldam, wabanakiak waldam
    Nizi waldam, wabanakiak waldam
    (*Refrain, sung with an increase in intensity.*)
    Alosada, a-oh-oh mik-wa-al-da
    Alosada, a-oh-oh mik-wa-da
    (*Chorus.*) Mikwalda kagwi, i-oh-dali
    Wabanakiak kagwi, i-oh-dali

(*It's a disturbing song.* MOLLY MARIE *shudders and slowly, hesitantly gets out of her chair. She pulls her clothes tighter around her shoulders, hugging herself, walking around cautiously, as though she is exposed and there is nowhere to hide.*)

MOLLY MARIE
    (*Plaintively.*) Hmmm ... it sure is cold in here.

(MOLLY MARIE *stands, wavering, her eyes near tears.*)

(MOLLY OCKETT *changes from singing to chanting, in a deep, warm voice. The chanting seems to calm* MOLLY MARIE, *who turns toward the singing and visibly relaxes.*)

From left: Shelly LaValley as Molly Marie and Marge Bruchac as Molly Ockett at Smith College. Photo by Kevin Downey, May 8, 1999.

Wlioni, N'mahom, wlioni Nigawes, wlioni, Nokomes, wlioni, Nemitongwes
Wlioni, N'mahom, wlioni Nigawes, wlioni, Nokomes, wlioni, Nemitongwes
Wlioni, N'mahom, wlioni Nigawes, wlioni, Nokomes, wlioni, Nemitongwes

(*Light starts to rise a little center and stage right. Blue light turns off.*)

(MOLLY OCKETT *sees that her singing reaches* MOLLY MARIE *more effectively than her words, and softly hums the tune of the "Indian Hollow Lament", in a kinder, warmer mode.*)

(*Humming gently.*) Mm-m mmm, mm-mmm....

(MOLLY MARIE *dreamily hums along with the song, as she carefully sits back down.*)

MOLLY MARIE
Mmm-mm, mm, mh-hm, mmm, mm-hmm....

(MOLLY MARIE, *still humming, puts the petition away and gingerly looks through her papers and books for something less grim. She takes a deep breath. Finding an old book that looks interesting, she opens it.* MOLLY OCKETT *perks up, sits up, interested, when she recognizes the story, and starts chiming in with* MOLLY MARIE, *adding her own comments.*)

(*Lights rise slightly overall.*)

MOLLY MARIE
> (*Pleased and relieved at finding this account.*) Here, what's this? Bethel, Maine, 1790.... "Molly had been out one day and gathered a pail of blueberries, which she carried to her friend, the wife of Eliphaz Chapman."

MOLLY OCKETT
> (*Also pleased, smiling.*) Hm-hm. Dat'd be a good story.

(*As the story continues, they fill in the text for, and with, each other, as noted.*)

MOLLY MARIE
> "Mrs. Chapman, upon emptying the pail found them very fresh, and asked Molly if she had been out picking them on Sunday.

MOLLY MARIE AND MOLLY OCKETT
> 'Certainly,'

MOLLY MARIE
> ... said Molly. 'But you did wrong,' was the reproof. Molly took offense and left abruptly...."

MOLLY OCKETT
> (*A little frustrated at the memory.*) Well, sure I did! Gotta pick berries when dey're offerin'—it'd be rude not ta! Stupid English!

(MOLLY MARIE *chuckles just a little.*)

MOLLY MARIE
> "... and did not make her appearance for several weeks, when, one day, she came into the house at dinner time. Mrs. Chapman made arrangements for her at the table but she refused to eat."

MOLLY MARIE AND MOLLY OCKETT
> 'Choke me!'

MOLLY MARIE
   ... said she;

MOLLY MARIE AND MOLLY OCKETT
   'I was right in picking those blueberries!'"

MOLLY OCKETT
   (*Explaining.*) I wuz right in pickin' dem blueberries on Sunday, it
   was so pleasant, 'n I wuz so happy dat Ktsinowask....

MOLLY MARIE
   "'The Great Spirit...

MOLLY MARIE AND MOLLY OCKETT
   ... had provided them for me.'

MOLLY MARIE
   Mrs. Chapman felt condemned for reproving this child of
   nature."

(*They both heave their shoulders and sigh.*)

MOLLY OCKETT
   (*Disappointed.*) Well, you wuz doin' fine 'til ya got ta dat "child a'
   nature" part....

(*They are both chuckling at the story and the comment.*)

MOLLY MARIE
   (*Sarcastically.*) "Child of nature!" Hah! (*Pause.*)

(*She looks around the room, acknowledging her isolation, wistfully.*)

   I don't even remember when the berry-picking times are, anymore ... (*wryly*) ... or where ... or when.... Heck, how long has it
   been since I've even tasted....

(MOLLY OCKETT *slowly gets up, sighing tenderly, walking toward* MOLLY
MARIE.)

MOLLY OCKETT
   (*Gently.*) Squassis, you be needin' a story. Lissen up, now.

(MOLLY OCKETT's *voice subtly changes tone, gently commanding attention.* MOLLY MARIE *sits in her chair, staring out at the audience, listening almost as though she hears the story, which* MOLLY OCKETT *spins out for her, and for the audience, as though working a spell.*)

(MOLLY OCKETT *circles clockwise around behind* MOLLY MARIE's *space, as she carefully relates the story, gesturing with her hands, with slight pauses, and occasional asides to* MOLLY MARIE *to see if she's listening. Phrasing of dialogue reflects pauses for emphasis.* MOLLY MARIE *sits, daydreaming, still, looking off into the distance, unfocused.*)

MOLLY OCKETT

When all th' critters wuz bein' shaped. (*Pause.*)
awaasak, siwask, sipsak, abaziak, nebisonsisak, e'en th' alakwasak. (*Pause.*)
Ktsinawask set ta' makin' th' two-leggeds.
Now th' first ones wuz made outa stone, but dey wuz so hard-hearted, tramplin' ever'thin' around, dat dey wuz broke up an' scattered 'bout.

(*She turns to* MOLLY MARIE, *questioning.*) Ya' ever wonder why dere's so many rocks aroun' Ndakinna, Moll?

(*Continuing the story.*) Now de next ones, made outa water, froze up so bad inna winter dey turned inta ice-hearts, not feelin' nothin'. (*Pause.*) So Ktsinowask sets an arrow ta th' bow an' lets loose inta th' ash tree, "maahlakws," tall 'n straight. Outta dat tree steps two two-leggeds, like halves ta one 'nother but differnt, woman an' man, th' "alnobak." Dese alnobak was gonna need a lot a' help, so's th' other bein's agreed ta take care a' dem.... All th' alnobak had ta do wuz care fer one another an' be respectful.

(*She has crossed to the front of* MOLLY MARIE's *desk, stage right, and turns back to see if* MOLLY MARIE *is listening.* MOLLY OCKETT *continues with the story. Her telling is so focused that the audience loses track of* MOLLY MARIE, *who is sitting, quietly, looking into the distance.*)

Now it seems dere wuz some kinda trouble 'twixt a brother 'n sister.... Dat girl started walkin', an' wan't turnin' back fer nothin'....
(*She points to the sky.*)

Kisos, th' sun, seein' dis trouble, an' bein' kinda tender-hearted, tried ta fix it.

(She gestures for each plant in the story, shaping with her hands the small blackberry vines, the blueberry bush, the strawberry plant as though they are growing into place in front of her. Then as she talks, she mimes the actions.)

Sendin' down some a' her rays ta th' ground in front a' dat woman's path, dere sprung up a plant, all tangled up wi' thorns an' li' l sweet black berries—these wuz th' first blackberries. Kisos was figgerin' dem thorns would ketch th' edge a' her skirt, and th' berries'd give 'er sumthin' good ta eat... .

(She mimes the woman's actions.)

But dat sister, steppin' o'er it, kept right on walkin'.... She wuz angry. So Kisos tried agin. Sendin' down some a' her rays 'til a bush sprung up, leaves branchin' out, wi' soft juicy-lookin' berries ... these wuz th' first blueberries. But she pushed right on through dem branches an' kept on goin', not stoppin' for nothin'. Now her brother wuz gittin' desperate.

(She reaches her arms up to the sky.)

Reachin' up ta th' sky, he's callin' out, "Kisos, ta wlioni ni, kizi n'mamihon!"
An' Kisos figgered out what ta do.

(She reaches out to one side and then the other, pulling toward her heart, like shaping a ball of light, which she then aims down toward the ground.)

Takin' some a' dat love th' brother had in his heart, an' some a' de love dat sister had, an' mixin' it up wi' some a' her rays ...

(She kneels, her hands reaching out to the ground.)

Kisos sent it down ta th' earth....where dat girl's tears wuz fallin'...

(Sudden spotlight, like a small ray of sunlight, hits the floor in front of the desk where MOLLY OCKETT's *hands are aimed. She lovingly gestures the plant into shape.)*

Where dem rays hit th' ground, a li'l plant come up ... wi' li'l green leaves an' red seedy berries. Mskikominsak.
Dese was th' first strawberries.

(*Standing up, she mimes the sister's reaction.*)

> Now dat girl looked down, saw all dem berries 'round her, an' she
> stopped!
> She bent down,

(MOLLY OCKETT *is bending down, intently focused, reaching out, just about to pick
that imaginary strawberry from the middle of the patch of sunlight.*)

> ... picked one a' dem berries....

(MOLLY OCKETT *picks a berry, and, smiling, slowly starts to bring it toward her
mouth.* MOLLY MARIE *suddenly gets up from the table, disturbed, and slams a book
down, scattering papers to the floor. Without saying a word, she stomps off, stage left.*
MOLLY OCKETT *stops moving and speaking, staring after her in shock.*)

(*All lights quickly fade off. End scene.*)

Scene 2

Introduction Song: "Gawi Squassis" Lullaby.

(*Stage and audience are in total darkness when the scene starts.* MOLLY OCKETT *is
sitting on the floor, stage right, singing.*)

MOLLY OCKETT
> Gawi squassis, squassis, gawi
> Gawi, squassis, abazi
> Gawi, squassis, wligawi
> Gawi, sguassis, wligwasi

(*Still in the darkness,* MOLLY MARIE *is heard stumbling in, half asleep. She trips over
a book and mutters a curse.*)

MOLLY MARIE
> Shit. Where is that light...? mmm....

(*She is heard fumbling along the back wall, groping for a light switch.*)
(*Suddenly, the desk lamp turns on by itself.*)

(MOLLY MARIE *looks up above her, her back to the audience, puzzled. She slowly turns, makes her way to her desk and sits down heavily. She groggily tries to concentrate and then starts to slumps at her desk, spilling over with papers.*)

(*Mumbling sleepily.*) Mmm … just a little nap … just … a little….

(*She drops her head to her arms, and, as she shifts her weight, falling asleep, first one paper, then a few more, then an old dusty book falls to the floor, nearly splitting its spine as pages fly out of it. She dozes, oblivious.*)

(MOLLY OCKETT *slowly gets up and stares at* MOLLY MARIE, *pondering what to do. She picks up* MOLLY MARIE's *coffee cup from the desk, sniffs it, and makes a face in disgust. She sets it down, reaches into her pouch, brings out a bag of herbs, and sifts some into the cup, stirring it with her finger.*)

MOLLY OCKETT
This'll do. A li'l snakeroot fer th' heart, an' some ginsen'll git ya up an' goin'….

(*She finds a bottle of spring water on the floor and reads the label.*)

(*Approvingly.*) Mmph. Poland Spring. I 'member dat place.

(*She pours a bit into the cup, stirs it with her finger, sets it down on* MOLLY MARIE's *desk, and sits on the bench to wait. She softly sings the "Greeting Feast Song," drumming with her fingertips.*)

MOLLY OCKETT
(*Singing.*) Hey, gwanudaaay (*pause*) ah-we-ah, gwanuday
Hey, gwanuday, ah-we-ah yok-yo way
Ah yok, yo way, ah-we-ah, we-ah yok, yo way
Ah yok, yo way, ah-we-ah, we-ah yok, yo way

(*As she sings, center stage and stage right lights slowly come up.*)

(MOLLY MARIE *slowly starts to wake; she stretches one arm across the desk, and a few more papers fall to the floor. She starts to groggily lift her head.*)

MOLLY MARIE
Mmmm … mm….

(*She sits up, looks around for her coffee mug, finds it, and, holding it expectantly in both hands, takes a sip.*)

(*Shocked.*) Mmph!

(*She makes a terrible face, abruptly bolts up out of her chair, and forcefully throws the mug away in disgust! It loudly shatters into her wastebasket.*)

(*Disturbed.*) Unhh! God, that was disgusting!

(*Plaintively.*) Mph ... coffee. I need coffee....

(MOLLY MARIE *stands, still half asleep, surprised and a little dismayed at the mess, realizing the loss.* MOLLY OCKETT *shakes her head, solemnly, smiling. She pulls an identical mug out of her pouch and sets it carefully down in the same spot on the desk. She reverently pours something else into the cup, fills it with the same spring water, and stirs it with her finger. She sits back down on the bench, waiting expectantly.*)

MOLLY OCKETT
> (*Indulgently and matter-of-factly.*) Snakeroot or bitter root, don' matter to me. Drink it up, girl. We got sum talkin' ta do.

(MOLLY MARIE, *still in somewhat of a daze, turns and sees her cup, on the desk, whole again! She stares at the shattered pieces in the basket, and gestures between the two, one whole, one broken, puzzling. She sits down, and slowly, suspiciously, turns the new cup in her hands, wondering. Holding it carefully with both hands, she sniffs it approvingly, takes a cautious sip, slowly savoring it, and then hungrily drains it.*)

(MOLLY OCKETT *is watching carefully, waiting.* MOLLY MARIE *starts talking to herself, trying to figure out what she's feeling.*)

MOLLY MARIE
> (*Disappointed.*) What the hell am I doing? This isn't relevant—none of it....

(*She starts to pace, gesturing at her desk, searching for words, confused.*)

> This is just folklore, fantasy, settlers and Indians pseudo-drama bullshit. (*Strained.*) I've got real work to do!
>
> (*Running her fingers through the papers, idly.*) All these texts ... I don't need this! Who wants it? I had it down, clear! I need to be clear....

(*She hesitates, and then suddenly slams her fist on the table, justifying her anger.*)

> I don't wanna know! All these papers, all this stuff—if I look at those words and get any kind of meaning behind 'em, it'd be my

responsibility! (*Slapping her palm on her chest.*) Mine! I don't want that responsibility!

(*Blue light up on small bench backstage left.*)

(*She walks away from the desk, to the stage left back corner, and sits on the bench, like a little girl, uncomfortably. Throughout this speech she is nervous, frustrated, searching for some way to shake off the memories, the responsibility, the history. She becomes so strained that when she collapses in tears at the end of this speech there is a tangible sense of old, conflicted, grief.*)

(*Scornfully gesturing.*) What good did knowing any of this do for them? Any of them....
I don't want people looking down at me like they did Grandpa! Momma didn't need it. Ask her yourself.

(*Sarcastically, imitating her mother's voice.*) "Me, I'm jes' a li'l white girl, don't nobody ask no questions."

(*Her voice cracking.*) Who's gonna care! ... or even notice. You don't know—none a' you know!
(*Painfully.*) God, it was easier when I didn't know.

(*She goes back to her desk and slumps into the chair, disheartened, bitter. She continues to argue, searching for some way to shake off whoever she thinks is driving her.*)

What if ...

(*She sits upright.*)

... all right, what if I'm not Indian enough?
What if nobody believes me, and that full-blood bitch starts dragging my ass through the mud ... who's gonna claim me then?

(*She angrily throws her hands out, as if forcing someone away.*)

Get off me! Go find another Indian to kick around! I don't want your stories!

(*She sits defiantly at her desk, arms tensing on the chair.*)

(*Frustrated.*) Damn. This isn't where I wanna be! It's easier just being white.... Let someone else be the Indian!

(*With a grand sweep, she knocks most of the papers and books off the desk. They slam and crash to the floor. She slumps at her desk again, head on her arms, sobbing heavily with frustration.* MOLLY OCKETT *watches quietly for a moment, and then gets up and starts walking around behind her, speaking soothingly but firmly to* MOLLY MARIE.)

MOLLY OCKETT
      (*Softly.*) Gawi, gawi, squassis ... wli nanawalmezi ... hushhhh ...
      Old Mali has somethin' she's been wantin' ta say ta ya ... th'
      ancestors did th' choosin', girl ... ain't your responsibility
      nohow....

(*She gestures to upper stage right. She is speaking the words of* OLD MALI *to comfort* MOLLY MARIE.)

      Ol' Mali, she sez, yer th' young one now....
      She sez, yer th' voice a' th' old ones....
      (*Smiling lovingly.*) Uh huh, she's right there beside ya, always has
      been ... holdin' ya up since ya wuz small.... She sez, now yer th'
      one holdin' pen an' paper....

(MOLLY OCKETT *softly starts to put her arms around* MOLLY MARIE, *then gently restrains herself. Instead she hums the lullaby, softly, until* MOLLY MARIE *starts hesitantly humming it with her as she stops crying.* MOLLY OCKETT *drifts away, exiting stage left. After a moment,* MOLLY MARIE *stops crying and sits up slowly, looking around confused.*)

MOLLY MARIE
      Hm-mm, mm-mmm....

      (*To herself.*) Wake up ... wake up!

(*A little dazed, as though coming out of a trance, she stretches. She reaches out for a letter that sits folded on her desk. As she unfolds it, she remembers it as something needing her attention.*)

      Oh ... yeh ... I wanted to read this poem that Shelly LaValley sent
      me.

      (*Skeptically.*) LaValley? Yeh, right. That doesn't sound Indian.

(*She reads the poem, musing over its words, thinking about her feelings.*)

For a fleeting moment, I recognized myself ...
Then it vanished away ... the image turned cloudy, and gray
A snowy TV station, the image wouldn't cooperate
I smiled, I laughed, but all in vain ...
I couldn't escape the thought of myself turning gray.

(*She touches her face, shifts her weight—this is bringing up uncomfortable feelings.*)

Who was I, this self in the process of such change?
Who did I want to be?
Where am I going?
Maybe insane ...

(*She cautiously glances off to her side, then shakes her head no.*)

The old self is probably laughing, looking the other way.
The new self is confused, and needs answers to explain.
To explain the transformation and fear of the dark.
The new self sees images and hears voices beating on my head like
     a drum
not relenting or giving up ...
The voices almost whispering in my ear—
"Hear me!" they say, but I shrug them off in fear.
Then I glimpse a reflection of my old self
And for a moment I grasp it,
and feel clear ...

(*She turns the pages over and starts to read the first line again.*)

For a fleeting moment, I ...

(*She sets the papers down and looks straight out toward the audience, remembering.*)

(*Slowly, sadly.*) When I was a little girl, I used to hear drumming.
Drumming, at night when I was alone and trying to sleep ...
drumming, and voices ...

(*She shifts her weight, and sits firmly upright, no longer soft and vulnerable. She sets her palms determinedly on the desk.*)

(*Confidently, bitter.*) I had to work really hard to make them go away.

(M OLLY M ARIE *gets up, straightens her shoulders, and walks away, exiting stage left.*)

(*All lights down immediately after she exits, end scene.*)

Scene 3

Introduction Song: "Quaboag Rock House"

Stage and audience are in total darkness during the song. No characters on stage. M OLLY O CKETT *is singing offstage.*

M OLLY O CKETT
    Hey, kwa hu-wa, kwa hu-wa, wa he-ey-ya
    Hey, kwa hu-wa, kwa hu-wa, wa hey
    Kwa hu-wa, wa he-ey-ya, kwa hu-wa, wa he-ey-ya
    Kwa hu-wa, kwa hu-wa, kwa-hu-wa, wa hey
    Kwa hu-wa, kwa hu-wa, kwa-hu-wa, wa hey

(*When the song ends, light come up stage right on the bench. Center light on desk comes up about halfway.*)

(M OLLY M ARIE *walks jauntily in with a book in her hand and a newspaper under her arm, singing along to herself, beating out a rhythm on the book. Her mood is upbeat, playful, as though she's just come in from a long walk outside. She walks behind the desk and starts to pull the chair out to sit, then stops herself abruptly, making it clear that's not really where she wants to be. She looks around for a different place to sit, and goes to the bench stage right. She sits facing the audience, opens the newspaper, and starts to read, still humming cheerfully.*)

M OLLY M ARIE
    Hmm huh-hmm ... la la la la la....

(*She scans the page, reading headlines and dismissing them. Note: Any contemporary headlines of ethnic tension, refugees, war, and genocide may be substituted for the given dialogue.*)

    (*Matter-of-factly, with no emotion.*) Kosovo. Refugees. War and destruction ... nope. Israel and Palestine? Unh-unh.

(She noisily flips the page, reading other headlines as they come up.)

More refugees. Ethnic Albanians....
(Sarcastically.) See! That's where "displaying your culture and tra-ditions" gets you—erased!

(She flips the page again.)

Editorials ... nah. Ah, theater! Let's see....
(Pompously.) "molly has her say—the voices of Abenaki women, past and present...." Mmph. Boring. Is there anything worth reading in here? Anything at all?

(Center stage light rises slightly.)

(MOLLY OCKETT walks somberly and soundlessly in, wearing a green French–and–Indian–War–style wool regimental coat. She casually sets herself cross–legged, Indian style, on top of MOLLY MARIE's desk, amid the papers and books, facing the audience and turned slightly toward MOLLY MARIE. She looks for a particular book, finds it, and carefully opens it up. MOLLY MARIE shudders slightly, as though a cool breeze just blew through, but she doesn't see MOLLY OCKETT. Then MOLLY OCKETT waves her left hand above the desk lamp without looking up, and it turns itself on.)

(MOLLY OCKETT reads intently, quietly. MOLLY MARIE discovers something in the paper that surprises her. Her mood changes abruptly, and she snaps the newspaper.)

MOLLY MARIE
    Whoa!

(MOLLY OCKETT starts reading phrases aloud from her book, an account of Rogers' Raid, an attack on the Abenaki village of St. Francis in 1759, when MOLLY OCKETT was a young girl. MOLLY MARIE reads from the newspaper, an account of the Vermont Eugenics program in the 1920s and '30s that judged many Abenaki men and women as "degenerate" and "unfit to breed," and sterilized and institutionalized them. The two readings of colonial efforts at extermination, past and present, alternate, and resonate with each other.)

MOLLY OCKETT
    "Rogers' Raid. 1759. Destruction of an Indin Village. Passin' up the Hudson...." *(She looks up, reminding herself, nodding.)* That'd be th' Mahicanituck. Den up th' lake, Champlain, Bitawbakw, an' on ta th' north....

"Rogers wuz seven days in reachin' Missisquoi Bay, seekin' a revenge on th' Indins...."

MOLLY MARIE
"The Perkins Solution. 1925. A Half Century Ago, University of Vermont's Henry Perkins Proposed to Cleanse the Vermont Gene Pool by Sterilizing Those He Considered Unfit...."

MOLLY OCKETT
(*Reading from the book.*) "Concealin' his boats, he pushed on thru th' woods ta Saint Francis.... (*She looks up at the audience.*) Th' Indins was wholly unsuspicious a' th' danger."

MOLLY MARIE
"In 1925 ...

(*She hesitates, as if the date is familiar, and writes it down.*)

... In 1925, there seemed nothing sinister about the Eugenics Survey, combining research and education with a plan for the betterment of the white race." Hmph?

MOLLY OCKETT
(*Bitterly, as she looks toward* MOLLY MARIE.) "Th' conquest would insure safety ta th' frontiers a' New England."

MOLLY MARIE
"The survey singled out certain families in particular for scrutiny ... among them the so-called 'gypsies' whose Indian blood contributed to their degeneracy."

MOLLY MARIE AND MOLLY OCKETT
"Radical measures ..."

MOLLY MARIE
"Perkins wrote ..."

MOLLY OCKETT
(*Wryly.*) "... was needed ta protect th' King's colonies."

MOLLY MARIE
"... would reduce the number of costly, degenerate people."

MOLLY OCKETT

(*Bitterly angry, spoken immediately after* MOLLY MARIE.) Degenerate people! (*Reading.*) "Disguised as Indins, Rogers an' his men went on ta reconnoiter, sneakin' inta the village ...

MOLLY MARIE

"Tribal members told stories of government encampments, field hospitals...."

MOLLY MARIE AND MOLLY OCKETT

"... luring Indians ..."

MOLLY MARIE

(*Blandly.*) "for free medical care." Hmm.

MOLLY OCKETT

(*Angrily.*) "... ta their death!" (*Reading sarcastically, she waves her hand in a grand gesture.*) "Th' enterprise convinced th' Indins that th' hand a' vengeance wuz upon 'em, an' th' frontiers wuz safe from savage attacks!" (*Disgusted.*) Nobody wuz safe wi' dem soldiers!

MOLLY MARIE

(*Sad, puzzled.*) "Free medical care. Sterilization, hospitalization, and institutionalization. Eliminating unwanted births. Breeding better Vermont citizens."

(MOLLY MARIE *slams down the newspaper in disgust and shifts around, uncomfortably.* MOLLY OCKETT *slowly closes the book and looks sadly over at* MOLLY MARIE.)

MOLLY OCKETT

(*Softly, insistently.*) Ya forgot ta read th' names, Squassis.

(MOLLY MARIE *looks around, dazed for a moment, and reluctantly picks up the paper again, finds the article, and starts slowly reading the list of names, mispronouncing them awkwardly, pausing after each one, wondering at who these people are.* MOLLY OCKETT *recites the names along with her, half a beat ahead or behind. For her, speaking each name clearly conjures up vivid and distinct memories of particular people and families.*)

MOLLY MARIE AND MOLLY OCKETT

(*Slowly.*) Tamakwa, Michel, Taxus, Obomsawin, Sabattis, Portneuf, Saint Francis, Capino, Sadoques, Lavelle....

(MOLLY MARIE *is shocked at the realization that her mother's maiden name is among those on the list. She stands up at the shock, newspaper still in hand. She is running dates around in her head, struggling to piece the memories together.*)

MOLLY MARIE

(*Surprised.*) Lavelle? (*Reciting from memory.*) Flora Lavelle, 1925. Lavelle ... 1925.... (*Shocked.*) Momma was born then! God, her mother must have escaped!
Is that why she'd never go back?

(*She steps sideways, and suddenly shifts into her memory of her mother, talking back, stubbornly.*)

"Unh-unh, yer not getting me back ta that Indin place," she'd say, "Too many spirits there...."

(*Sadly.*) Oh, mamma....

(MOLLY MARIE *looks lost. She stares down at the newspaper in her hand as if it is to blame for her disturbance, and then abruptly and viciously shreds the newspaper into pieces, scattering them, trying to make them go away. She slumps back down on the bench, despairingly.*)

(MOLLY OCKETT *calmly watches. She slowly steps down from her perch on the desk as she starts talking. She gestures to* MOLLY MARIE, *as she describes the scene the night before Rogers' Raid, explaining the various strategies for coping with the impending threat.* MOLLY MARIE *just sits, staring sadly ahead, not reacting to* MOLLY OCKETT's *words.*)

MOLLY OCKETT

(*Reminiscing, smiling sadly at the thoughts.*) Me, I wuz jus' a young'un, hidin' in th' bushes 'roun' de meetin' house....

(*Gesturing around.*) Some of 'em wuz dancin', some wuz singin', some drinkin' rum th' Francois brung 'em ... when th' message come, wa'n't no agreement among 'em....

(*She leans toward* MOLLY MARIE, *and then lunges suddenly across the stage in front of the desk, toward the audience, with her hand raised like a weapon.*)

Some got weapons an' run off hollerin'....

(*Savagely shouting.*) "Le's kill all de English!"

(*She gestures away, behind the desk, into the darkness.*)

> (*Sadly, solemnly.*) Lot of 'em took th' childr'n an' hid in de ravine out back....

(*She leans down conspiratorially to* MOLLY MARIE.)

> Dey didn' wanna believe it, neither, Moll, same's you.... (*Sarcastic.*) Some thought speakin' French an' bein' "civilized" wuz protection enuff.

(MOLLY OCKETT *stands, waiting for a reaction.* MOLLY MARIE *kneels down and starts to pick up the papers. She drops them in a pile, frustrated, and starts to walk back toward the desk, gesturing, pointing at the papers and the desk.*)

MOLLY MARIE

> Why can't I just get away from this stuff?

(*Light on bench stage right goes down when* MOLLY MARIE *moves away.*)

> What good are these stories? All these books, all these words....

(*She gestures straight at* MOLLY OCKETT, *although it is clear she does not see her.*)

> All these dead people!

(MOLLY MARIE *tries to walk around behind the desk, to get into her chair, but* MOLLY OCKETT *is standing in her way, and* MOLLY MARIE *stops, sensing the barrier.*)

MOLLY OCKETT

> Some thought schoolin' wuz th' answer—git th' alnobak readin' an' writin' like th' English. But schoolin' gits ya too far off course, less'n ya know where yer goin'....

(MOLLY MARIE *looks longingly at her desk, standing behind and slightly stage left of it.* MOLLY OCKETT *stands in the way, with her back to the audience, facing* MOLLY MARIE.)

MOLLY MARIE

> (*Pleading, her arms out.*) Where can I go with any of this?

(MOLLY OCKETT *takes off the green coat, and, turning to face the audience, throws it stage left, to land in front of* MOLLY MARIE's *path.* MOLLY MARIE, *shocked, sees the coat fall to the ground, and stares unbelievingly at it.*)

MOLLY OCKETT
(*Soothingly.*) 'Member de story Nokomes used ta tell ya?

(*As* MOLLY OCKETT *is speaking,* MOLLY MARIE *slowly walks around the desk, from rear stage left, toward the space in front of the desk, as though entranced.* MOLLY OCKETT *follows her like a shadow, walking in step behind her. The two move slowly, synchronously.*)

'Bout two sisters followin' th' sun all afternoon, lookin' fer berries?

(*Light on floor in front of desk comes up.* OLD MALI *light also turns on.*)

(*When they are both in front of the desk,* MOLLY MARIE *suddenly stops, her enchantment broken, and turns back.*)

MOLLY MARIE
(*Assertively.*) Maybe I should start over. A different thought. A different thesis. Something less grim.

MOLLY OCKETT
(*Gently, continuing the story, calming and guiding* MOLLY MARIE *with her voice.*) The sun wuz goin' down, ever'thin' lookin' dark.

MOLLY MARIE
(*Musing.*) What would Momma say?

MOLLY OCKETT
(*Singing.*) Hey yanna, hey yanna, hey yanna hey....

MOLLY MARIE
What kind of a story would mamma tell if she were here?

MOLLY OCKETT
(*Laughing.*) Dem two lazy girls'd been talkin' an' laughin', eatin' more'n they wuz pickin'. Badger come along sayin' "there be more berries in t'other meadow."

(MOLLY MARIE *stares at her desk.* MOLLY OCKETT *keeps drawing her into the story.*)

MOLLY MARIE
Maybe it's just too much.

MOLLY OCKETT
An' now dey be so busy rangin' dey wuz lost....

MOLLY MARIE
(*Longingly.*) But where can I go?

(*As* MOLLY OCKETT *talks, she slowly, gracefully lowers herself down to sit cross-legged in front of the desk, stage left, angled toward the audience.* MOLLY MARIE *simultaneously lowers herself to the floor, although more wobbly, to sit cross-legged stage right, angled toward the audience, mirroring* MOLLY OCKETT.)

MOLLY OCKETT
But e'en dem young girls know how ta make a wigwam, lay a bed a' spruce boughs, make a safe an' warm place ta sleep. (*Singing.*) Hey yanna, hey yanna, hey yanna hey....

MOLLY MARIE
(*Sadly smiling at the memory.*) When Momma used ta read ta me.... (*Brightening, she picks up the thread of the story* MOLLY OCKETT *is trying to tell her.*) Let's see, how'd that one go about Badger and the two sisters? Badger ... and two sisters ... and somethin' about bein' lazy.

(*She laughs a little, and puts her head back, telling the story from memory.* MOLLY OCKETT *gestures along with the telling, to indicate the badgers sunning in the meadow, the girls picking berries, the sun going down, and wandering off. As* MOLLY MARIE *relaxes into the telling, her gestures start to mirror those of* MOLLY OCKETT.)

One day Badger and his brother were sunning themselves in a meadow when along came two foolish girls. They'd been sent to pick blueberries, but, being lazy, spent the whole morning talking....

(*She waggles her finger in disapproval, smiling knowingly.*)

"You're not lookin' in the right place," said Badger, grinning.

(*Both women gesture the sun going down.*)

"Follow the sun to the going-down place....

(*Both women spread their arms to indicate fields full of berries.*)

There you'll find more berries than you ever imagined!"

From left: Shelly LaValley as Molly Marie and Marge Bruchac as Molly Ockett, performance at Smith College. Photo by Kevin Downey, May 8, 1999.

(*Eagerly.*) "Quick," cried younger girl. "Let's find 'em 'fore someone else does!" and away they went!

(MOLLY OCKETT *picks up the thread of the story, enjoying the fact that, finally, they are on the same track.*)

MOLLY OCKETT
(*Shaking her head.*)

Yer mother should a' warned ya! Now, in th' mornin' dem two girls wake and dere be two men, big shining eyes, black hair, handsome bucks ... jes' like yer father, Molly ... and dey be sayin', "We be tired a' livin' alone."

MOLLY MARIE
(*Chuckling sarcastically.*) I never did understand that. "Two handsome men, tired of livin' alone." Hah!

MOLLY OCKETT
> Now dem two girls get ta thinkin' husbands takin' care of 'em sounds like a good thing ... an' off dey go, wit' dem two men, ta live wit' 'em in a blue land, no trees, no water, nothin' but sky all 'round....

MOLLY MARIE
> (*Dreamily.*) That sky land had lodges, clothes, food, all they needed. But they were told, "Never look under that flat rock...."

MOLLY MARIE AND MOLLY OCKETT
> (*Boldly, smiling.*) ... but bein' smart Indin girls, sure tha's jus' what they do!

MOLLY OCKETT
> Under dat rock dere be a hole, lookin' way down ta trees an' earth an' rivers below. Den dey know dey been turned inta....

MOLLY MARIE
> What was it they turned into?

MOLLY OCKETT
> Alakwasak.

MOLLY MARIE AND MOLLY OCKETT
> Sky land people.

MOLLY OCKETT
> Wit' stars for husbands. An' den dey be hungry for dirt under th' feet. (*Sadly.*) But dey don' know th' way back.

(MOLLY OCKETT *abruptly stops speaking, and gets up.* MOLLY MARIE *senses the break in the flow of the story, and also gets up, alarmed.*)

MOLLY MARIE
> (*Surprised and disappointed.*) Hey! Is that the end of the story?

MOLLY OCKETT
> (*Tenderly.*) Wid'out th' songs, dem girls can't git home. Only a gran'mother kin call one a' dem lost girls back, an' if she ain't listenin'....

(MOLLY OCKETT *turns her head as though she hears something calling her. She turns back.*)

(*Apologetically.*) My time's runnin' out, girl.

(MOLLY MARIE *looks despairingly around the stage, not knowing what to do.*)

MOLLY MARIE
But I'm sure there was more to the story.... (*Forlornly.*) Time's runnin' out.

(MOLLY MARIE *walks over to the bench stage right, and sits down, disheartened.* MOLLY OCKETT *hesitates, and then moves slowly toward her, as though she has very little energy left, and kneels down in front of* MOLLY MARIE *to share one last memory. She gestures expressively as she tells the story, hoping* MOLLY MARIE *can hear her.*)

(*Lights up slightly on bench stage right.*)

MOLLY OCKETT
Molly, 'member dat day in th' meadow? You an' dat sister a' yourn out pickin' berries when dat bear roared up outa nowhere?

(MOLLY OCKETT *lifts both arms up and out to represent the bear.*)

(*Sarcastically.*) She went screamin' off—her wit' all her supposed powers....

(*She flings her left arm aside to represent the sister running off, and then gestures tenderly with open palm toward* MOLLY MARIE.)

(*Proudly.*) But you, you started singin' ta old Awassos....

(MOLLY MARIE *starts absentmindedly humming a lullaby.*)

MOLLY MARIE
(*Humming.*) Mm-hmm, hm-mmm, mm, mm, hm-mmm....

MOLLY OCKETT
Dat ol' lullaby ... dat's right, th' one Flora taught ya. (*Nodding approvingly.*) An' ever'body watchin', wide-eyed, while dat big ol' bear set right down and let ya dump dat whole basket a' berries in front a' him, not growlin' or e'en takin' a swipe 'til you walked away, still singin'....

(*She pauses, savoring the memory.*)

(*Smiling ruefully.*) You Indin girls don' e'en know what you got....

(MOLLY OCKETT *creakily gets up and very slowly, looking surprisingly tired and old, turns and starts to walk away, toward front stage left.* MOLLY MARIE *shakes herself out of her reverie, and gets up.*)

(*Light suddenly goes down stage right.*)

MOLLY MARIE

> (*Dismissing the memories.*) Well, it's just another one of those old Indian folktales.

(MOLLY MARIE *turns toward her desk, about to shift back into her scholarly mode.* MOLLY OCKETT *is bending down, picking up her green coat from the floor.*)

> I'd best get back to work.

(MOLLY MARIE *starts toward her desk.* MOLLY OCKETT *suddenly stands and turns, flinging the coat back to the floor stage left. She reaches dramatically back toward* MOLLY MARIE, *both arms outstretched, and, with enormous effort of will, catches her attention very much by surprise.*)

MOLLY OCKETT

> (*Loudly, urgently.*) Skwamiskwa!

(MOLLY MARIE *stops, frozen, startled like a deer caught in the headlights, and stares straight at* MOLLY OCKETT, *actually seeing her for the first time. Her eyes are locked on her, and her shoulders are hunched up in surprise. She slowly relaxes as* MOLLY OCKETT *speaks to her.*)

MOLLY MARIE

> (*Timidly, eyes wide.*) What?

(MOLLY OCKETT *smiles, knowing she finally has* MOLLY MARIE's *conscious attention.*)

MOLLY OCKETT

> (*Gently.*) Skwamiskwa....

(*She speaks very slowly, clearly, gesturing with her hand to her ear, and to her mouth.*)

> When it gits dark, squassis, lissen.
> Lissen fer th' stories.

(MOLLY OCKETT *sits slowly on the floor, stage left, cross-legged, watching and wait- ing.* MOLLY MARIE's *vision blurs, and she loses sight of* MOLLY OCKETT. *She looks*

cautiously around, wonderingly, and then, slowly, sits down in her chair, at her familiar desk, pondering. She moves a book and discovers a small sweetgrass basket on the desk. It is the same one that MOLLY OCKETT *had in her hand at the beginning of the play.*)

MOLLY MARIE
(*In a very small voice.*) Oh!

(*Slowly,* MOLLY MARIE *picks up the basket and turns it over and around, studying it.* MOLLY OCKETT *watches her carefully , and then starts talking, picking up where she left off in telling the First Strawberries story at the end of Scene One, timing the telling to match* MOLLY MARIE's *exploration of the sweetgrass basket.*)

MOLLY OCKETT
Now dat woman saw dat li'l plant, an' she stopped!

(MOLLY MARIE *opens the basket. Inside is a single red strawberry.* MOLLY MARIE *takes it out and holds it up, between thumb and forefinger, examining it in such a way that her thought, "Should I taste it?" is clear to the audience.*)

She bent down ... picked one a' dem berries ...

(MOLLY MARIE *gently bites into the strawberry, eyes closed.*)

... an' tasted it. An' it wuz th' sweetest taste.

(MOLLY MARIE *smiles, savoring the taste.*)

Th' taste a' forgivin' an' rememberin' all mixed together.
Anhaldamawi kassiwi palilawlakwa.
Wlibomkanni, skwamiskwa.

(MOLLY MARIE *opens her eyes, and slowly pans her gaze across the audience, with a knowing, gentle look, as though seeing beloved friends and relatives who are long past. When her gaze reaches* MOLLY OCKETT, *she smiles a gentle, apologetic half-smile of recognition. They are still smiling, eyes locked on each other, unmoving, as the lights fade.*)

(*All lights slowly fade to total darkness.*)

END

Historical Sources

The text of *molly has her say* includes quotations from historical writings about the Abenaki, personal experiences, regional memories, and traditional songs and stories. Following are some notes on particular sources and additional background information.

QUOTATION: "Amid all this stillness ... unpronounceable language, strike his ear."
SOURCE: Oliver N. Bacon, *History of Natick* (Boston, Damrell and Moore Printers, 1856), 20.

Reverend John Eliot ministered to the eastern Massachusetts Indians in the mid-seventeenth century, founding "praying villages" where Indians adopted English dress and political organization, and helped Eliot translate biblical texts into the Indian language. But settlements of Christian Indians, like the Nipmuc at Natick during King Philip's War, and the French Catholic Abenaki at St. Francis in 1759, became easy targets for attacks by white soldiers.

QUOTATION: "It was a new light when my guide gave me Indian names."
SOURCE: Henry David Thoreau, March 5, 1858, *The Journal of Henry D. Thoreau*, edited by Bradford Torrey and Francis H. Allen (Boston, Houghton Mifflin Company, 1949), 295.

Henry David Thoreau, like many early travelers to New England, found Algonkian languages to be more sophisticated than expected. Anthropologists and linguists still puzzle over the complexities of proto-Algonkian origins, dialects, and languages, and the concepts and beliefs imbedded in traditional words and place names. The words and definitions in this text come from a variety of printed and oral sources.

QUOTATION: "Warriors way on back, reduced to lumberjacks and basketmakers...."
SOURCE: Personal and regional family oral histories.

Native families throughout the Northeast, my own included, survived the nineteenth and twentieth centuries in part by marketing their skills at medicine, hunting, lumbering, guiding, and basket-making to their Anglo-American neighbors. Yet northeastern Native peoples who remained in their homelands, rather than moving to western reservations, were often mistakenly labeled as "remnants of vanishing tribes," rather than viable communities. If they looked or acted stereotypically "Indian," they were typically labeled "the last of their tribe."

> QUOTATION: "Story of Molly Ockett and Sabattis. Molly Ockett often boasted of her noble descent ... white man gaining the supremacy of the Indian in this section of Maine."
> SOURCE: Arthur D. Woodrow, *Metalluk, the Last of the Cooashaukes* (Rumford, Maine: Rumford Publishing 1928), 71.

Molly Ockett, c. 1740–1816, was a Pequawket Abenaki "Indian Doctress," an herbal medicine woman. As a young woman, she witnessed Robert Rogers' bloody raid on the Abenaki mission of St. Francis in 1759. She spent most of her adult life traversing northern New England, ministering to whites and Indians alike. She was especially fond of relating historical events from her parents' and grandparents' time, from the Indian point of view, emphasizing the savage behavior of white invaders in Indian homelands.

> QUOTATION: "O, come on ye painted Redskins.... And Lovewell closed his eyes in death."
> SOURCE: Anonymous, 1726, excerpted in Ernest E. Bisbee, *The State O' Maine Scrap Book* (Lancaster, New Hampshire: Bisbee Press, 1940), 26.

In the late-nineteenth and early-twentieth centuries, towns throughout New England reenacted local history with frontier pageants that depicted Native peoples as primitive savages, attacking civilized white heroes. These stereotypes, preserved in dramatic pseudo-historical plays, novels, and poetry, still color modern perceptions of regional history.

QUOTATION: "Petition to the General Court of Massachusetts ...
Dunstable, 1724."
SOURCE: J. W. Meader, *The Merrimack River* (Boston: B. B. Russell,
1869), 228.

During times of Indian warfare, English and American colonists
placed bounties on Indian scalps. Although scalping had been practiced by some indigenous peoples prior to European contact,
European colonists turned scalp-hunting into a source of profit.
After killing ten Indians in Wakefield, Lovewell and his crew, including the local minister, stalked a peaceful encampment of Pequawkets
that included Molly Ockett's kin. They were surprised by Paugus, and
the event was poeticized into a "duel" in this popular ballad.

QUOTATION: "Molly had been out one day and gathered a pail of
blueberries."
SOURCE: Arthur D. Woodrow, *Metalluk, the Last of the Cooashaukes*
(Rumford, Maine: Rumford Publishing 1928), 71.

This anecdote has been retold by many firsthand sources who knew
Molly personally. Molly Ockett was generous to her white friends,
although she found their religious restrictions curious. She was fond
of visiting churches, and speaking up wherever white women were
expected to remain quiet. She often ignored English and French
manners, despite long familiarity with white customs, demonstrating
a savvy play of innocence in order to do just as she pleased. Historian
Jo Radner cleverly labels this coded resistance, "the revenge of the
genteel squaw."

QUOTATION: "She walked outa that lodge ... picked one a' them
berries, an' tasted it."
SOURCE: Original adaptation of "The First Strawberries,"
inspired by versions told by Princess Redwing (Narragansett),
Gayle Ross (Cherokee), and Paulla Dove Jennings
(Narragansett).

The traditional story of "The First Strawberries" illustrates the importance of ritual forgiveness, practiced at the time of "Strawberry Thanksgiving," when fresh strawberries are shared among friends and relatives. Molly Marie's initial unwillingness to even hear the story reveals her inability to listen to, or forgive, the past.

> QUOTATION: "What if I'm not Indian enough? What if nobody believes me?"
> SOURCE: Personal and regional family oral histories.

Molly Marie is expressing the dilemma of indigenous people who have been subjected to Anglo-American definitions of political and cultural identity. In the late nineteenth century, the U.S. government, claiming sole right to determine Indian entitlements, started measuring Indian blood mixtures in order to "cleanse the white race" of mixed-bloods, remove Native people to reservations, and claim Indian lands. Algonkian peoples in New England have continued to identify each other primarily through traditional family and regional groupings, rather than government labels. Only a few Nations in the northeast are federally recognized as Native Americans, despite their persistent presence in traditional homelands.

> QUOTATION: "For a fleeting moment, I recognized myself ... I grasp it, and feel clear."
> SOURCE: Original poem by Shelly LaValley, April 1999 .

Shelly wrote this poem during early rehearsals, while the script was still a work in progress. It turned out to be the perfect expression of Molly Marie's inner conflict, and Shelly's growing awareness of her own Indian identity.

> QUOTATION: "Rogers' Raid 1759. Destruction of an Indian Village...."
> SOURCE: Numerous written and oral records.

Robert Rogers was employed by Sir Jeffrey Amherst to attack St. Francis (Odanak), a mission village near the St. Lawrence River in

Canada, as retribution for Indian raids on white settlements. His rangers wore distinctive green regimental coats with Indian leggings. The village had become a refuge for Abenaki and other New England Algonkians forced out by white settlement. Oral traditions of numerous survivors contradict Roger's inflated accounts of hundreds dead, and reveal multiple responses—some fled, some hid, and some fought.

> QUOTATION: "The Perkins Solution ... stories of government encampments, field hospitals."
> SOURCE: James Bandler, "The Perkins Solution," *The Sunday Rutland Herald*, Sunday Magazine, Rutland, Vermont, April 9, 1995.

Efforts at Abenaki extermination continued into the twentieth century under the guise of the Eugenics Survey, a project aimed at sterilizing criminals, the insane, and people of color in Vermont. The records were sealed for decades, and, when opened, revealed many Abenaki families, often listed by pseudonyms like "gypsies" or "pirates." Many families moved into neighboring states, changed their names to escape identification and prejudice, out of sight of the mainstream American society. The names listed in the play represent the primary families associated with the areas from Lake Champlain to Pequawket Country across Vermont and New Hampshire. In the late twentieth century, writers, researchers, and storytellers like myself gain our revenge by bringing into the open the stories, traditions, and histories our ancestors were forced to hide.

> QUOTATION: "Badger and the Two Sisters ... with stars for husbands."
> SOURCE: Original adaptation of "Badger and the Two Sisters" inspired by numerous written and oral versions.

This story, of two women who are so enchanted by the idea of an exotic new world that they become lost, serves as a metaphor for American Indian women who become lost in modern American culture. Without a grandmother to "call her home," Molly Marie's best hope of finding her way is to listen to the stories and learn the songs of the ancestors, so she can safely follow whatever track she chooses.

Published Plays by Native Women Playwrights in the United States and Canada

Compiled by
Ann Haugo
Illinois State University

Arkeketa, Annette. *Hokti*. In *Stories of Our Way: An Anthology of American Indian Plays*, edited by Hanay Geiogamah and Jaye T. Darby. Los Angeles, California: UCLA American Indian Studies Center, 1999.

Benjamin, Cheryl. *Change of Heart*. In *Both Sides: New Work from the Institute of American Indian Arts, 1993–1994*, edited by Cheryl Benjamin, Bunky Echo-Hawk, Patrice Farmer, Frank Hyde, Bessie Ann Joseph, Grace Lego, and Pat Natseway. Santa Fe: Institute of American Indian Arts, 1994.

Blue Spruce, Paula (Carol DuVal Whiteman). *Katsina*. *Quarterly Review of Literature*. Vol. 34 (1995).

Bouvier, Vye. *Teach Me the Ways of the Sacred Circle*. In *The Land Called Morning: Three Plays*. Saskatoon, Saskatchewan: Fifth House Publishers, 1986.

Charles, Monica. *Yanowis*. *The Indian Historian*. 4, no. 3 (1971): 46–51.

Clements, Marie Humber. *The Age of Iron* (excerpt). In *Taking the Stage: Selection from Plays by Canadian Women*, edited by Cynthia Zimmerman. 1994. Toronto: Playwrights Canada Press, 1995. 225–27.

Clements, Marie. *"Now Look What You Made Me Do (Black Lights)."* In *Prerogatives: Contemporary Plays by Women*. Winnipeg: Blizzard Publishing, 1998.

Clements, Marie. *The Unnatural and Accidental Women*. *Canadian Theatre Review* (Winter 2000): 53–88.

Colorado Sisters, The. *1992: Blood Speaks*. In *Contemporary Plays by Women of Color*, edited by Kathy A. Perkins and Roberta Uno. New York: Routledge, 1996.

Dauenhauer, Nora Marks. *Raven Loses His Nose*. In *Life Woven With Song*. Sun Tracks, Vol. 41. Tucson: University of Arizona Press, 2000.

Endres, Robin. *Ghost Dance*. In *Women and Words: Anthology/Les Femmes et les Mots: Anthologie*. Madeira Park, British Columbia: Harbour, 1984. 140–143.

Flather, Patti, and Leonard Linklater. *Sixty Below*. In *Staging the North: Twelve Canadian Plays*, edited by Sherrill Grace, Eve D'Aeth and Lisa Chalykoff. Toronto: Playwrights Canada Press, 1999. Originally published by Playwrights Canada Press, 1997.

Glancy, Diane. *American Gypsy: Six Native American Plays*. Norman: University of Oklahoma Press, 2002. Collection includes *American Gypsy*, *Jump Kiss*, *Lesser Wars*, *The Toad (Another Name for the Moon) Should Have a Bite*, *The Woman Who Loved House Trailers*, and *The Woman Who Was a Red Deer Dressed for the Deer Dance*.

Glancy, Diane. *Bull Star*. Aboriginal Voices 2, no. 3 (Fall 1995). See also Diane Glancy, *War Cries*.

Glancy, Diane. *Halfact*. SAIL: Studies in American Indian Literature 5, no. 1 (Spring 1993). See also Diane Glancy, *War Cries*.

Glancy, Diane. *The Truth Teller*. In *Stories of Our Way: An Anthology of American Indian Plays*, edited by Hanay Geiogamah and Jaye T. Darby. Los Angeles, California: UCLA American Indian Studies Center, 1999. See also Diane Glancy, *War Cries*.

Glancy, Diane. *War Cries*. Duluth, Minnesota: Holy Cow! Press, 1997. Collection includes the plays *The Best Fancy Dancer the Pushmataha Pow Wow's Ever Seen*, *Bull Star*, *Halfact*, *Mother of Mosquitos*, *One Horse*, *Segwohi*, *Stick Horse*, *The Truth Teller*, and *Weebjob*.

Glancy, Diane. *Weebjob*. In *Contemporary Plays by Women of Color*, edited by Kathy A. Perkins and Roberta Uno. New York: Routledge, 1996. See also Diane Glancy, *War Cries*.

Glancy, Diane. *The Woman Who Was a Red Deer Dressed for the Deer Dance*. In *Seventh Generation: An Anthology of Native American Plays*, edited by Mimi Gisolfi D'Aponte. New York: Theatre Communications Group, 1999.

Gomez, Terry. *Intertribal*. In *Contemporary Plays by Women of Color*, edited by Kathy A. Perkins and Roberta Uno. New York: Routledge, 1996.

Gomez, Terry. *Reunion*. In *Gathering Our Own: New Work from the Institute of American Indian Arts*, edited by Dana Dickerson, Brian Lush, and Ti Stalnaker. Santa Fe: Institute of American Indian Arts, 1996.

Hail, Raven. *The Raven and the Red Bird: Sam Houston and His Cherokee Wife*. Reprint. Mesa, Arizona: Raven Hail Books, 1993.

Howe, LeAnne, and Roxy Gordon. *Indian Radio Days*. In *Seventh Generation: An Anthology of Native American Plays*, edited by Mimi Gisolfi D'Aponte. New York: Theatre Communications Group, 1999.

Isom, Joan Shaddox. *Act Four: Four Plays for Special Days*. Oklahoma City, Oklahoma: Melody House, 1990.

Isom, Joan Shaddox. *Free Spirits*. Boston: Plays, Inc., 1975.

Isom, Joan Shaddox. *The Halloween Visitor: A One Act Play for Children*. Oklahoma City, Oklahoma: Melody House, 1978.

Isom, Joan Shaddox. *The Living Forest: A One-Act Play for Children*. Oklahoma City, Oklahoma, 1978.

Isom, Joan Shaddox. *Paint Me a Memory: A Short Thanksgiving Play for Children*. Oklahoma City, Oklahoma: Melody House, 1978.

Isom, Joan Shaddox. *A Pound of Miracles: A One-Act Christmas Play for Elementary Children*. Oklahoma City, Oklahoma: Melody House, 1978.

Kane, Margo. *Moonlodge*. In *An Anthology of Canadian Native Literature in English*, edited by Daniel David Moses and Terry Goldie. Toronto and New York: Oxford University Press, 1992.

Keams, Geraldine. *Flight of the Army Worms*. In *The Remembered Earth: An Anthology of Contemporary Native American Literature*, edited by Geary Hobson. Albuquerque: University of New Mexico Press, 1981.

Keeshig-Tobias, Lenore. *Quest for Fire: How the Trickster Brought Fire to the People* (excerpt). *Canadian Theatre Review* 68 (Fall 1991): 86–87.

Kneubuhl, Victoria Nalani. *The Story of Susanna*. In *Seventh Generation: An Anthology of Native American Plays*, edited by Mimi Gisolfi D'Aponte. New York: Theatre Communications Group, 1999.

Linklater, Leonard, and Patti Flather. *Sixty Below* (excerpt). In *Beyond the Pale: Dramatic Writing from First Nations Writers & Writers of Colour*, edited by Yvette Nolan, Betty Quan, and George Bwanika Seremba. Toronto: Playwrights Canada Press, 1996.

Manuel, Vera. *Strength of Indian Women*. In *Two Plays About Residential School*. Vancouver: Living Traditions Writers Group, 1998. Excerpt originally published in Nolan, Yvette, Betty Quan, and George Bwanika Seremba. *Beyond the Pale: Dramatic Writing from First Nations Writers & Writers of Colour*. Toronto: Playwrights Canada Press, 1996.

Mojica, Monique. *Princess Pocahontas and the Blue Spots*. *Canadian Theatre Review* 64 (Fall 1990). See also Monique Mojica, *Princess Pocahontas and the Blue Spots: Two Plays by Monique Mojica*.

Mojica, Monique. *Princess Pocahontas and the Blue Spots: Two Plays by Monique Mojica*. Toronto: Women's Press, 1991. Collection includes *Princess Pocahontas and the Blue Spots* and *Birdwoman and the Suffragettes: A Story of Sacajawea*.

Mojica, Monique. *This Is for Aborelia Dominguez*. In *Beyond the Pale: Dramatic Writing from First Nations Writers & Writers of Colour*, edited by Yvette Nolan, Betty Quan, and George Bwanika Seremba. Toronto: Playwrights Canada Press, 1996.

Nolan, Yvette. *Annie Mae's Movement*. Toronto: Playwrights Canada Press, 1999

Nolan, Yvette. *Blade, Job's Wife, and Video: 3 Plays*. Toronto: ArtBiz Communications, 1995.

Nolan, Yvette. *Child.* Toronto: Playwrights Canada Press, 1994. Excerpt also published in *Beyond the Pale: Dramatic Writing from First Nations Writers & Writers of Colour*, edited by Yvette Nolan, Betty Quan, and George Bwanika Seremba. Toronto: Playwrights Canada Press, 1996.

Nolan, Yvette. *Everybody's Business*. Toronto: Playwrights Canada Press, 1991.

Nolan, Yvette. *A Marginal Man*. Toronto: Playwrights Canada Press, 1994.

Proffitt, Rebecca. *The Good God Debate*. In *Both Sides: New Work from the Institute of American Indian Arts, 1993–1994*, edited by Cheryl Benjamin, Bunky Echo-Hawk, Patrice Farmer, Frank Hyde, Bessie Ann Joseph, Grace Lego, and Pat Natseway. Santa Fe: Institute of American Indian Arts, 1994.

Shorty, Sharon. *Trickster Visits the Old Folks Home*. In *Staging the North: Twelve Canadian Plays*, edited by Sherrill Grace, Eve D'Aeth and Lisa Chalhioff. Toronto: Playwrights Canada Press, 1999.

Spiderwoman Theater. *Power Pipes*. In *Seventh Generation: An Anthology of Native American Plays*, edited by Mimi Gisolfi D'Aponte. New York: Theatre Communications Group, 1999.

Spiderwoman Theater. *Reverb-ber-ber-rations*. *Women and Performance* 5, no. 2 (1992): 184–212.

Spiderwoman Theater. *Sun, Moon, and Feather*. In *Stories of Our Way: An Anthology of American Indian Plays*, edited by Hanay Geiogamah and Jaye T. Darby. Los Angeles, California: UCLA American Indian Studies Center, 1999. Originally published in *Contemporary Plays by Women of Color*, edited by Kathy A. Perkins and Roberta Uno. New York: Routledge, 1996.

Spiderwoman Theater. *Winnetou's Snake Oil Show from Wigwam City*. In *Playwrights of Color*, edited by Meg Swanson and Robin Murray. Yarmouth, Maine: Intercultural Press, 1999. Originally published in *Canadian Theatre Review* 68 (Fall 1991): 56–63.

Whiteman, Carol DuVal. See Paula Blue Spruce.

Williams, Wende. *Indian Game Show*. In *Gathering Our Own: New Work from the Institute of American Indian Arts*, edited by Dana Dickerson, Brian Lush, and Ti Stalnaker. Santa Fe, New Mexico: Institute of American Indian Arts, 1996.

About the Playwrights

Sierra Adare

Sierra Adare, Cherokee and Choctaw, is the author of eleven books, including her award-winning *What Editors Look For: How to Write Compelling Queries, Cover Letters, Synopses & Book Proposals*. She has worked as a staff reporter for *News from Indian Country*, and is currently a regular contributor to *Wild West* magazine. Additionally, she has taught Contemporary Issues of the American Indian for Haskell Indian Nations University, Cherokee History and Creative Writing as a Visiting Fellow for Cornell University's American Indian Program, and was an assistant instructor of Cherokee Language for the University of Kansas's Upward Bound Program.

Adare's articles on American Indians, travel, outdoors, history, how-to topics, and cooking have appeared in both regional and national publications. She is a mentor in Wordcraft Circle of Native Writers and Storytellers and is currently working on a series of American Indian history books with her husband, Tasiwoo Pa ápi, who is Comanche and Mohawk. The idea for this book series grew out of the couple's article, "The Last Comanche Code Talker," which appeared in *World War II Magazine*.

Annette Arkeketa

Annette Arkeketa is an Otoe-Missouria/Muscogee playwright, poet, and writer. Her play *Hokti* has been produced by the Tulsa Indian Actors' Workshop in Tulsa, Oklahoma and the Thunderbird Theatre at Haskell Indian Nations University in Lawrence, Kansas; the published play appears in *Stories of Our Way: An Anthology of American Indian Plays*. *Ghost Dance* was read by Tulsa Indian Actors' Workshop at the Gilcrease Museum, Tulsa, Oklahoma in January 2001 and at Tulsa University May 2002. Arkeketa's poetry appears in numerous anthologies, magazines, and journals, and she has one book of poetry entitled *The Terms Of A Sister*. She is the producer of the video documentary, *Intrinsic Spirit: The Artway of Jimmy Pena*. She is a Second Circle Board member for ATLATL, a Native American arts organization, and a member of Wordcraft Circle of Writers and Storytellers.

Arkeketa makes her home in Norman, Oklahoma. She holds a bachelor of business administration degree from Central State University, Edmond, Oklahoma and a master of arts degree in Interdisciplinary Studies at Texas A & M University, Corpus Christi. She is currently employed as a contract negotiator at Tinker Air Force Base in Oklahoma. She conducts creative writing workshops in poetry and playwriting throughout the United States.

JUSTIN KENNICK

Marge Bruchac

Margaret (Marge) Bruchac, Abenaki, has spent fourteen years working in historical research, design, and museum consulting. As the Native American consultant to Old Sturbridge Village, Bruchac created the character of Molly Geet, the Indian Doctress, based on extensive study of early nineteenth-century Native healers. While working as a Smith Scholar at Smith College from 1995 to 1999, Bruchac won a Five College Theater Playwriting Award for *Staging the Indian*, performed at the Five College Word Festival, and was twice awarded the Jeanne McFarland Women's History Prize. In her role as an adviser for the Wampanoag Indian Program at Plimoth Plantation, she coauthored *1621: A New Look at Thanksgiving*, published by National Geographic in 2001. Bruchac is now pursuing graduate study in cultural anthropology at the University of Massachusetts, Amherst, funded by the Sylvia Forman Fellowship for Minority Scholars and a Graduate School Fellowship.

With her brother Joe Bruchac and nephews Jim and Jesse, she sings on two Dawnland Singers recordings of traditional and contemporary Abenaki music: *Abenaki Cultural Heritage Celebration* (1993) and *Alnobak* (1994). Bruchac and her husband, Justin Kennick, recorded *Zahkiwi Lintow8ganal/Voices in the Woods* (1998) and have performed at festivals in the northeast and northern Europe, including the First People's Festival in Montreal; Mystic Seaport Sea Music Festival, Sagakwa; and Oost-Friesland Folk Fest in Kellinghusen, Germany, among others. In 2000, Bruchac was chosen Storyteller of the Year for public speaking by the Wordcraft Circle of Native American Writers and Storytellers.

NICK SEIFLOW

Marie Clements

Marie Clements is an award-winning writer, performer, and artistic director of urban ink productions. Her nine plays including *Age of Iron*, *Now look what you made me do*, *The Unnatural and Accidental Women*, and *Urban Tattoo* have been produced and presented on stages across Canada, the United States, and Europe, and published in a variety of anthologies and books.

Her latest play, *Burning Vision*, was commissioned by Rumble Theatre and developed in collaboration with Playwrights Workshop Montreal where it was produced by Rumble Theatre in association with urban ink and nominated for six Jessie Awards. *Burning Vision* and *Copper Thunderbird*, a commission by Les Ondinnok Theatre, have evolved over the last two years through residencies at Rumble Theatre, Playwrights Workshop Montreal, The National Theatre School, The Banff Playwrights Colony, and The Firehall Arts Centre. Last season Marie worked in the writing department of Davinci's Inquest and she is currently working on the film adaptation of her stage play, *The Unnatural and Accidental Women* for the British Columbia Film Commission, as well as contributing a regular commentary for CBC Radio's Morning Edition. *Burning Vision* and *The Unnatural and Accidental Women* will be published by Talon Books in spring 2003 and fall 2003.

PHILIP CHANNING

**Daystar/
Rosalie M. Jones**

Born on the Blackfeet Reservation in Montana, **Daystar** is of Pembina Chippewa ancestry on her mother's side. She holds a master's degree in dance from the University of Utah and studied at the Juilliard School in New York. She was a member of the performing arts faculty at the Institute of American Indian Arts in Santa Fe, New Mexico during the 1960s and again in the early 1990s, when she served as chair of the department. Daystar was a Distinguished Visiting Artist at the American University in Bulgaria (1997), the Chancellor's Visiting Professor in the Dance Department at the University of California, Irvine (1998), and Artist in Residence in the School of Arts and Performance at the State University of New York-Brockport (1999–2001). She lectured and performed as the featured keynote speaker at the 23rd Annual American Indian Workshop conference in Dublin, Ireland, March 2002.

Daystar is the founder and artistic director of DAYSTAR: Contemporary Dance-Drama of Indian America. The company was founded in 1980, and has performed throughout the United States and Canada, and in Germany, Bulgaria, and Turkey. Daystar's creative process is both personal and tribal. Some of her major choreographic works include *Tales of Old Man* (Blackfeet), *Wolf: A Transformation* (Anishinabe), *The Woman Who Fell From The Sky* (Six Nations), *Sacred Woman, Sacred Earth* (Lakota), and *Prayer of the First Dancer*. Daystar was asked by editor Dr. Charlotte Heth to write the chapter "Native Modern Dance: Beyond Tribe and Tradition" for the publication *Native American Dance: Ceremonies and Social Traditions* (1992). In 1995, she received a two-year NEA Choreographer's Fellowship, the first Native American to receive the award.

During the past thirty years, Daystar has taught in Native American schools, communities, and colleges throughout the country, encouraging and promoting Native American talent in the arts. Today she remains active as a dancer, choreographer, actress, teacher, and writer. Her website is daystardance.com.

DAVE SCHEELE

Diane Glancy

Diane Glancy is professor of English at Macalester College in St. Paul, Minnesota, where she teaches Native American literature and creative writing including scriptwriting She has received the Cherokee Medal of Honor from the Cherokee Society. Her book of nine plays, *War Cries*, was published by Holy Cow! Press in Duluth, Minnesota. She recently completed a second collection of six plays called *American Gypsy*. Her plays appear in various anthologies including *Seventh Generation* (Theater Communications Group), *Contemporary Plays by Women of Color* (Routledge), and *Stories of Our Way* (UCLA American Indian Studies Center). An award-winning author, Glancy also has published several novels and collections of poetry, essays, and short stories. Her awards include: American Book Award, Five Civilized Playwriting Competition Award, Jones Commission and Many Voices Playwriting Fellowship from the Playwrights' Center in Minneapolis, Minnesota State Arts Board Fellowship, National Endowment for the Arts Fellowship, and North American Indian Prose Award.

LEWIS LAKEY

Marcie R. Rendon

Marcie R. Rendon, White Earth Anishinabe, is a mother, grandmother, writer, and sometimes performance artist. In 2001, BAPA Imagination Stage in Bethesda, Maryland produced her children's play, *Rough-Face Girl*. Rendon was the 1998–99 recipient of the St. Paul's Company's LIN (Leadership in Neighborhoods) Award and a former recipient of the Loft's Inroads Writers of Color Award for Native Americans. Additional awards include a 1996–97 Jerome Fellowship from the Minneapolis Playwrights' Center and an Intermedia Arts Emerging Artists' Installation award in 1995–96.

Rendon's nonfiction children's books include *The Farmer's Market* and *Pow-wow Summer*, published by Carol Rhoda Books. *Dreaming Into Being* is a self-published poetry chapbook. Her poetry appears in a number of publications including the anthologies, *Nitaawichige*, published by Poetry Harbor, and *Re-Inventing the Enemy's Language*, edited by Joy Harjo and Gloria Bird.

MARTHA SWOPE ASSOCIATES

Spiderwoman Theater

Spiderwoman Theater's work has appeared in various publications such as *500 Years of Chicana History*, *Theatre Journal 52: Mythical Performativity: Relocating Aztlan in Chicana*, *Feminist Cultural Productions*, *Chicanas/Latinas in Performance on the American Stage*, *Journal on Dramatic Theory and Criticism*, *Beautiful Necessity: The Art and Meaning of Making Women's Altars*, *Ollantay Magazine*, *Contemporary Plays by Women of Color*, *Tulane Drama Review*, and *Heresies Magazine*. Their latest play,

Chicomoztoc Mimixcoa — Cloud Serpents, will be published next year by the University of Illinois Press in a new anthology. They are working on a new play based on the stories of the Zapatista women.

Lisa Mayo, Kuna/Rappahannock, was born into a Native American family who lived in Brooklyn, New York and who were performers in powwows, parades, civic events, and Snake Oil shows with other Native American families. Sometimes she ballyhooed for John Wayne movies or performed at carnivals. Mayo left that work at the age of ten feeling that she was destined for better things. She took voice lessons and became a classically trained mezzo-soprano, and studied acting with Herbert Berghof, Uta Hagan, Walt Witcover, and Bobby Lewis. She became a performing member of Masterworks Laboratory Theater, singing the role of Anina in the opera *La Traviata* at the Actors Studio under the direction of Lee Strasberg and Walt Witcover. For the last twenty-five years Mayo, as a founding member of Spiderwoman Theater Workshop, has been performing all over the United States, Canada, Europe, Australia, New Zealand, and China. In 1998 in New York City she was cast by Conway and Pratt Productions in their unique theater piece, *A Woman's Work Is Never Done*, which had a run in Boston, September and October 2001. She serves on the board of directors of the American Indian Community House in New York City as board secretary. She has also been awarded an honorary doctorate in fine arts from Miami University in Oxford, Ohio, where the Native Women's Playwrights' Archives are kept. Mayo is especially excited about "Persistence of Memory" which includes the next two generations of performing artists in her family.

Gloria Miguel, Kuna/Rappahannock, studied drama at Oberlin College, Ohio and is a founding member of Spiderwoman Theater. She has worked extensively in film and television, toured the United States in *Grandma*, a one-woman show by Hanay Geiogamah, toured Canada as Pelajia Patchnose in the original Native Earth production of Tomson Highway's *The Rez Sisters*, and performed in the Canadian play *Son of Ayash* in Toronto and *Bootlegger Blues* at the Arbour Theater in Peterborough. She performed as Coyote/Ritaline in *Jessica*, a Northern Lights Production in Edmonton, Canada, for which she was nominated for a Sterling award for outstanding supporting actress. She was a drama consultant for Minnesota American Indian Youth AIDS Task Force to develop a play on AIDS. When not on tour she taught drama at the Eastern District YMCA in Brooklyn, New York and was a visiting professor and drama consultant at Brandon University, Canada. She performed in Beijing, China at the 4th World Woman's Conference. She and Lisa Mayo received a Rockefeller grant, as well as funding from the Jerome Foundation to create *Nis Bundor: Daughters from the Stars*, which premiered at Dance Theater Workshop. She was also a judge and teaching consultant for an annual theater festival at Greyhills Academy, a Navajo high school in Arizona. In 1999, Miguel performed as Maria in an adaptation of Louise Erdrich's book *Love Medicine* in Chicago. She also taught drama at Red Winds College in Red Mesa, Arizona. She is the recipient of an honorary doctorate in fine arts from Miami University in Oxford, Ohio, and has a lifetime membership at the Lee Strasberg Institute.

Muriel Miguel, Kuna/Rappahannock, is a founding member and artistic director of Spiderwoman Theater, the longest running Native American feminist theater group in North America, which has toured internationally for twenty-five years. She has directed all of Spiderwoman's shows, which are created from original scripts. She has directed for Native Earth Performing Arts and Nightwood Theatre in Toronto, for Coatlicue, and at New York Theatre Workshop in New York City. She choreographed *Throw Away Kids* as the guest choreographer for the Chinook Winds Aboriginal Dance Program at the Banff Centre. As an actress, Miguel was an original member of Joseph Chaikin's Open Theatre, one of the leading alternative New York theater groups in the 1960s. She originated the role of Philomena Moosetail in *The Rez Sisters* for Native Earth Performing Arts, the role of Aunt Shadie in *The Unnatural and Accidental Women* for the Firehall Theatre in Vancouver, and the role of Spirit Woman in *Bones: An Aboriginal Dance Opera* at the Banff Centre 2001 Summer Festival. Miguel has created two one-woman shows, *Hot'N'Soft* and *Trail of the Otter*. She studied with Alwin Nickolai at the Henry Street Playhouse as well as Eric Hawkins and Jean Erdman. She is the cofounder of the Thunderbird American Indian Dancers in New York City and a founding member of Shy Woman Singers and Dancers, a traditional women's drum and dance troupe. She teaches extensively in a variety of settings, including as an assistant professor of drama at Bard College. She teaches on an ongoing basis at the Centre for Indigenous Theatre in Toronto and the Aboriginal Arts Program at the Banff Centre where she has been instrumental in training Native youth in theater and dance. She has developed two shows for The Minnesota Native American AIDS Task Force in Minneapolis, working with inner city Native youth on HIV/AIDS and its impact on their lives. In 1998, Miguel was selected for the Bread and Roses International Native Women of Hope poster. She has also been awarded an honorary doctorate in fine arts from Miami University in Oxford, Ohio, the site of the Native Women's Playwrights' Archives. She was recently honored by the Brothers of the Sisters of ASTRAEA as an elder and role model for two spirit women of color.

Hortensia Colorado, Chichimec Otomi, is a storyteller, performer, playwright, community activist, and cofounder, together with her sister Elvira, of Coatlicue Theatre Company. Coatlicue is the Mexican deity of earth and creation. Together they write and perform personal stories which are interwoven with creation stories and issues that affect indigenous communities. These stories have the power to transform and heal. They have performed and given storytelling theater workshops throughout the country and Mexico for more than fifteen years at universities, reservations, museums, and cultural centers. Their theatrical productions serve to educate as well as entertain while reaffirming and celebrating their survival as indigenous women. They have received a NYFA Fellowship for playwriting, NYSCA Artists Theatre Fellowship, and a Lila Wallace Grant. They have given storytelling theater workshops and performances in the indigenous communities in resistance in Chiapas and Oaxaca, Mexico.

Colorado is a board member of the American Indian Community House in New York City where she organizes cultural events such as Day of the Dead celebrations. As one of the founding members of the New York Zapatistas she organizes festivals of resistance to create an awareness of the indigenous Mexican communities' struggles; she works with women's cooperatives; and she uses pirate radio to distribute community and Indian Country news. As a member of Danza Cetiliztli, a Mexican dance group, she works to empower youth through traditional dance.

Deborah Ratelle, stage manager, has worked as the production manager for Spiderwoman Theater in New York since 1990 and has traveled throughout Canada, the United States, Europe, Australia, and New Zealand with them. She also has had a longstanding relationship with Native Earth Performing Arts in Toronto, working as both production manager and stage manager. She was the stage manager for The Chinook Winds Aboriginal Dance Program at the Banff Centre for two summers. On April 1, 1999, she stage managed the gala performance for the opening of the Nunavut Territory in Iqaluit, *The Unnatural and Accidental Woman* for the Firehall Theatre in Vancouver, and *Bones: An Aboriginal Dance Opera* for the Banff 2001 Summer Festival. She has been the coordinator for the Banff Centre playRites Colony at the Banff Centre for the last five years and is the program/production manager for the Aboriginal Dance Program at the Banff Centre.